TILL DEATH
DO US PART

TILL DEATH DO US PART

·

Bendix vs. Martin Marietta

·

HOPE LAMPERT

HARCOURT

BRACE   San Diego

JOVANOVICH,   New York

PUBLISHERS   London

Library of Congress Cataloging in Publication Data
Lampert, Hope.
Till death do us part.
1. Consolidation and merger of corporations—United
States—Case studies.   2. Bendix Corporation.   3. Martin
Marietta Corporation.   I. Title.
HD2746.5.L36   1983   338.8'362904'0973   83-8546
ISBN 0-15-190310-7

Designed by Joy Chu

Printed in the United States of America
First Edition 1983
A   B   C   D   E   F   G   H   I   J

TO MY PARENTS

CONTENTS

•

•

•

ACKNOWLEDGMENTS

•

This book could not have been written without the encouragement of Harry Anderson, Marty Lipton, Bill Marbach, and Brian Schneider. Chris Pagano at Allied, Roy Calvin and Bill Harwood at Martin Marietta, Tom Drohan and Bill Blase at United Technologies, and the library staff at Wachtell, Lipton, Rosen & Katz were always patient. I would like to thank them and everyone else who helped and encouraged me along the way.

•

AUTHOR'S NOTE

•

This book is based primarily on extensive interviews, total-
ing more than 250 hours, with the main participants. I have
used quotation marks to indicate dialogue that the participants at each meeting remember having happened. The
quotations fairly reflect the substance and flavor of what
the participants told me was said; they do not necessarily
indicate the exact words used.

I conducted two rounds of interviews. Many of the sessions were taped. First, I asked each participant to consult
his desk calendar and telephone logs; if necessary, I reminded the participant of meetings that had occurred.
Where appropriate, I prompted him by telling him parts of
what other participants had already told me. I asked each
interviewee to focus on what he had said and done; what
others had said and done in his presence; and to confirm or
correct what I had been told by others. I checked what each
person told me with others who had been present for that
meeting.

When I had finished the first round of interviews, I
drafted a preliminary manuscript. In that manuscript I reported the events and the dialogue on the basis of what I
had been told. In almost all cases, I quoted each participant as speaking the words he himself remembered having

•

•

used or, failing actual recall, thought he was likely to have used. The exceptions were those cases in which an interviewee's statement to me conflicted with what others who were present remembered. Reinterviewing eliminated all but a few conflicts. I resolved remaining discrepancies in a second round of personal interviews with the participants.

During this second round I showed each interviewee the pages of the preliminary manuscript referring to him or describing events at which he was present. In some cases, I showed the interviewee the entire manuscript. I asked each to comment on accuracy. Seeing my typescript often jogged the memory of the participant. Each made specific comments on accuracy and phrasing; unless there was still a conflict between statements of interviewees, I made the suggested revisions. To resolve the remaining conflicts, I relied on those participants, almost invariably more than one, whose statements I found to be more credible in the circumstances.

In addition to the personal interviews with participants and their review and comment on the preliminary manuscript, I read thousands of pages of documents, including all the SEC filings in the transactions and documents filed in related legal proceedings. I read public materials relating to the four companies involved; portions of the minutes of certain board meetings were read to me. I also read the day-by-day reports on the drama that appeared in the *New York Times*, the *Wall Street Journal*, the *Detroit Free Press*, and the *Detroit News*, as well as other news reports. I reported the battle as it occurred for *Newsweek* magazine and have reviewed the notes that I made at the time.

Of course, only fragments of all the thinking, planning, conversations, meetings, and events that were a part of this complex and controversial matter can be included in a book. Within that constraint, I have aimed for accuracy, balance, and comprehensiveness.

PRINCIPAL
PARTICIPANTS

•

Investment Bankers: Salomon Brothers and First Boston
Law Firms: Hughes Hubbard and Reed and Fried, Frank,
   Harris, Shriver & Jacobson
William M. Agee—chairman
Harold Barron—general counsel
W. Michael Blumenthal—former Bendix chairman
Marc Cherno—litigator, Fried, Frank
John Cooke—vice-president for human resources
Mary Cunningham—executive assistant to Agee, vice-
   president for corporate affairs, then for strategic plan-
   ning—moved to Seagram's and became Mrs. Agee
George Davidson—litigator, Hughes Hubbard and Reed
Coy Eklund—chairman, The Equitable Life Assurance So-
   ciety, on Bendix board
Arthur Fleischer, Jr.—lawyer, Fried, Frank
John Fontaine—lawyer, Hughes Hubbard and Reed, on
   Bendix board
Stephen Fraiden—lawyer, Fried, Frank
Tony Grassi—investment banker, First Boston
John Gutfreund—chairman Salomon Brothers
Ira Harris—investment banker, Salomon Brothers Chicago
   office

Jay Higgins—investment banker, Salomon Brothers
Stuart Katz—lawyer, Fried, Frank
Donald Kayser—chief financial officer
Alonzo McDonald—president
Charles Nathan—lawyer for Salomon Brothers
Peter Peterson—chairman, Lehman Brothers
Richard Pogue—lawyer for Bendix at Jones, Day, Reavis
    & Pogue
Nancy Reynolds—vice-president, Bendix Washington
    office
Michael Rowny—vice-president
Donald Rumsfeld—president, G. D. Searle, on Bendix
    board
Donald G. Speyer—vice-president
Robert Strauss—Washington lobbyist
Harold Tanner—investment banker, Salomon Brothers
William Tavoulareas—president, Mobil, on Bendix board
Hugo Uyterhoeven—Harvard Business School professor,
    on Bendix board
Bruce Wasserstein—investment banker, First Boston
Martin Weinstein—arbitrageur, Salomon Brothers
Anne Wexler—lobbyist

MARTIN MARIETTA

Investment Banker: Kidder, Peabody
Law Firm: Dewey, Ballantine, Bushby, Palmer & Wood
Laurence Adams—chief operating officer
Griffin Bell—former attorney general, on Marietta board
Barry Biggar—lawyer, Dewey, Ballantine
Frank Bradley—president, Halco Mining, on Marietta
    board
Doug Brown—investment banker, Kidder, Peabody
George Bunker—former chairman

John J. Byrne—chairman, Geico, on Marietta board
Roy Calvin—vice-president for public affairs
Robert Fullem—lawyer, Dewey, Ballantine
John Hanigan—chairman, Genesco, on Marietta board
Richard Katcher—lawyer for Kidder, Peabody; Wachtell,
    Lipton, Rosen & Katz takeover specialist
Melvin Laird—former secretary of defense, on Marietta
    board
Leonard P. Larrabee, Jr.—lawyer, Dewey, Ballantine
Charles Leithauser—chief financial officer
Frank Menaker—general counsel
Joe Morrow—head proxy solicitor
Robert Powell—treasurer
Thomas G. Pownall—president
J. Donald Rauth—chairman
Doris Rush—pension lawyer
Wayne Shaner—assistant treasurer
Martin A. Siegel—investment banker, Kidder, Peabody
James Simpson—vice-president
Carol Trencher—ERISA lawyer, Dewey, Ballantine
Peter Wood—investment banker, Kidder, Peabody
Eugene Zuckert—former air force secretary, on Marietta
    board

UNITED TECHNOLOGIES

Investment Banker: Lazard Frères
Law Firm: Wachtell, Lipton, Rosen & Katz
Stillman Brown—chief financial officer
Robert J. Carlson—executive vice-president in charge of
    Pratt & Whitney
Harry Jack Gray—chairman
Pehr G. Gyllenhammer—managing director, Volvo, on
    UTC board
Alexander Haig—former UTC president

Edward W. Large—executive vice-president for legal and
   corporate affairs
Martin Lipton—lawyer, Wachtell, Lipton
James Lyons—vice-president
Clark MacGregor—senior vice-president
Felix Rohatyn—investment banker, Lazard Frères

ALLIED

Investment Banker: Lehman Brothers and Kuhn Loeb
Law Firm: Skadden, Arps, Slate, Meagher & Flom
Harold Buirkle—chief financial officer
Joseph Flom—lawyer, Skadden, Arps
Brian Forrow—general counsel
Eric Gleacher—investment banker, Lehman Brothers
Edward L. Hennessy, Jr.—chairman
J. Tomlinson Hill—investment banker, Lehman Brothers
William M. Kearns—investment banker, Lehman Brothers
   partner in charge of Allied account
Robert Kilpatrick—president, Cigna insurance, on Allied
   board
Morris Kramer—lawyer, Skadden, Arps
Paul Thayer—chairman, LTV, on Allied board

TILL DEATH
DO US PART

•

THE CALL

(Wednesday, August 25, 1982)

•

The meeting was scheduled for eight o'clock in the morning at the law offices of Hughes Hubbard and Reed. It had been raining for hours and the streets of lower Manhattan were already clogged with taxis, but John Fontaine made sure that he got to his One Wall Street office early. He was the host. Fontaine was on the Bendix board. His firm, Hughes Hubbard and Reed, was the company's principal legal counsel. Arthur Fleischer, Jr., a gray-haired takeover specialist from the law firm Fried, Frank, Harris, Shriver & Jacobson, arrived with the papers. Jay Higgins, the investment banker from Salomon Brothers, was right behind him. The three talked. A lawyer came in. Then another. The bells of Trinity Church across the street chimed eight o'clock. Bill Agee was late.

Fontaine read over the press release. Fleischer glanced at his timetable. Higgins made a phone call. The receptionist buzzed. Agee was there. Fontaine escorted him to a small conference room. The others were sitting with their papers, waiting.

Agee stood at Fleischer's side at the head of the oval table. Fleischer flipped through the pages in front of him.

•

•

He read the key paragraphs out loud one final time. Fleischer wanted to make sure that Agee knew exactly what the documents said. When he had finished, Fleischer looked at his watch. The call had been scheduled for eight forty-five. It was ten to nine.

"Time to call," said Fleischer.

"Okay," said Agee. "This is what I'm going to say if he answers the phone: 'Tom, as you know, we've had an interest in your company for a long time. Yesterday, the board authorized me to make you an offer. That offer will go out tomorrow. If you're amenable, I want to come down and talk about it. I will get on my plane now and come down to your office this afternoon if you say so. I want to do this as friends.' "

Agee looked around the table. The lawyers and bankers nodded in approval.

Agee and Fontaine walked into the corner office. Agee picked up the phone. The switchboard placed the call. Agee asked for Pownall.

"I see. Thank you," he said. "Tell him I'll wait for his call."

The phone rang. It was the Hughes Hubbard lawyer waiting in a phone booth across the street from Pownall's office. The lawyer had been told to check in every five minutes. He had a letter for Pownall. He couldn't deliver it until Agee told him to. Agee said deliver.

"Tom wouldn't take the call," said Agee as he walked back into the conference room. The lawyers swung into action. One called the New York Stock Exchange. Another called the lobbying team in Washington. Someone called the lawyers around the country who were waiting to file their lawsuits against Pownall's company. Someone else called Dow Jones with the press release. A few minutes later, the stock ticker began to click.

•

2

•

Southfield, Mich. Bendix Corp. announced a tender offer as a first step to acquiring all of the common shares of Martin Marietta Corp. . . . Bendix said it informed Martin Marietta of its offer this morning. It said Bendix chairman William M. Agee indicated his willingness to meet with Martin Marietta.

•

Martin Marietta president and chief executive officer, Thomas G. Pownall, arrived at the company's modern headquarters complex in the hills of suburban Washington at quarter to eight that morning. Canada geese floated tranquilly on the glassy surface of the company's duck pond. Pownall skimmed the morning papers. He strolled down the hall and around the corner to talk to Frank Menaker, his general counsel. They discussed Bendix. There had been rumors the week before that Bendix was about to make a pass at Martin Marietta.

At nine o'clock, Pownall and Lawrence Adams, Martin Marietta's chief operating officer, sat down in the conference room next door to the boardroom to talk about long-range planning. Before they could begin, Pownall's secretary, Eleanor, came in. "There's a Bill Agee on your line," she said. "He wants to talk to you immediately."

Pownall could guess what Agee wanted. "Tell Mr. Agee that this is an inopportune moment to call," he said. "I am at a meeting away from my office and I can't take his call. I will call him back."

Pownall walked out to talk to Roy Calvin, the vice-president for public affairs. "Get the strike team together in the conference room," said Pownall. Pownall walked on to Menaker's office.

"Bill Agee just called me," he said. "I didn't take the

call. I wanted to talk over what to say first. I will call back later."

Pownall and Menaker were still talking when Pownall's secretary buzzed. "There is a to-be-receipted letter for you at the front desk," she said.

"Go get it immediately," said Pownall. He guessed that it came from Agee. Pownall and Menaker walked into the conference room. Five of the other executives on the strike team were waiting. J. Donald Rauth, Martin Marietta's chairman, wasn't there: he was at his beach house in Ocean City, New Jersey.

Before Pownall could begin the meeting, his secretary came in with the letter. The logo said Bendix. Pownall slit the envelope and skimmed the cover note. Attached was a press release.

"Oh, hell," he said. "Here we go."

Pownall read the letter out loud. Bendix offered to buy Martin Marietta for $43 a share. According to the press release, Bendix owned 4.5 percent of Martin Marietta. The release said that Bendix chairman William Agee had contacted Martin Marietta that morning.

"We've got to get moving," said Menaker. "We've got to react quickly."

The executives went back to their offices. Menaker called Martin Marietta's legal counsel in New York. Charles Leithauser, the chief financial officer, called the investment bankers. Pownall tried to reach Rauth at his beach house, but he couldn't get through. Pownall called the other directors of the company. There will be an informal board briefing tomorrow, he told them.

THE STRATEGY

·

There is a giant Norman Rockwell painting on the wall of Bill Agee's office. It is called *The Connoisseur.* A bald man in a gray suit stares up at an abstract, paint-splattered painting. His hands are crossed behind his back. He is wearing gray gloves and holding a gray hat, a long black umbrella, and a copy of the *Saturday Evening Post.* It's clear that the man wants to understand the painting in front of him, but he is confused. Agee and his wife bought the picture on their honeymoon in Hawaii. They like its irony.

Agee calls himself a "contrarian by nature." "I've always been the kind of person who starts to become suspicious when the conventional wisdom, whatever it might be, starts to take on unanimity. When everyone starts to say something, that is the time to start thinking about something else, because whatever it is that everyone thinks, is obvious. The world never stays that way."

Bill Agee grew up in Boise, and he never quite lost the touch of Idaho sunshine. He likes Norman Rockwell. He doesn't like formality. He doesn't have an imposing desk in his office. Instead he works at a round table in a comfort-

·

5

·

able chair. He prefers not to wear a jacket. He keeps a photograph of his wife beside the telephone.

Agee's most distinguishing feature is an engaging smile. He is of average height. He has brown hair. He wears wire-rimmed glasses. He smiles a lot and he has an infectious kind of enthusiasm. He loves to talk. He philosophizes for hours in what he calls "Idaho speech." While he talks he tends to gesture a lot with his hands. He radiates self-confidence and he radiates pride. "Ever since I was a little kid and I used to dig dandelions and take out coal clinkers for the neighbor ladies, I've always wanted people to like me and I've always wanted them to respect me," he says. "At the same time, I've always wanted to be at the top."

Bill Agee got to the top quickly. He went to Harvard Business School and graduated with distinction. He got job offers from W. R. Grace, TWA, and Ford Motor Company, but Agee chose to go to work for a small forest products company called Boise Cascade. Agee thought he would have better opportunities there, and he did. Boise had just embarked on an acquisition binge. By 1969, Agee was named chief financial officer at the age of thirty-one. When the recession of 1970 set in, the Boise empire started to crumble. Agee realized that there would be no more growth and that he would not be named the next Boise chairman. When a headhunter called with a job offer at Bendix, Agee said he was interested. W. Michael Blumenthal, chairman of Bendix, had just set up a four-man office of the chairman; Blumenthal wanted Agee to be the chief financial officer. Agee liked the idea, and in 1972 he took the job.

Soon Agee was number two all by himself. Blumenthal dissolved the office of the chairman and named Agee president of Bendix. Just one month later, Jimmy Carter asked Blumenthal to be his secretary of the treasury. Blumenthal went to Washington and Agee was elected chairman of Bendix. He was thirty-eight years old.

.

.

The Bendix that Agee inherited was a $1.8 billion con-glomerate, one of the one hundred largest companies in America. It was founded on the ingenuity of one man: Vin-cent Bendix. Until Vincent Bendix had invented the starter drive, the way to turn a car on was to crank the engine. Bendix had a better idea. He designed an innovative starter transmission system and convinced Chevrolet to install it in their "Baby Grand" touring car. Soon, almost every car on the road was outfitted with a Bendix starter drive. Ben-dix later expanded into the budding airplane parts busi-ness. By the time Agee took the helm, Bendix also owned an industrial winch-making company, a forest products company, and some timberland; Bendix made Fram filters, Autolite spark plugs, airplane wheels and steering gears. It made cutting tools for the Big Three car manufacturers. There had once been a company called Bendix that made washing machines. Bendix was strong and financially healthy. In 1976, *Dun's Review,* the financial journal, named Bendix one of the five best managed companies in America.

Agee quickly moved to change the Bendix style. He abolished the executive dining hall. He removed the re-served places from the company parking lot; he even took the ponderous table out of the boardroom. Agee scheduled regular review meetings with middle management. The air at Bendix became electric with enthusiasm.

In April 1978, Agee bought a 20 percent stake in Asarco, a copper and silver refiner with mines in the White Clouds region. The $128 million purchase was the largest that Bendix had ever made, and since Asarco was losing money, Wall Street analysts wondered what Agee was up to. Agee explained that copper and silver were inflation hedges and that he thought that the consumer price index and the price of metals were both about to take off. That would increase the price of Asarco stock; it would increase the dividends Asarco paid to Bendix, and because Bendix owned so much

·

7

·

of Asarco, Bendix was allowed to count some Asarco earnings as Bendix earnings: any boost to Asarco profits was also a boost to Bendix.

A year and a half later, Agee bought the Warner & Swasey Company, a major supplier of automated factory equipment like numerically controlled presses and lathes. The price of the company was high, $291 million, and Agee was criticized for having overpaid. But Bendix already made some machine tools, so Warner & Swasey was a good match. Now Bendix was number two in the market.

Bendix's bread-and-butter business was still the auto aftermarket—filters, spark plugs, brake shoes—which Agee felt was in the winter of its life. He wanted to get Bendix into newer, more high-technology fields with greater growth potential. In June 1979, six months before he bought Warner & Swasey, Agee hired a twenty-seven-year-old executive assistant straight out of Harvard Business School to help him develop a new strategy for Bendix. Her name was Mary Cunningham. Cunningham studied Bendix. She studied the industries that Bendix was in. She studied the industries that Bendix wasn't in. She studied companies that Bendix might want to buy. With Agee she developed a three-part strategy:

1. *Corporate Reorganization.* Decisions should be made at the divisions—not at headquarters. More autonomy and more flexibility could mean higher profits.
2. *Product Mix.* Bendix should get rid of its cyclical commodity businesses like forest products. It should sell the Asarco stock. It should buy new higher-technology businesses.
3. *Research and Development.* Internal spending should be increased. Bendix should buy small "windows on technology," innovative companies that are in the

process of developing risky but potentially profitable new products.

During most of 1980, Agee and Cunningham continued to work on their road map for Bendix. They called it The Strategy. Agee and Cunningham quickly became close friends. They both had apartments in the same suburban Detroit complex. They went to the U.S. Tennis Open together. They were seen in a television pan of the crowds at the Republican National convention, sitting with former president Gerald Ford. Cunningham is a strawberry blonde with blue eyes.

At the time, Mary Cunningham was separated from her husband, an executive at The Chase Manhattan Bank in New York City. In June 1980, Agee promoted Cunningham to vice-president for corporate and public affairs.

A week and a half after Labor Day that year, Agee announced the resignations of William P. Panny, president of Bendix, and Jerome Jacobson, the Bendix vice-president for strategic planning. Agee explained that he was reorganizing Bendix management—and that Panny didn't fit into the new structure. Agee said that Jacobson had been offered a job at Burroughs that Bendix couldn't match. One week later, Agee announced that he had made a deal to sell the Bendix forest products operations. Kohlberg Kravis Roberts & Company, a group of private investors, had offered him $435 million for the unit. Agee said that he was thinking about selling Bendix's Asarco stock. The stake was now worth $330 million, more than twice what Agee had bought it for two years before. Agee said that he would use the money to buy a high-technology company.

The timing of the sales turned out to be impeccable. The stock never traded above what Agee sold it for. By then the price of timber had fallen through the floor; forest products companies were in trouble.

In late September 1980, the day after he announced that he was selling forest products, Agee gave out the details of his corporate reorganization. Two hundred fifty of the eight hundred Southfield headquarters employees were going to the divisions. Agee named Mary Cunningham vice-president for strategic planning. She had been at the company for only fifteen months. Later that day, Agee had a talk session for six hundred employees. At the end of the meeting, Agee tried to quell some rumors that he had heard making the rounds at Bendix. He said that he had not fired Panny or Jacobson. He said that although he was an active Republican he was not going to go into politics even if Ronald Reagan were elected president in November. Then he talked about Mary Cunningham. "I know that it has been buzzing around that her rise in this company has been unusual and that it has something to do with a relationship between us. Sure it's unusual, because she's a very unusual and talented individual. It is true that we are very close friends and she's a very close friend of my family, but that has nothing to do with the way that I and others in this company evaluate her performance. Her rapid promotions have been totally justified."

Agee knew that there were reporters in the audience. He had invited them. But since all that he had meant to do was deny a rumor, Agee had not expected any headlines. He and Cunningham left on a business trip to San Francisco. Two days later, the story of the "romance" was national news. Agee hurried back to Southfield to deal with the controversy. He only made it worse. First he said that he and Cunningham would make a joint announcement the next day. Then he canceled the announcement on the grounds that there was nothing more to say. Cunningham told reporters that she would resign temporarily. The Bendix board refused her request because they didn't want to buckle to the media. In October, Cunningham did resign.

Six months later she took a job as a vice-president in strategic planning at Joseph E. Seagram & Sons. In June 1982, she married Bill Agee.

After Cunningham's resignation Agee continued to press forward with The Strategy. Within a few weeks he sold the Asarco stock, bringing the Bendix cash hoard to more than $770 million. Some observers predicted that Agee would buy a high-technology company quickly, but Agee didn't. He thought that the stock prices of the companies he was looking at were too high. He hired Lehman Brothers, Kuhn Loeb, a New York investment banker, to help him manage his portfolio, and he appointed a committee of three Bendix directors to oversee his investment decisions. The cash went primarily into Treasury notes that earned spectacular interest rates.

Agee's divestitures had by then made him the darling of the business community. But there was still trouble inside Bendix. Employees grumbled about corporate favoritism. Two days after the annual meeting in January 1981, one of the directors got an anonymous letter from "a loyal Bendix executive" who claimed to be a corporate officer. The letter said that Agee no longer enjoyed the trust of "most of us in management" and alleged that Agee had tried to sell two profitable Bendix businesses, the Fram Company and the Heavy Vehicle Systems division. The directors were worried about employee morale and called a special meeting for early March to discuss management.

At the end of February, Agee called a special board meeting of his own. He told the board that he was planning to buy a large technology company. He asked the four Bendix directors who also sat or had sat on the Burroughs board to choose either Burroughs or Bendix. One chose Bendix. The other three dual directors—one of whom had resigned from the Burroughs board eighteen months earlier—resigned. Another director was upset and considered resigning, but stayed on; he wanted to see if Agee would really make a major acquisition.

Despite Agee's statement that the resignations were tied to acquisition strategy, there was nasty speculation that the real reason that Agee had purged the board of Burroughs directors was to strike a blow at Mike Blumenthal. Blumenthal had resigned from the Carter cabinet in July and come back to Detroit as the vice-chairman of Burroughs. Agee did not ask Blumenthal to rejoin the Bendix board, and Blumenthal criticized Agee's handling of the Mary Cunningham rumors. Agee's supporters thought that Agee was on the verge of making his long-promised major acquisition. But the months went by and Agee did not.

Instead, Agee bought blocks of stock in small high-technology companies. He purchased 19 percent of Maxwell Laboratories, the maker of pulsating power technology; he invested in Enertec, an energy windmill manufacturer; he bought part of VLSI, an innovative maker of integrated circuits. Agee also increased Bendix's research and development budget and opened a new technology center in Columbia, Maryland. But he still kept more than a quarter of the Bendix assets invested in the money market. It was a smart move: interest rates were at almost record highs.

Some businessmen in Detroit began to grumble. They said that Agee didn't have a strategy and that he was really running a financial holding company. Bendix was itself an attractive target because of its cash. In March 1981 Agee bought back some of his own shares. "Folks," said Agee, "you have to stay tuned and see what we do."

●

By the summer of 1981, Agee's list of target takeover companies was down to sixteen, but only five of those—code-named Silver, Freedom, Yellow, Georgia, and Dog—were serious options. Agee's staff kept charts on the hourly stock prices of the takeover targets, and in August, Agee decided to move. The stock prices of the companies he had been watching had dropped as much as 70 percent. He thought that the market had just about bottomed out, that interest rates were going to fall, and that stock prices were going to rise. This was the time to buy that high-technology company at a bargain-basement price.

So at the end of August, Agee began buying Freedom (Lockheed) stock through Lehman Brothers, and he put out feelers to both Silver (RCA) and Georgia (Martin Marietta). Agee called Thornton Bradshaw, who had just been named chairman of RCA. RCA was in financial trouble. Its profits fell 82 percent in 1981: the NBC broadcasting subsidiary was on the rocks; the Hertz division was barely breaking even; the CIT financial division was pinched by high interest rates. But RCA did have television and satellite technology.

"Is there anything we can joint-venture?" Agee asked Bradshaw when the two sat down to talk. "Would you like to sell any of your businesses? Is there any way we can help you out? We have some cash. Why don't the two of us figure out a way that Bendix can do something."

Bradshaw wasn't interested. "It's too early to do any of this," he said. "Let's get together at some later date."

"Okay," said Agee. "But you ought to know in the meantime that Bendix intends to take an investment position in RCA. I don't know how big it will be, but it will be important, because we happen to think that your stock is undervalued."

Five days later, Goldman, Sachs & Company, a second New York investment banker working for Agee, began to buy RCA stock.

About the same time, Peter Peterson, chairman of Lehman Brothers, which managed part of the Bendix portfolio, called J. Donald Rauth, chairman of Martin Marietta. Rauth was an old friend of Peterson's and the two sat on the board of the Black & Decker tool company. Because of the recession, Marietta earnings were down and the stock price was at a record low. Peterson asked Rauth if he wanted to have lunch with Bill Agee. Rauth said that he did not.

By the beginning of November, Bendix owned 4.1 percent of Freedom (Lockheed). Agee went to see Roy Anderson, chairman of Lockheed, at his office in Burbank, California. Agee and Anderson had talked about the possibility of a Lockheed-Bendix merger several times before. Agee brought up the idea again, but Anderson demurred. Later Anderson called back with a definite no. Agee called several times after that. Anderson didn't want to sell. In December, Lockheed announced that it was going to cancel the Tri-Star airplane. The TriStar program had been a big money-loser, and without it Lockheed was a very profitable company. The price of Lockheed stock soared. Lockheed was now an expensive company to buy. Agee sold his shares for a profit.

All the while, Bendix quietly accumulated RCA stock through Goldman, Sachs. By February, 1982, Bendix owned almost 5 percent of the company. As soon as it hit the 5 percent ownership level, Bendix would have to file a 13-D report with the Securities and Exchange Commission, saying how much stock it owned, how much it had paid to buy it, and what it intended to do with the block. If Bendix filed, the news would be out. Agee got geared up to make a move. He asked Alonzo McDonald, the new Bendix president who had been chief of staff during Carter's last eighteen months to get a publicity and lobbying campaign ready. McDonald, Nancy Reynolds, head of the Bendix Washington office, and Anne Wexler, a highly respected lobbyist, worked up two binders full of tactics: a red defensive book and a black offensive book. Inside were call lists and information distribution schedules. There were sample texts of what to say about a Bendix investment or a Bendix raid. There were ideas for tactics if another company tried to buy Bendix.

At the beginning of March, Agee met again with Thornton Bradshaw of RCA. After the meeting, Bendix issued a press release stating that it had bought 7.3 percent of RCA as an investment. Bradshaw was prepared. He had hired Martin Lipton, a topflight takeover specialist from the law firm of Wachtell, Lipton, Rosen & Katz, to advise RCA, and he had two investment bankers on retainer: Felix Rohatyn of Lazard Frères, who was an old close friend of Bradshaw's, and Peter Peterson, another old friend and an RCA board member, and until then Bendix's banker. RCA quickly issued its own press release: "The purchase of RCA stock by Mr. Agee's Bendix is not welcomed by RCA. Mr. Agee's action in secretly accumulating a block of RCA stock shows that his only purpose is to further his own ambitions and not the interest of RCA stockholders or even Bendix and its stockholders. Agee has not demonstrated the ability to manage his own affairs, let alone someone else's."

Bradshaw had adopted a standard tactic in fighting off a potential takeover: shame your opponent into withdrawing. It worked. Later that week, Bendix signed an agreement with RCA promising not to buy any more RCA stock for thirty days and to give RCA at least forty-eight hours notice if it decided to buy more RCA stock after that.

•

Two weeks after Agee signed the standstill agreement with RCA, Al McDonald, the president of Bendix, called John Gutfreund, chairman of Salomon Brothers, to set up a lunch for Bendix with some of the top Salomon Brothers staff. Bendix was now using three investment bankers (Salomon, Lehman, and Goldman, Sachs) in pursuit of its big acqui-

•

•

sition. On March 30, Agee and McDonald flew into New York to meet Gutfreund, Harold Tanner, a partner in the corporate finance department and a business school classmate of Al McDonald, and two other Salomon senior partners. Jay Higgins, the partner who heads the firm's mergers team, was in Europe on business.

"I'm thinking of asking Salomon Brothers to look at some investment and acquisition candidates for me," said Agee at the end of the meal. "I've got a list that my staff put together for me."

Agee recited a half dozen names. Gutfreund listened. One of the companies was RCA. Another was Gould. A third was Martin Marietta. "Salomon Brothers does corporate financing for RCA," he said. "We can look at the company for you, but we can't represent you in a hostile bid. We are extremely close to Gould, so we won't even look at it. The others are fine."

Agee explained that he was interested in companies that had a high technology applied to their core businesses. He wanted to do his buying in two steps. First: buy a 5-to-10 percent stake in several companies. Agee liked the idea of a minority interest. He didn't have to pay a premium over the market price to purchase the shares, and he could make a good profit. Second: buy a company and do it without weakening the Bendix balance sheet. Gutfreund said he'd get a team started. On his way out, Agee asked Gutfreund to have Salomon Brothers start to accumulate a position in Martin Marietta. Soon, Salomon was buying Martin Marietta stock.

In March, Agee had asked Lehman Brothers to begin to buy stock in Yellow (Gould). By the end of April, Agee had bought a big enough block that Gould chairman William T. Ylvisaker began to wonder if someone was planning to make a raid. The company tried to cut the aggressor off by buying the 5 percent stake in Gould that Borg-Warner owned.

Agee had wanted to buy that block of shares, but he kept thinking about a Gould merger even after Gould had bought it back. In June, Agee called Ylvisaker.

"Bendix is a Gould shareholder," said Agee. "I want to sit down and talk."

Ylvisaker assumed that meant talk about a merger. He knew what to say. His investment banker Martin A. Siegel of Kidder, Peabody and his lawyer Marty Lipton had told him to be explicit. Ylvisaker told Agee he did not want to meet. He did not mince his words.

"You're not too happy about this, are you?" asked Agee.

"No," said Ylvisaker.

A few weeks after Agee's lunch, Salomon Brothers began the broad acquisition study that Agee had asked for. Higgins, back from Europe, looked over Agee's list. By then it had become two lists. There was a long list of companies, including RCA, that Agee thought were undervalued and a shorter list of potential targets: Cessna, an aircraft maker; General Dynamics; Lockheed; McDonnell Douglas; and Martin Marietta. Agee told Salomon Brothers to focus on the short list. Higgins added several ideas of his own and had his staff run some numbers on the balance sheets and income statements of each possible merger. The team quickly eliminated every company on the list but RCA and Martin Marietta. Higgins talked to Agee. Agee asked for a financial feasibility study of the two takeovers. "Emphasize RCA," he said. "Concentrate on financials. I don't want legalities. I just want your input on banking issues."

Higgins set his staff to work on a top secret study of whether Earth (Bendix) could buy either Wind (RCA) or Fire (Martin Marietta). Indeed, they concluded, Earth could quench Wind or Fire. At the end of the month, the study was ready, and on July 27, Agee and McDonald came into New York to take a look. Higgins went over a fat book of tables.

•

•

"You can try RCA," said Higgins, "but it wouldn't be our recommendation." Higgins explained that if press reports of Agee's meeting with Thornton Bradshaw in March were anywhere near accurate, RCA would put up an enormous fight against any takeover attempt by Bill Agee. That might be personally embarrassing for Agee. It might drive up the cost of buying RCA by as much as $1 billion. "And after you buy," said Higgins, "the merger might not be a success. You could sell CIT and Hertz, but they have both been on the block for months, and RCA doesn't seem to be able to get the prices it wants. To make this deal work, you'd have to turn NBC around. No one at RCA seems to know how to do that."

"This study is good," said Agee. "Do this same kind of study on Martin Marietta."

•

On Wednesday, August 18, Agee flew into New York to look at the Salomon study of Fire (Martin Marietta). Agee had said to stress financials, so the Salomon Brothers partners spent an hour and a half of the two-hour meeting talking about the Marietta businesses and how they fit with Bendix.

"This one makes good financial sense," said Higgins. "Their aerospace business is extremely attractive." Marietta makes missiles like the Titan and the Pershing. "Their other businesses—cement and aluminum—are good businesses in decent times, but they are in difficult straits right now. But the crown-jewel defense business is so good that it is carrying the other parts of the company, and Martin Marietta is still making profits. If you could stem the losses in aluminum and hold on in cement, you could be in excellent shape."

Agee said that he was worried about the Marietta aluminum company. Higgins offered to take a look at the financial structure of the merged Bendix and Martin Marietta, assuming that Bendix sold both divisions. Agee told him that he didn't want to think of selling either cement or aluminum just yet.

"Your willingness to hold on to the sick divisions is a plus," said Higgins. "I can't think of anyone else who is likely to bid for the whole operation. I can't tell you that their aerospace technology is state-of-the-art in every respect, but we can get a consultant to look at that."

Higgins's staff had prepared a spread sheet comparing the Bendix balance sheet if Bendix bought Martin Marietta at three different prices. Companies buy each other by buying stock from shareholders, so the price tag for Martin Marietta had to be higher than the stock market trading price. That was now $29 a share. Higgins had run three possible purchase prices through the computer: $35, $40, and $45 a share. Agee said that $38 might be right.

"What about timing?" asked Agee. The stock market had gone wild the day before. The Dow Jones Industrial Average had risen 39 points that Tuesday, the biggest one-day jump in history.

Agee and Higgins talked about the market for a minute.

"Martin Marietta looks good," said Agee. "I'm not ruling out RCA, but keep your eye on Marietta stock. I'm comfortable with Marietta's business fit with Bendix. We may want to do something right after Labor Day."

"What do you mean 'something'?" asked Higgins. "Labor Day is only two and a half weeks away. Are you thinking of making a hostile offer?" There are two ways to buy a company: a "friendly" deal that both companies agree is a good idea and work out together, or a "hostile" one that the target company opposes and does what it can to stop.

"I'm thinking of making an offer," said Agee. "It may have to be hostile. I'll let you know when I decide."

"Wait a minute," said Higgins. "You can't just make a hostile offer. You have got to think about strategy. You have to think about how Marietta is going to react."

"We are going to consider all of our options with regard to Martin Marietta," said Agee. "We have not ruled out an unfriendly offer. Our clear preference is to keep discussions friendly."

"If you make an unsolicited offer, it might not be friendly," said Higgins. "There are a hundred things Marietta might do. They might try to sell off the crown jewels." That winter, Whittaker Corporation, a medical and chemical products company, had tried to buy Brunswick, a diversified maker of leisure products and medical supplies. What Whittaker had really wanted was Brunswick's Sherwood medical division, and Brunswick had sold that to American Home Products before Whittaker could buy the whole of Brunswick. "Marietta might try a personal attack. I don't know what will hapen. I repeat: there are a hundred things that Marietta could do."

"I'll be ready," said Agee.

"You know, Bill, bidding for Martin Marietta might draw in a bidder for Bendix," said Higgins. "Bendix is an attractive target. You've got some good businesses and you've got that cash. You're probably on everyone's hit list. If someone wants you without Martin Marietta, they might try to buy you as soon as you surface as a bidder for Martin Marietta."

Higgins and his partner Ira Harris, the famous dealmaker who heads the Salomon Chicago office, talked over with Agee just who might come out of the woodwork with a bid for Bendix—and what to do about it. Bendix would be in a stronger defensive position against a raid if it had "shark repellents" in its corporate charter, provisions that made it procedurally difficult to take over. Some companies have rules that say a merger has to be approved by

two-thirds of the shareholders, and there are other varia-
tions. Shark repellents have to be approved by the stockholders—rather than just be endorsed by the directors—and
they are often difficult to get.

"Look, Bill," said Higgins, "if you want to think about
bidding for Martin Marietta around Labor Day, you've got
to put together a team. You've got to have a sophisticated
legal counsel." The laws about buying companies are complicated. A minor legal gaffe can mean the difference between winning or losing a takeover battle. "We've got to
have a bidding strategy. We've got to sit down and talk."

"We've got a lawyer," said Agee. "I haven't been completely open with you, but I've had Fried, Frank working
for me for quite a while. We're using Arthur Fleischer."
Fleischer was one of the leading takeover lawyers in the
country. He had joined the Bendix team in March to negotiate the RCA standstill. "We are actually quite a bit more
organized than we told you. Bendix has been looking at this
for quite some time, and we're ready to go. It's just a question of deciding whether or not to pull the trigger."

"The Washington effort is organized and ready to
move," said McDonald. By now Bendix had three professional lobbyists on its team.

"Great," said Higgins. "Let's have a meeting."

"We'll have a meeting when I decide," said Agee. "We
don't need to do that now."

"We need a meeting," said Higgins. "We need to talk
about how the legal and banking issues work together."

"We love you guys and respect your work," said Agee.
"But we really want you to concentrate just on finance. I
just want your assessment of value."

"At Bendix, we want to know the options individually
from our advisors to understand our full range of options,"
said McDonald. "We don't like precooked compromises
thrashed out between our lawyers and investment bankers

without our participation. We want a strategic opinion from each firm so that Bendix management can make the final decisions."

"Look, Bill," said Higgins. "Once we make an offer, we can't predict exactly what will happen, but you can expect not only personal assaults, but lots of rough stuff like lashback tenders. We saw that twice this year."

"I remember that," said Agee.

In the spring of 1982, the American General financial company bid for the NLT insurance company. NLT responded by bidding back for American General. American General then upped its price and NLT agreed to merge. At the beginning of June, the Cities Service oil company heard a rumor that little Mesa Petroleum was going to make a bid. Citgo launched a preemptive bid for Mesa; days later, Mesa made its offer for Citgo. Mesa wasn't able to line up enough credit to pay for more than 15 percent of the Citgo stock, and Citgo convinced Gulf Oil to make a much better offer than Mesa's. Gulf later backed down and Occidental Petroleum bought Citgo at the end of the summer.

If all things are equal legally, the countertender won't work, since the first company to bid will be the first to be able to take control. But things aren't always equal legally. Some states have laws that force a raider to wait before he can take control. Some companies can't be bought without local or federal approval. Bendix, for example, needed clearance from the Federal Communications Commission before it could buy RCA.

"Countertenders are rare," said Higgins. "Those that have been tried haven't worked. But in this case there are important differences in the state laws." Agee had told Salomon Brothers not to consult a lawyer for the acquisitions study, but Higgins had asked his outside takeover attorney a couple of questions on a no-names basis all the same.

"I do not believe that Marietta is going to tender for

us," said McDonald. "No board that I sit on would consider making a countertender with this kind of unfavorable economics. It would be an irresponsible corporate act."

"It may be irresponsible," said Higgins. "It isn't likely, but it has happened."

"Jay," said McDonald. "Our tender will be the result of lengthy and serious acquisition studies. Theirs would be a knee-jerk reaction to save their jobs. That won't work."

"If they're out there with a bid for us at the right price, $80, $85 a share," said Agee, "maybe we should go out and get 'em."

Everyone laughed.

"Does that mean you would consider letting someone else buy the company?" asked Harris. "Is Bendix for sale?"

"Absolutely," said Agee. "I'm a manager. I'll consider a sale at the right price. But the merger is the first priority. I want to buy Martin Marietta."

"Okay," said Higgins. "A hostile tender is going to mean a lot of negative publicity. Look what happened to you with RCA. Why don't you try to make a friendly approach. Why don't you call them and talk first?"

"We tried to contact Marietta," said Agee. "Pete Peterson called them a year ago. You don't need to worry about that."

"That was a year ago," said Higgins. "Maybe things have changed."

"Look, Jay," said Agee. "I've been thinking about this a great deal, and I've been discussing it with a lot of people. I think calling before we bid will only give them time to prepare against me. I'm going to make an offer and then try to negotiate."

"Marietta may make a personal attack," said Higgins. "You should be prepared for extra voltage because of your reputation in the business community. You know what happened when you bought that RCA stock."

"I'm not worried about that," said Agee. "I've already had everything dug up about me that possibly can be." Agee laughed. "I even had to be cleared by the FBI for a presidential commission I'm on."

Agee looked at his watch. "I've got a lunch," he said. "I like your suggestion about getting an outside specialist to look at the aerospace business. Why don't you try to set something up. We can take a look at technology. We will revisit this whole topic within the next week or two for a go-no-go decision no later than just after Labor Day."

•

The price of the stocks of the defense contracting companies started to move up rapidly on Thursday, August 19. Friday morning, Agee called Bill Ylvisaker at Gould to say that he wanted to sell his Gould block back to Gould. Ylvisaker agreed and the two decided to negotiate a price on Monday. Agee scheduled a board meeting for the next Tuesday to decide on a bid for Martin Marietta. He called Jack Fontaine at Hughes Hubbard and Reed. He told Fontaine to draft the documents for a tender offer. Before Agee could call Jay Higgins at Salomon Brothers, Higgins called Agee.

"The consultant I talked to can't do the Marietta study because of a conflict," said Higgins. "Do you want me to try a large firm like Booz Allen or McKinsey?"

"No," said Agee. "That might cause a leak. Since our people have already done an extensive study, that won't be necessary. I have called a board meeting. Get ready for a go-no-go on Tuesday."

"Okay," said Higgins. "Can we have a meeting with all the advisers before that?"

"I'll tell Art to make sure that he gets together with you so you'll know we've done our homework," said Agee.

The Hughes Hubbard and Fried, Frank lawyers spent

the weekend drafting the reams of legal papers that Bendix needed to launch the raid. First there were the suits. A standard delaying tactic for a target company is to try to convince a local judge to enforce a rigorous state takeover law. The standard raider response is to ask a federal judge to declare the state law unconstitutional before the target gets to the state court. Then there is the "offer to purchase" that explains the terms of the bid. The text is basically legal boilerplate, but there are a couple of key sections that have to be delicately written. Bendix had to tell Martin Marietta shareholders where it was going to get the money to buy their stock and what it would do with the company after it bought. The Marietta lawyers would try to poke holes in the text of the offer; the smallest misstatement or omission would be labeled an attempt to mislead shareholders—and Marietta would sue to block the bid until those facts were set straight. At best that suit was a stalling tactic, since Bendix could always amend the offer, but in the merger game a twenty-four-hour delay could mean the difference between winning and losing. Bendix didn't want to give Martin Marietta an opportunity to gain precious time.

Another legal problem was antitrust. The Justice Department would look at the proposed takeover to see if it violated the Clayton Act. Bendix had to submit information on its businesses; so did Martin Marietta. Justice looked at the material; the department had fifteen days to figure out if the merger was legal. If Justice needed more time, it would ask for a ten-day extension. Bendix couldn't buy until it got the government green light. Martin Marietta would probably sue Bendix on the grounds that a Bendix–Martin Marietta merger did violate the antitrust laws. If the case was plausible, Marietta might be able to convince a court to delay the bid. The Bendix lawyers were worried that Justice would want an extension and Marietta would manage to block the bid. Bendix had just been given preliminary approval to bid for missile contracts, and it already did subcontracting for Martin Marietta. Bendix might be considered by Justice a potential Martin Marietta competitor.

In the course of putting together the papers, the lawyers discovered that there was a difference between the Maryland and Delaware corporate laws. Martin Marietta was a Maryland corporation. After Bendix bought the majority of Marietta shares, Bendix would have to call a special shareholder meeting to elect a new board of directors, and Bendix would have to wait a minimum of ten days to do that. Bendix was a Delaware corporation. If Martin Marietta made a counterbid for Bendix and bought the majority of the Bendix shares, Marietta could change the Bendix board of directors just by writing a letter. Marietta wouldn't have to wait. That legal nicety meant that if Marietta decided to bid back for Bendix, Marietta could control Bendix before Bendix could control Marietta. Still, Marietta's making a counterbid meant waiving what looked like its strongest legal defense: Martin Marietta couldn't claim that a Bendix–Martin Marietta merger violated the antitrust laws but that a Martin Marietta–Bendix one didn't.

Agee spent most of the day Monday going over documents with the lawyers. The Bendix public relations staff put together a list of questions and answers about the raid on "Georgia." Tuesday morning, Agee held a staff meeting at the Hughes Hubbard offices for all of the advisers. He introduced the Bendix team. "McDonald will be the point man. Rowny will help him." (Michael Rowny, a Bendix vice-president in strategic planning.) "Barron will handle the legal work." (Harold Barron, the Bendix general counsel.) "Kayser will run the numbers." (Donald Kayser, the chief financial officer.)

Then Agee named the chief outside advisers: Fleischer,

Fontaine, Higgins, and Tanner. "I'm proud to have you all on board," he said. "There's a lot of work to do on this and I sure hope it will be worth it. We are going to win.

"We are undertaking a major, possibly historic, effort to merge two great companies into an even greater one. It fulfills a business strategy we have been implementing for over two years. I hope the effort will be friendly, because it makes such great economic sense. If it isn't friendly, we will need to be ready to push ahead anyway, because it is right."

•

Tuesday afternoon, the Bendix board of directors met at the Bendix International headquarters at the General Motors Building in midtown Manhattan. Just before the session began, Higgins and Tanner pulled Agee aside for a last minute conference. Higgins took out the spread sheet on pricing that his staff had put together comparing bids of $35, $40, and $45 a share.

"Don't even think about starting this if you aren't willing to pay a good price," said Higgins. "The market is going crazy. Martin Marietta closed yesterday at $33, up from the last couple of days. Don't bid $35. Don't bid $40."

Agee cut Higgins off. "Don't worry," he said. "Everything is under control."

"Bill, the defense stocks are rolling," said Higgins. "Last week, you were talking about $38. Marietta and the market will laugh at you if you start at anything below $40."

"I'm going to bid $43," said Agee. Higgins had been ready to suggest $45. Agee walked into the boardroom.

The directors were already sitting around the long, rectangular table. Among them: McDonald; Jack Fontaine from Hughes Hubbard; William Tavoulareas, president of Mobil; Donald Rumsfeld, president of G.D. Searle; and Coy Ek-

lund, president of The Equitable Life Assurance Society.
Agee said that he had called them together to consider bidding for Martin Marietta. When he started to hand out a fat
information booklet on Martin Marietta that the Bendix staff
had put together, Eklund stood up. Equitable owned a large
block of Martin Marietta. Equitable would make a big profit
if Bendix bid. Eklund had a conflict of interests; he couldn't
help Bendix make a decision.

After Eklund left, Agee talked about Martin Marietta.
He described the Marietta businesses. He talked about how
Marietta fit with Bendix. The combined company would
have more than half of its sales in aerospace; a quarter of
the sales would be automotive, a tenth would be industrial,
another tenth in primary materials.

Agee asked Gutfreund to come into the boardroom;
Gutfreund hadn't worked on the merger study, but he was
chairman of Salomon Brothers. Gutfreund talked for a few
minutes about the merger of Salomon Brothers with Phibro
the year before. Then Gutfreund called Higgins and Tanner
in.

Higgins explained that Bendix would offer to buy Martin Marietta half in cash and half in stock. That way Bendix
would not load up the balance sheet with debt, since it
wouldn't have to borrow so much to buy. Tanner said that
if Bendix did buy Martin Marietta half cash/half stock,
Bendix wouldn't lose its fine credit rating. Then Higgins
answered some questions about strategy.

"A number of congressmen are looking at front-loaded
offers very carefully," said McDonald. A common way to
try to buy a company is to pay a high cash premium for
the controlling shares of a target company and then force
the rest of its shareholders to sell out for a package of securities worth much less. Those offers are called front
loaded; many businessmen and politicians think they are
coercive.

"Front-loaded offers are controversial," said Higgins. "We aren't recommending one. The Bendix offer is going to be highly visible. We want to be safe."

"Do you think that someone else is going to come in and bid for Marietta?" asked one of the directors.

"No," said Higgins. "Not in this economy. If you are willing to hold on to the aluminum and cement divisions of Marietta until the recession turns, you will have a competitive leg up in the bidding. We can't see Martin Marietta selling off just its aerospace business—the crown jewels— because that *is* Martin Marietta. Bendix will be able to buy Marietta for the price of its aerospace division."

"There are companies that might be potential white knights for Martin Marietta," said Agee. "United Technologies, Allied, GTE."

"Do you think that Marietta will countertender?" asked a director.

"It's conceivable, but unlikely in Salomon Brothers' opinion," said Higgins. "We know that Martin Marietta doesn't have the resources to buy all of Bendix. They can tender for a big hunk of us, but if they do they will throw away the antitrust defense and then we can start negotiating over terms. We've seen several of these lash-back tenders recently, and it might happen. If it does, we'll deal with it then. As I said to Bill earlier, once this thing starts, I can't predict what will happen, but it ultimately will be one of three things: we buy Marietta; a white knight buys our block and all of the rest of Marietta at a premium over our bid; or there's some sort of peace treaty which will involve our selling our block back to Martin Marietta at a profit. Each way we win if we keep our eye on the ball."

A Hughes Hubbard lawyer made a presentation on the potential antitrust problem. Then the directors asked Agee a few final questions.

"The missile business is very attractive," he said.

"Marietta's aerospace sales have grown very quickly. I'm not sure that I want to be in either aluminum or cement for the long haul."

"Does that mean you are thinking of selling those divisions?" asked a director.

"I don't know," said Agee. "I don't know enough about them. I haven't seen the books. I can tell you that I don't plan to sell them now. Those businesses are very depressed. Now is certainly not the time to sell."

Agee called for a vote on the bid. "The objective that I have in mind in this situation is to maximize shareholder value," said Agee. "We should not allow ourselves to be surprised to see tender, white knights, black knights, and other tactics that could well start happening."

The directors voted to make the offer.

DON'T GIVE UP
THE SHIP

2 Tom Pownall looks purposeful. He is just under six feet tall, with wiry gray hair and a jutting chin. His steel blue eyes spark when he is angry and dance when he smiles. He smokes heavily and grinds his jaw as he works. He tells jokes well and has an earnestness that wins devotion. When he can, he hunts—ducks to elephants; when he can't, he plays golf.

Pownall is not an "armchair" executive; he thinks of himself as just another member of the team, and he likes to be right in the middle of the action. Martin Marietta recruited Tom Pownall in 1963 as a vice-president for marketing. Selling defense systems to the Pentagon really means strategic planning, and Pownall had a flair for that. He had been on the job at the aerospace company for five years when, at eleven o'clock one morning, his boss, J. Donald Rauth, president of Martin Marietta Aerospace, called him from Washington.

"Can you get down here for lunch with Bunker and me?" asked Rauth.

George Bunker was chairman of the company, but Pownall had a heavy schedule that afternoon. His office was near Baltimore. He didn't want to waste the time driving to Washington and back. "It's sort of inconvenient," he said. "I'm busy today."

"It's important," said Rauth. "Get down here regardless of how busy you are."

"Certainly," said Pownall. "I'll be there." Pownall couldn't imagine what was wrong, but it sounded serious. Pownall drove to Washington. He met with Bunker and Rauth. They chatted. Bunker seemed to be in a good mood. So did Rauth. But Pownall was apprehensive.

"Don's going out to run the aluminum company," said Bunker. Martin Marietta had just bought control of Harvey Aluminum. "How would you like to run aerospace?"

It took Pownall a minute to answer. He said yes. Two years later in 1970, he became a Martin Marietta director. In 1977, he became president of the entire company. Four months before Agee called, Pownall had been made chief executive officer at age sixty; he would be elected chairman in January 1983, when Donald Rauth retired.

As president of the aerospace division, Tom Pownall had been the point man on Martin Marietta's proudest project: the Viking spacecraft. The Marietta-made Mars explorer is still the most sophisticated aerospace project ever completed, and by the time it touched down on Mars in 1976, Pownall felt as if he had been in the control room for years. Martin Marietta also put astronauts into orbit; it developed a laser-eyed shell called the Copperhead; it designed and produces the Titan, the Pershing, and the MX missiles. Martin Marietta headed the Pentagon's list of research and development contractors in 1981; it was also America's fourth-largest cement maker, its sixth-largest aluminum producer, and a major supplier of specialty chemicals, dyestuffs, and aggregates—the crushed stone, sand, and gravel used in building roads. Until Bill Agee launched his bid, Martin Marietta was hardly a household name. It didn't want to be.

●

Glenn Luther Martin built his first airplane in 1909, just six years after the Wright Brothers flew at Kitty Hawk. For half a century the Martin Company led the way in airplane innovation: Martin built the first all-metal plane and the first night-mail plane. Martin built the first trans-Pacific seaplane, the *China Clipper,* for the fledgling Pan American Airways. Martin built more than 10,000 planes for the Air Force during the Second World War, mostly the famous B-26 Martin Marauder attack plane.

In October 1961, the Glenn L. Martin Company merged with the American-Marietta Company, a diversified chemical company that made auto paints, kitchen mops, and cement. At the time, the merger was one of the largest in corporate history. The new Martin Marietta Corporation ranked 33 on the Fortune 500 list of industrial companies. Martin Marietta quickly sold off the Marietta consumer divisions and used the cash to buy control of Harvey Aluminum.

Martin Marietta has always focused on internal growth. Although aerospace is not a capital-intensive industry—the government owns the plants and leases them to contractors—Marietta's other businesses are. During the seventies, J. Donald Rauth, Marietta's chairman, had set the company on an intense capital-spending program. Marietta built a huge new plant in Davenport, Iowa, that produces more cement than the one it replaced—but with only half the energy. It built another giant cement plant outside Salt Lake City, where cement demand outstrips supply. Marietta expanded capacity at its Kentucky aluminum rolling mill by 50 percent. It expanded its Goldendale, Washington, aluminum reduction plant by 75 percent. At the same time,

Martin Marietta built new chemical plants. It upgraded its aggregate processing centers. It plowed dollars into aerospace research. From 1977 to 1982, capital spending totaled almost $1.7 billion. "It is the long term that commands our concentrated attention," explained Rauth. "We build confidently for that. In most of our businesses, we invest with the expectation that our plants will produce favorable returns for long periods—two to three decades or longer."

By the late seventies, Martin Marietta had reached the limits of growth in aerospace, aluminum, and cement. The top executives started to think about getting into new industries and made plans for a major acquisition. In the summer of 1981, Charles Leithauser, the chief financial officer, hired Kidder, Peabody & Company, a New York investment banking firm, to help him look. He put together a hit list.

Bendix was on it. Bendix aerospace was a defense subcontractor whose businesses seemed to mesh well with Martin Marietta's own systems work. The Bendix automotive division was profitable, and it ran on a different cycle than the Martin Marietta divisions. The Bendix machine tools business seemed distinctly grubby. But Leithauser didn't know much about it. He moved Bendix to the hold list.

Then, at the end of 1981, the economy began to sour. Marietta aluminum sales slumped. Cement and chemical sales dropped. Cash flow was pinched. All acquisitions plans were put on the back burner.

Other companies were suffering too, and some of them became targets. Dupont, Seagram's, and Mobil battled over Conoco. U.S. Steel bought Marathon Oil. Rauth began to worry that Martin Marietta might also be an attractive target. At the beginning of September 1981, Rauth put together a team to deal with a crisis: Rauth, Pownall, Calvin,

Leithauser, Menaker, and the company's secretary, Mary Jane LaBarge. At the end of the month, Rauth called the team into his redwood-beamed and brick lounge to talk about takeover defenses. Martin Marietta had made almost no formal preparations. Rauth thought that it was time to do that.

About the same time, Kidder, Peabody, the investment bankers who had been looking at acquisition candidates for Martin Marietta and who were also on the defense for Gould, began to nag Leithauser about strengthening the company's own defenses against attack. Leithauser had told the bankers to go ahead with some preliminary analysis at the end of the summer. Then they were invited to make a formal presentation to the board in October. Kidder put together a slide show, and at the end of the month, Marty Siegel flew down to Washington to give the presentation.

First Siegel explained just what it was that the company was worried about: what he termed an "unnegotiated" takeover attempt. "Basically you are dealing with someone who takes a look at the public information on the company—the annual report, news clippings, stock analysts' reports—and decides what *your* company is worth to *his* stockholders. Then he tries to put pressure on your shareholders to sell out by making a tender offer to pay cash for their stock. Legally he can purchase the company after fifteen business days. That's not much time for anyone to make an informed judgment about price. Obviously if you are going to face this problem, it is better to prepare before the bid than after it.

"And you should be concerned about this. Martin Marietta is a classic takeover target," explained Siegel. "There are probably a number of companies looking at you. Let's review why."

The lights dimmed and Siegel snapped on the first slide. "There are four kinds of reasons that a company is attractive or vulnerable. First: business. Martin Marietta is a diversified company with a leading position in each of its industries. That means you are attractive to lots of different kinds of companies. You are decentralized. That means that it is easy for an aggressor to sell off the parts of the company that he doesn't want and use the proceeds to help pay for the parts that he does."

Siegel flashed to the second slide. "Second: financials. Martin Marietta has generated a very high return on assets. You don't have much debt. Any aggressor can use your debt capacity to borrow to buy you. You're at the low point in your earnings cycle and on top of that you're well into a capital-spending program which will increase future earnings." Siegel snapped to the third slide. "Third: stock price. It's depressed. You're a good value. This is the time to make a bid." Siegel moved on to slide four. "Ownership. Martin Marietta is owned mostly by big investors like banks and pension funds. Those institutions will sell quickly whenever they can make a profit. If someone makes a bid for you, he will get most of your stock overnight."

Then Siegel ticked off some suggestions for getting ready for a raid. "You need to have an ongoing evaluation of how much the company is worth. That way you can decide quickly whether an offer is acceptable or not. You don't want to be surprised, so you should watch for approaches to directors. If any of you gets a call, you should report it to Don Rauth. You should start a stock watch to detect if anyone is accumulating a big cache of your shares. You have to talk to investors about the company, because the more people know, the higher is the price of the stock. You have to update your banking relationships so that you can borrow money quickly during a crisis. Think about golden parachute employment contracts that guarantee salaries after a change in control. You have to hold on to your key people through a crisis. Otherwise you might 'win' the battle and have no one left to run the company—the only people who will call more than stock traders during a takeover fight are corporate recruiters. And you should start thinking about amending the corporate charter with shark repellents to make it harder for a raider to take control of the company quickly.

"The most important thing is to remember that you can never be too explicit when a raider calls. You want to make yourself perfectly clear about your lack of interest or he will hear what he wants to hear. The more profane you are the better. Sometimes you can deflate them by saying *no* in no uncertain terms. People who make these kinds of approaches tend to have big egos." Siegel had given the same advice to Gould. It had worked.

The directors told Rauth and Pownall to take a closer look at each of the things that Siegel had suggested. Menaker drafted the golden parachute contracts and hired the New York law firm Dewey, Ballantine, Bushby, Palmer & Wood to help prepare antitrust defenses. Menaker signed on Morrow & Company, an experienced proxy solicitor. Leithauser put Kidder, Peabody on defense retainer and assigned several members of his financial staff to help Kidder keep tabs on just how much Martin Marietta was worth. Rauth appointed an "ad hoc" committee of four outside directors to handle a crisis, and he formalized the internal strike team that he had appointed the month before.

For months, there was not even a rumor of a bidder. The directors never got around to giving golden parachutes to their key employees or adopting shark repellents. In March 1982, an alarm bell sounded. After the RCA battle with Bendix, *Newsweek* magazine published a Bendix-watcher's best guess at the Bendix hit list. Martin Marietta was on it.

Rauth called the strike team into his office. "You can't believe what you read in a newsmagazine," he said, "but we ought to be prepared."

Leithauser called his sources in the investment community and discovered that the Bendix rumor was running rampant on Wall Street. He bought 100 shares of Bendix stock so that Martin Marietta would be able to sue Bendix as a shareholder if that became necessary. Menaker asked the legal staff to figure out if there were any antitrust overlaps between Bendix and Martin Marietta that could be used as a defense. Rauth read the *Newsweek* article to the directors at the March board meeting.

Nothing happened. The rumor died down and disappeared. Leithauser sold his Bendix stock. Menaker put the Bendix antitrust study back into the file cabinet. In April, Leithauser noticed that Salomon Brothers was amassing a cache of Martin Marietta stock. The stock watch showed that the brokerage house bought thousands of shares every day. Salomon seemed to be the only buyer. Leithauser didn't like that. He called Siegel.

"Do you think that Salomon Brothers is fronting for a raider?" he asked. "Can you call someone there and find out?"

"They might be," said Siegel. "You should make the call, not me. If I called it would raise eyebrows."

Later that month one of the Marietta investor relations staffers called a source at Salomon Brothers. All that the source would say was that the cache was "for investment purposes only."

Through June and July, Leithauser and Siegel watched the Salomon Brothers holding of Martin Marietta grow to 3, 4, 4½ percent. At the end of July, it leveled just below 5 percent. Whoever was buying the stock wanted to keep his name a secret.

In the middle of August, only three weeks after Salomon Brothers' appetite for Martin Marietta was suddenly sated, the rumor that Bendix was after Marietta resurfaced. By Wednesday August 18, it had become so widespread that one professional called a Martin Marietta assistant treasurer named Wayne Shaner to find out if it were true. "I have it from a reliable source that Bendix is about to make a pass at Martin Marietta," said the trader.

Shaner passed the word back to his boss Robert Powell, Martin Marietta's treasurer. Powell called Siegel.

"Well, really, we are worried about whoever owns that Salomon Brothers stock," said Siegel. "Salomon Brothers doesn't normally work for Agee. Lehman Brothers does. Agee is looking at another Kidder client." Siegel meant Gould. "I know that Agee called the CEO of this other client to talk about a merger last June. As far as I know, Agee hasn't given up on my other client. You never know for sure though."

Powell called Leithauser, who was on business in San Francisco. Powell called Pownall, who was inspecting an aerospace plant in Orlando. Pownall told Powell to talk to Rauth.

"Assume that the rumor is reliable unless proven otherwise," said Rauth.

Leithauser in California had not been terribly worried when he heard that the Bendix rumor had resurfaced. He had heard it before and nothing had happened. Leithauser called Siegel. Siegel repeated what he had told Powell. The next day, Leithauser got a call from an investment banker he didn't know. The banker told Leithauser that he had heard the Bendix rumor and checked it out. One of the banker's staffers had called a junior man on the Bendix corporate planning team. The Bendix man had sidestepped the question of a Marietta raid, but he had admitted that the department had been working pretty hard. To Leithauser it was confirmation of what Siegel had told him.

Bendix must be working pretty hard for a raid on Siegel's *other* client.

Powell was scheduled to take his son college-visiting the next week. Friday afternoon, he called Leithauser again.

"You go ahead on vacation," said Leithauser. "I'll take over responsibility for this."

•

Monday morning, Siegel got a call from Bill Ylvisaker, chairman of Gould. Ylvisaker said that Agee wanted to negotiate selling back his Gould block. Siegel gave him a few pointers on the transaction. Then Siegel called Leithauser.

"Agee is selling back the block he owns of the other client's stock," said Siegel. "He isn't going after that other client that I told you about last week. He may be doing some house cleaning. He may be getting rid of the blocks of stock he owns to finance a bid. He may be getting ready to bid for you. Be prepared for a call."

Bill Agee didn't call Monday. He didn't call Tuesday. On Wednesday, Menaker decided to brief Larry Adams on takeover defense. Rauth had added Adams to the strike team when Adams was named chief operating officer in May, but there had never been any urgency about filling him in on how to fight a takeover attempt. At eight thirty that morning, Menaker outlined the defenses. At nine o'clock, Bill Agee finally called.

The investment bankers and lawyers began to arrive in Bethesda early Wednesday afternoon. Robert Fullem, the senior Dewey, Ballantine corporate partner advising Marietta, was on vacation in Martha's Vineyard and could not catch a plane to New York until Thursday afternoon. Siegel was in Memphis on business, and the Marietta jet could not get him back to Washington until the middle of the afternoon. Fullem's partner, Leonard P. Larrabee, Jr., and several other Dewey lawyers came down about one o'clock. Richard Katcher, a partner of Marty Lipton, who had been hired by Kidder, Peabody, was with them. So were Siegel's partners, Doug Brown and Peter Wood. Leithauser settled the bankers in the empty office between Pownall's and Adams's. The room was scheduled to be divided into two executive sitting rooms, but construction could be postponed. Brown immediately ordered two additional phone lines. The office became the war room.

As soon as Siegel arrived at four, Pownall, Leithauser, Menaker, Siegel, Katcher, and Larrabee sat down at the round table in Pownall's office to discuss what was happening and what Marietta could do. By law Bendix had to wait fifteen business days before it could buy any stock; for the first ten calendar days of that waiting period, Bendix had to collect promises to sell—tenders—from Marietta shareholders. Tenders are put into a "proration" pool. Anyone who tendered could change his mind up until the "withdrawal" date, the fifteenth day of the waiting period, but a shareholder who tendered during those first ten days and didn't withdraw was guaranteed of getting some cash. Bendix had to buy the same percentage of the stock that each shareholder brought into the pool. If Bendix got twice as many shares as it had asked for, it would buy half of everyone's stock.

The Martin Marietta board had to make a recommendation to shareholders on whether or not to sell to Bendix. Martin Marietta was 60 percent owned by institutions, and institutions would tender no matter what management said; institutions always did whatever they could to make a quick profit on the portfolio. Any recommendations would be almost meaningless.

Siegel ticked off a list of alternatives that Martin Marietta had if it decided that the Bendix price of $43 a share was too low.

- Martin Marietta could go to court and try to get a judge to stop Bendix from buying. The standard claim was that the raider had somehow misled investors by leaving key information out of the documents that it mailed to shareholders. Another common ploy was to claim that the merger would create antitrust problems.
- Martin Marietta could make a "defensive" acquisition buying either a company that competed with Bendix or one that it knew Bendix wasn't interested in.
- There were a raft of "scorched earth" defenses. Martin Marietta could pay out a huge dividend to get cash to the shareholders before Bendix bought. Martin Marietta could issue more stock to make it harder for Bendix to buy a majority of the shares. Martin Marietta could buy back some of its own stock at a higher price than Bendix was offering. It could sell off the aerospace crown jewel at a higher price than Bendix was paying for them.
- Martin Marietta could fully liquidate itself.
- Martin Marietta could sell itself to a "white knight" bidder who was willing to pay a higher price and might be a better business fit.

"That's just the standard list of defenses," said Siegel. "I'm not putting any faith in any of them. But there's another defense that looks interesting to me: the countertender."

Siegel explained that twice in the past six months target companies had tried to defend themselves by bidding for the raider. It hadn't worked; neither had stayed independent. NLT had merged with its raider, American General, at a higher price. Cities Service was eventually bought by Occidental Petroleum. "I haven't had a chance to take a really close look at Bendix," said Siegel, "but it seems to me that this is a unique situation and that a countertender might be an effective way to keep your independence. Bendix is about the same size as Martin Marietta. Your bank credit is good. You should be able to get financing."

Pownall wasn't sure about that. He didn't think that Marietta could possibly line up the six or seven hundred million in cash that it would need to bid for Bendix.

"Bendix is vulnerable," continued Siegel. "Bendix has $500 million in cash that you can use to pay off your debt after you buy the company."

"If we go down that road, can we change our mind later on?" asked Pownall.

"No," said Siegel. "If you make a countertender, you have to be ready to carry out the threat or it won't work."

"Take a look at it," said Pownall. "I'm not committing myself yet."

•

Thursday morning the directors came in for their briefing. Frank Bradley, president of Halco Mining, an aluminum company based in Pittsburgh, flew in from his vacation home in San Diego. Eugene Zuckert, a Washington attorney and former air force secretary, chartered a plane from Maine that morning. Griffin Bell, the attorney general under Jimmy Carter, interrupted his vacation in Sea Island, Georgia. John J. Byrne, chairman of Geico insurance, headquartered just down the road from Marietta, drove over for the morning.

"I just got a call from Bob Strauss this morning," said Bell. Strauss had run the Carter campaign and was now a Washington lawyer. "He told me he'd been employed by Bendix to assist them in the acquisition of Martin Marietta and that if there was anything he could do to answer my questions, he was standing by. I figure that was an attempt to establish what they call in intelligence a 'back channel.' "

The directors began to talk about Bendix and Bill Agee. No one mentioned Agee's highly publicized personal life. They understood that Tom Pownall would never bring it up and that the corporation would not attack it. But the directors were concerned about Agee as a businessman and Bendix as a company. Agee was known as a financial man not a systems man. Bendix was a parts company not a prime contractor. Bendix seemed to court publicity. And the price that Bendix was offering was less than the stock market high of a year ago. That seemed terribly low.

Pownall began the meeting by telling the tale of the Agee phone call and the hand-delivered letter. Then he introduced each of the New York experts. "The advisers are going to explain what they plan to do for us over the weekend," said Pownall. "If you don't like one of their suggestions, say so. We won't waste time exploring it."

While Pownall did the introductions, Jack Byrne looked down at his tie. He loosened the knot and slid it off his neck. He scribbled a note on the yellow tablet in front of him. Byrne wrapped the tie in the paper and passed it around the table. When Pownall sat down, Zuckert handed him the package. Pownall unwrapped it. He read the message:

> This tie was given to me when I faced a similar situation at Geico. I wore it every day until the crisis was over. It might be useful to you in this crisis. I therefore tender it to you.
>
> P.S. I need a tie. Will you pass yours down?

Pownall looked at the tie. It was red. It was covered with white naval pennants: "Don't Give Up the Ship." Pownall took off his own tie and put on Byrne's. He passed his tie around the table to Byrne with a note. "I won't wear another tie until this is over."

•

•

The Dewey, Ballantine antitrust lawyer gave a quick review of the antitrust overlaps between Bendix and Marietta. They were almost nonexistent. Some of the directors wondered why the company was wasting time investigating them.

"This is a pretty weak defense," said Menaker.

Siegel ticked off the same list of options that he had given Pownall the night before. "I think that the counter-tender might be a good strategy," he said.

After the meeting, Jack Byrne pulled Tom Pownall aside. Byrne had been so impressed with an editorial that Agee had written for the *New York Times* on "How Companies Should Use Their Cash" that he had xeroxed it for top Geico executives. By bidding for Martin Marietta, Agee wasn't doing what he had written about, but Byrne had an open mind. "This guy may be pretty smart," said Byrne. "Maybe you should call him."

Pownall said he'd talk to the advisers about it.

"Agee may be smart," said Zuckert, "but he is not even fit to carry Tom's bags in aerospace."

The investment bankers settled down in the war room to work. Kidder had updated its study on Martin Marietta value only that May, but the numbers had to be revised again. Leithauser started to help the bankers put together the information, and he got out the study that he had done on Bendix the year before. Kidder would have to update that as well.

Jack Byrne stuck his head into the Kidder war room. Geico had an extensive investment library.

"By coincidence, my investment department just asked me to approve buying some Bendix stock," said Byrne. "They've got a study on Bendix and a lot of information in the files. You're welcome to use that or anything else in our library."

The lawyers began to look through their books for legal

defenses or delaying tactics. Menaker's staff had already started to update their antitrust study. They finished that and then moved on to studying the laws that might affect a countertender. They discovered the same difference between the state statutes that the Bendix lawyers had discovered over the weekend.

As soon as the teams began to study Bendix, they realized that there was an important question that no one seemed to be able to answer. Almost a quarter of the Bendix stock was held in an employee profit-sharing plan called the Salaried Employee Saving and Stock Ownership Plan (SESSOP). The plan rules weren't in the Martin Marietta or Geico or Kidder files. The lawyers didn't know whether, if Martin Marietta made an offer, Bendix employees could tender their shares or if someone could tender for them and who that might be. Kidder did locate a copy of the Bendix self-tender made the year before. The employees had been able to sell their stock then. It wasn't clear that that would be the case this time.

Since Wednesday afternoon, the Martin Marietta treasury department had been busy putting together a financing package. Leithauser wanted to be ready to pay for a defensive acquisition or a bid for Bendix. The company already had a $300 million credit line from a group of banks, but even so it was going to be a herculean effort to line up the rest. Powell and his staff worked out the basic terms of an extension of the credit line to $900 million with a man from the Bank of America on Friday. On Sunday afternoon, they met with loan officers from thirteen Martin Marietta banks in a conference room at Dewey, Ballantine in New York.

While Powell met with the bankers to polish up the loan agreement, the rest of the team met at Dewey to run through the legal papers one last time. Siegel, Brown, and Wood stopped by to see how things were coming.

"Should I call Agee?" asked Pownall. The Marietta

·

·

strike team had talked through the idea for several hours the night before.

"I think it makes sense," said Menaker. "He might not be responsive, but there's a chance that he will withdraw if he knows how deadly serious this is about to become."

"I'm endorsing the idea," said Fullem, of Dewey, Ballantine.

Katcher, of Wachtell, Lipton, was dubious. Takeover battles were his speciality. "Any conversation that you have with Agee might make its way to the press," he explained. "If the traders hear that you are talking about pulling the offer, they aren't going to believe you are serious."

"I don't think calling Agee makes sense," said Siegel. "You want to convince him that the countertender is not just a bargaining ploy. If you call Agee and offer to pull out, your bid is not going to be very convincing. The time to call is after you have made the offer."

Pownall thought about it. "I won't make the call,"

At one o'clock on Monday morning, Powell signed the new credit agreement in a conference room at Dewey, Ballantine. Martin Marietta had lined up $900 million in cash to buy Bendix.

•

The Monday board meeting began at ten o'clock at the midtown offices of Dewey, Ballantine on the corner of Park Avenue and Forty-first Street. Menaker had been so worried about security in New York City that he had hired a consultant to search the conference room for listening devices just before the meeting began. There was a guard stationed in the annex room next door with an electronic surveillance microphone to check the room for interference during the meeting.

The first item on the agenda was golden parachutes. The directors were worried that the company's key management and research staff would be lured away by the likes of Lockheed and Raytheon in the course of the battle. They awarded twenty-seven salary guarantees.

Next came the Bendix offer for Marietta. Leithauser stood up to talk about the value of the company.

"Can we close the blinds?" interrupted Menaker. He pointed to the window. Leithauser turned around. There was a photographer on the roof of the next building. It looked like he was pointing his camera at the skyline behind him, not into the conference room. Menaker pulled the blinds.

"It's not really a photographer we ought to be worried about," said Mel Laird, the former defense secretary. "It's someone with a directional microphone. Those things pick up the vibrations on the surface of glass. They can hear through windows and blinds."

Leithauser finished his presentation. Siegel stood up. Over the weekend, the Kidder staff had put together a fat binder of facts on Martin Marietta. Now Siegel flipped through the pages.

"The Bendix offer is inadequate," he said. "Marietta stock is now trading at $33 a share. Agee is offering $43. That is a premium, but any raider has to pay a premium for control. You have to look at two things before you decide to accept an offer. First, is this the time to sell the company? Second, is this the price at which to sell it?

"The answer to the first question is no. Marietta's stock price is depressed because of the slump in aluminum and cement. When the economy turns, those industries will pick up dramatically and the stock price will soar. Marietta is very well positioned for a recovery. Over the past five years, you have spent $1.6 billion in plant and equipment. You have made yourself a low-cost producer of cement and aluminum. You've taken aerospace research and development into the profitable production stage. Your stockholders are just about to get the benefit of all that capital spending. The price of your shares could easily be $75 in two years. You are currently at the bottom of the earnings cycle. Now is definitely not the time to sell the company.

"And even if it were, this is not the right price. Marietta stock is one of the most undervalued stocks on the market, so the premium that Agee is offering is over something that is already abnormally low. It is a premium of only 30 percent over market; the average premium for control is about 60 percent. The break-apart value of the company—the value of the separate businesses added together—is $75 to $90 a share. Book value at cost is $71 a share. The recent high is $51. Kidder doesn't think that this is the time to sell. But if you want to do that, the Bendix bid is inadequate."

Mel Laird spoke up. "We've got a particularly outstanding group of people with some unusual defense programs. What is going to happen if Bendix takes over? What is that going to do to morale? Our people are not high-exposure people. I am not sure I want to get involved with a company that is anxious to have a lot of PR."

"It is more than that," said Rauth. "Martin Marietta could be hurt if it is taken over by Bendix, which has no experience in big systems operations."

"I'm not sure we want someone with short-term goals to take over Martin Marietta," said a director. "Our company has a long-term focus."

Rauth called for a vote on the offer.

"You have to look at this in terms of the future prospects of the company," Fullem reminded the directors. "You can't just compare the offering price to the stock price. Bendix has to pay a premium for control: control has value. If the offer is fair and reasonable in terms of future earnings, then you have a duty to accept it. If the offer isn't fair, then you have a duty to reject it."

·

·

The directors voted unanimously to reject the offer. Rauth appointed a steering committee of seven directors— Rauth, Pownall, Griffin Bell, and the four directors who live in the Washington area—to act for the board on questions about the takeover battle whenever a decision had to be made quickly and the full board could not get together on short notice.

Siegel returned to his presentation. "We have to do something strong to signal our determination to fight the bid. We've got to have an active rather than a passive defense. I said last week that one option was a white knight. We could get you a white knight. Goodyear and Litton and Combustion Engineering have all called. But I don't think that this is the time to sell the company to anyone, for all the reasons I've already given. The lawyers say that there is no antitrust defense. If there is no antitrust and no white knight, then there is probably going to be a combination of the two companies. And if there is going to be a combination of Martin Marietta and Bendix, it ought to be on terms that make sense to Marietta shareholders. That means that the best defense is to countertender for Bendix. If we decide we want to do this, we have to do it soon. Marietta is 60 percent owned by institutions like banks and insurance companies. They will tender because the laws say that they have to act like a 'prudent' individual. Bendix will have half our stock within ten days."

"Why don't we get in touch with all our stockholders and explain that we're trying to keep the company independent and offer them a dollar a share more than Bendix to sell to us," suggested Griffin Bell.

"That doesn't make sense," said Siegel. "You're talking about going private."

"I'm not talking about going private," said Bell. "I'm talking about going partially private. If we explain why we don't want to sell the company, some shareholders won't sell. I imagine half will sell to us."

"You can't go partially private in the middle of a takeover war," said Siegel. "If someone wants to take you over, going partially private helps him. Say we offer to buy our own shares. Bendix will let us buy the stock, then Bendix will make a new offer. There will be less stock for them to buy to have control of the company. The idea will just backfire on the shareholders who did sell to us, because they will get less than the ones who later sold to Bendix. Timing is very important here. I think the best defense for us is to countertender."

"That's what NLT tried to do when American General made its hostile bid last spring," said John L. Hanigan, chairman of Genesco. Hanigan lived in Nashville, where NLT is based, and knew the company's top executives. "The countertender didn't keep NLT independent."

"That's right," said Siegel. "The countertender has been tried before as a defense, but it has never been successful at keeping a company independent. In this case I think there is a good chance that it will. This is a unique situation. Bendix is vulnerable because of Agee's reputation and because of its $500 million cash pool. Martin Marietta is about the same size as Bendix. There is a SESSOP, but no single person owns a large block of Bendix stock that we won't be able to get. And our board has the resolve to stick by an offer.

"There are four possible outcomes if we countertender: our offer for Bendix puts Bendix in play and draws in another bidder; we negotiate a settlement on our terms; Bendix backs down and withdraws its offer completely; both companies buy each other's stock. That last isn't necessarily a disaster. If Marietta buys Bendix after Bendix has bought Marietta and then Marietta sells the Bendix automotive and industrial divisions and the Marietta cement company to pay off some of the debt, the effect will be the same as swapping Bendix aerospace for Marietta cement. Conceptually that's a very attractive proposition."

Larry Adams of Martin Marietta and Peter Wood, of Kidder, Peabody, made a presentation on Bendix. Adams had boned up on Bendix over the weekend. He made a good case for the aerospace match. Bendix was a respected subcontractor. It did parts work for Martin Marietta on the Pershing missile. It had some aerospace contracts that appealed to Martin Marietta. "Bendix has a good position in the automotive aftermarket," said Adams. "They make brakes, filters, and spark plugs. The business isn't badly depressed in a recession."

One of the directors said he didn't think so highly of the automotive business.

Adams continued. He was not very convincing when he talked about the fit between Martin Marietta and the Bendix industrial division. "We already do work in artificial intelligence," explained Adams. "We're interested in robotics. We don't know how much of that Bendix has."

When the presentation on Bendix was done, Rauth asked Fullem to talk about the legal issues. "We have an advantage," said Fullem. "The Maryland corporate laws say that Bendix has to call a shareholder meeting to take control of Marietta and that it has to wait at least ten days to do that. We can take control of Bendix the day we buy the stock, because in Delaware you don't have to call a meeting. You can take control by written consent of the majority of the shareholders—which will be us. There are some risks involved. There is a Delaware statute that says a subsidiary can't vote the shares of its parent. There is a Maryland law that says the same thing. If both companies buy each other, each is a subsidiary of the other. There is no case law on what happens next. There is a substantial risk that if that happens, neither company will be able to vote.

·

·

There is a chance of a Mexican standoff."

Rauth asked Siegel to talk about pricing. "Bendix stock is held 22 percent by the SESSOP, an employee profit-sharing plan, 26 percent by institutions, and 52 percent by the retail market," said Siegel. "I'm not sure that the SESSOP can tender. We looked at a self-tender that Bendix did a year and a half ago, and the SESSOP shares could be tendered in that. But I don't know. What's important is the institutions. Institutions tender. And Bendix isn't owned by institutions. We've got to change the Bendix ownership profile."

Siegel explained that there is a group of professional stock traders called arbitrageurs, who make a living buying the stock of takeover targets from retail owners and then reselling the same shares to the raider. The higher the cash premium that the raider offers over the market price, the more eager the arbs are to buy and tender. When the arbs start to buy, of course, the price of the target's stock starts to rise. "We've got to offer a high cash premium," said Siegel. "Bendix is worth about $65 a share. If we make a front-loaded offer and pay more cash per share for the controlling half of the company than we pay in stock for the rest, we can end up paying the right average price and still be sure that enough shares get tendered. I'm recommending a cash offer of $77 to $80 a share."

"Seventy-five is our best offer," said Leithauser. Powell had lined up plenty of credit to pay for that. "Can the offer be done at $75?"

"I think so," said Siegel. "Bendix stock is trading at $50. Seventy-five ought to get it moving. If we make that offer, Bendix stock will start to trade up. We're calling about twenty companies that may want parts of Bendix."

The directors discussed what they had heard. Rauth called for a vote on the motion to countertender for Bendix at $75 a share. It was unanimous—in favor.

COUNTERING THE
JONESTOWN DEFENSE

•

From the very day that Agee had called Tom Pownall, Bendix had sensed that Martin Marietta was going to fight. As soon as he got back from the meeting at Hughes Hubbard Wednesday morning, Jay Higgins had called Marty Siegel. Siegel wasn't in—he was in Memphis and later in Bethesda—and Higgins had left a message: "Merry Christmas. My guys want to talk about *everything* including price. Remember, it's just business. Nothing personal."

Siegel didn't call back until Friday.

"We're willing to negotiate everything," repeated Higgins.

"We'll talk," said Siegel, "but only if you terminate the tender offer. We aren't going to negotiate with a gun at our heads."

Higgins stiffened. "Come on, Marty," he said. "Get serious. We're not going to agree to that."

"I need an answer," said Siegel.

"I'll call you back," said Higgins.

Higgins called Agee and Agee told Higgins to tell Siegel no. Higgins called Siegel again. "We're not pulling the tender," he said. "If they want to negotiate, great, but the bid stays out."

"Well, then, we've got some work to do here," said Siegel. "My boys are serious people."

•

Jack Byrne had gone up to New York after the meeting at Martin Marietta Thursday morning to see John Gutfreund of Salomon Brothers on Geico business. Gutfreund and Byrne were old friends, and Geico was a longtime Salomon client. After the meeting at the Waldorf-Astoria Hotel, Gutfreund asked Byrne to wait behind in the conference room.

"What do you think about the Bendix offer?" asked Gutfreund.

"The board hasn't met yet," said Byrne. He didn't say that there had been a briefing that morning. "Don't expect it to be easy. These guys are serious. They are very resolute people."

Gutfreund passed the message on to Higgins and Higgins called Agee. "Why don't we try to see if Byrne will talk to us," suggested Higgins. "He's a Marietta director. He's a financial guy. He is very close to Salomon Brothers. We can't ask him to join our squad, but there's a chance that he might open up to us about what they are thinking and what they might want to do to make this deal friendly. Do you want me to try to talk to him?"

"No," said Agee. "I don't want you to talk to him or anyone else. We're on course. Contacts are going to be made."

"By whom?" asked Higgins.

"I can't go into that with you now, Jay, but don't worry," said Agee. "I don't want you to try to contact Byrne or anybody else."

"Bill, that sounds odd," said Higgins. "It is not the traditional way to do it."

•

•

By Friday afternoon, the Salomon Brothers traders had begun to pick up the rumor that Martin Marietta was planning a "transactions-oriented" defense. Higgins had never heard the jargon before; it sounded like selling the crown jewels. That didn't make sense. There were three other possibilities: a self-tender, a defensive acquisition, or a lash-back bid. Higgins discussed the possibility of a countertender with McDonald and Fleischer. As Higgins had told the board on Tuesday, he didn't think that Martin Marietta could line up the cash to bid for all of Bendix. McDonald said that he didn't think they could try it; making a countertender with their balance sheet would be irresponsible. Fleischer pointed out that making a countertender meant waiving the antitrust defense.

Late Friday, Hal Tanner, of Salomon Brothers, called Al McDonald with a market wrap-up. Tanner was worried that Marietta might be getting ready to lash back.

"They'll be looking at that in Southfield over the weekend," said McDonald. McDonald was going to Nashville on Saturday to settle his daughter at college. Agee was headed for Cape Cod with Cunningham. Wednesday was Cunningham's birthday and they were celebrating early.

"I'll come out to Michigan for a strategy meeting," offered Tanner.

"You don't need to do that," said McDonald.

Sunday morning Tanner called Michael Rowny, Bendix's contact man for the Detroit team over the weekend. Rowny told Tanner that Bendix was holding a strategy meeting at two in the afternoon.

"If I catch the next plane from New York, I'll be there in time for the meeting," said Tanner.

"That won't be necessary," said Rowny.

Tanner called McDonald again on Sunday night. "There are strong rumors about this countertender," he said.

"No responsible company would do that," said Mc-

Donald. "Not with Martin Marietta's balance sheet."

"They may," said Tanner. "They may."

Higgins was working at his desk on Monday afternoon when the announcement of the Martin Marietta counter-tender came across the wire at twenty after four. Higgins called Agee.

"Mr. Agee is not available," said Agee's secretary.

"Switch me to McDonald," said Higgins.

"How are the stocks doing today," said McDonald as he picked up.

"Martin Marietta just tendered for Bendix," said Higgins. "Let me read you the wire."

> Martin Marietta Corp. said its board authorized a cash tender offer for 11,900,000 shares of The Bendix Corp.'s common stock at $75 per share. . . . The board also voted unanimously to recommend to shareholders that they reject Bendix's offer for up to 15,800,000 shares of Martin Marietta common stock at $43 per share. . . . Martin Marietta has also commenced litigation against Bendix alleging among other things various violations of the federal securities laws in connection with Bendix's offer.

"There's a board meeting scheduled for tomorrow?" asked Higgins. Agee and McDonald had scheduled regular board meetings twice a week during the battle. It was easier to cancel on short notice than to schedule.

"Yes," said McDonald.

"We'll get all cranked up," said Higgins.

•

Monday afternoon, Fleischer met with his team in New York. Outside counsel had flown in from Delaware and Maryland to talk to the New York team about key legal

•

5 7

•

questions like litigation strategy. Fleischer had just introduced the lawyers to each other when the Marietta announcement crossed the wire. The lawyers immediately began to talk about how Bendix should react to the counteroffer.

One possibility was to try to add shark-repellent amendments to the Bendix charter. If Bendix made it harder for Martin Marietta to take control, Marietta might drop its offer, or at least start to negotiate. Fleischer had thought about the possibility of shark repellents as soon as the rumors about a Marietta countertender had surfaced. One of the lawyers had drafted several of them over the weekend.

"We've got to decide whether to go ahead with the shark repellents," said a lawyer. "If we do, we should call the stock exchange." Companies had to tell the New York Stock Exchange that they were planning to hold a shareholder meeting and why.

"I think we should," said Stuart Katz, one of Fleischer's partners at Fried, Frank. "It's a no-lose situation. The amendments probably won't pass—they rarely do in the middle of a battle—but it won't hurt us if they don't. There is no downside risk. The worst thing that can happen is that the charter would stay just the same as it is now. And maybe the fact that we are trying to change the charter will put some doubt in the minds of the arbs about the Marietta offer. That uncertainty can only help us."

"Is there time to get a meeting date before Martin Marietta can buy?" asked one of the lawyers. There are laws about how long a company has to wait to call a meeting.

"I don't know," said Katz. He got out his pocket calendar and began to count off the days. The New York Stock Exchange rules said that the exchange had to have ten days advance notice that a company was setting a "record date," a day on which it made an official list of shareholders. Today was August 30. That meant that the "record date" would be September 10; perhaps September 9 if Labor Day counted as a calendar day; anyone who owned Bendix stock when trading stopped that day would be allowed to vote at the meeting. The Delaware corporate laws say that a company has to spend at least ten days collecting absentee ballots, called proxies, between the day of the meeting and the record date. That meant that the first day that Bendix could hold a shareholder meeting was September 21; at midnight on September 21, Martin Marietta would be able to buy Bendix stock under its counteroffer.

Katz looked at his watch. It was almost five. He and two of the lawyers from Hughes Hubbard called the stock exchange.

"Bendix would like to hold a shareholder meeting on September 21," Katz told the NYSE official. "I know that the stock exchange recommends a thirty-day notice period, but we're going to ask you to waive that. The point of the notice period is to give shareholders a chance to make a decision. In this case, they can't make a decision unless the notice period is shorter, because otherwise Martin Marietta will buy before the meeting. Then the game will be over."

"I don't know what to tell you," said the official. "I'll make a note that you called, and we'll have to call you back when we decide if that is okay."

While Katz was talking to the stock exchange, Fleischer and the litigators started to figure out what kind of suit Bendix should file against Martin Marietta to try to block the bid. The obvious answer was to claim that the Marietta counteroffer was fraudulent, a hastily conceived attempt to keep Bendix from buying in order to preserve the lucrative jobs of the Martin Marietta management.

"Martin Marietta doesn't have the money to do this," said Marc Cherno, the senior litigating partner from Fried, Frank. "If Martin Marietta borrows $900 million to pay for Bendix, that will cost $120 million a year just in interest payments. Martin Marietta only made $52 million in the first half of this year. Martin Marietta might not make enough in the whole year to pay for interest on the new debt. And Martin Marietta might not be able to vote the shares that it buys. Marietta will be a Bendix subsidiary. Legally, a subsidiary can't vote against the wishes of its parent. This offer just doesn't make sense."

Monday night, Agee called John Gutfreund of Salomon Brothers.

"I've scheduled a board meeting for ten tomorrow morning," he said. "I want to take a bigger role in running things. There will be a strategy meeting every morning at eight o'clock from now on. I want to see your team in my office tomorrow."

•

All of the advisers were at the General Motors Building for the meeting Tuesday at eight o'clock. They couldn't fit in Agee's office, so they sat around the table in the Bendix boardroom. The *Wall Street Journal* had called the counter-bid a "Pac-Man" that morning. The bankers and lawyers laughed about the label. Then Agee came in.

"Let's talk about this bid," said Agee. "Let's start with the legal side." He looked at Fleischer. "How do you see things, Art?"

"The most important thing for Bendix legally is to get through the court without a delay," said Fleischer. "Anti-trust isn't going to be a problem after all. Marietta gave that up by bidding."

Fleischer explained that his team was working on a lawsuit. He said that the lawyers had drafted some shark repellents over the weekend and that Katz had already called the stock exchange. "We've talked to the proxy so-licitors," said Fleischer. "It's always tough to pass shark repellents in the middle of a takeover battle, but the proxy solicitors say that with so much stock in the SESSOP the odds that these get passed are about fifty-fifty."

"What about strategy?" asked Agee. "What do we do now? Do we raise our bid? How do you see things, Jay?"

"We don't want to raise our offer now," said Higgins. "If we change our bid for Marietta before the prorate pool closes, then the day that we can buy the stock will be moved back. And since timing is the key in these things, that is silly. We should think about raising our bid after the proration date, to keep the stock in the pool. Fleischer is right. The top priority is to make it through without a delay. We have to watch in case a white knight comes in for Martin Marietta."

"How much Martin Marietta stock do you think is going to be tendered to us?" asked Agee.

"Sixty percent," said Martin Weinstein, the Salomon Brothers arbitrageur. "More than half of the Martin Marietta stock is held by institutions and 75 percent of all institutional stock is almost always tendered. The rest of the stock is retail. Half of the retail stock will be tendered."

Agee looked surprised that Weinstein thought that so much stock would come in.

"I'll give you a bottle of champagne if we get that much stock," said Tanner to Weinstein.

Everyone laughed.

"Tendered doesn't mean sold," said Weinstein. "Smart investors know that tendering isn't a commitment. They get their shares into the prorate pool so that they can get cash, and they wait until the last day to make a decision. The best thing that could happen is that we get exactly as much stock as we asked for. Then there will be no proration risk to the arbs. They will know that they were getting one hundred cents on every dollar of stock that they tendered. They won't withdraw."

"So the key date is the withdrawal date?" asked Agee.

"That's right," said Weinstein. "That's when you can start buying."

Agee asked some other questions about strategy.

"Look at their offer," interrupted McDonald. "Look how front-loaded it is."

"It makes sense," said Higgins. "If they want anyone to tender, they have to front-load. It's all the money they've been able to beg or borrow. If the bid were for all the stock at half the price, the market would laugh."

"Front-loaded offers are unethical and grossly unfair to employee shareholders," said McDonald. "We've got 23 percent of our shares held by employees whom we have to protect. Front-loaded offers are illegal."

"They aren't illegal," said Charles Nathan, Salomon's lawyer. "The SEC frowns on them, but they aren't illegal."

"They should be," said McDonald "I'll bet there are a hundred congressmen who believe that front-loaded offers are unfair. I think we should run a press campaign to build up some negotiating pressure against them. We should get a letter and an ad on every congressman's desk."

"Hold on, Al," said Higgins. "The day may come when we might need a front-loaded offer ourselves."

Agee reached up and put his hand on McDonald's shoulder. "We'll talk about this later," he said.

Agee asked a few more questions. Then the meeting broke up. Agee and McDonald left the boardroom. McDonald came back. "This meeting had too many people," he said. "Agee doesn't like to operate that way. From now on he wants there to be only two bankers and two lawyers."

The Bendix directors met at ten o'clock. Higgins began by explaining Martin Marietta's offer.

"The lash-back is designed to make Bendix raise its offer for Marietta or drop out of the bidding altogether," said Higgins. "It isn't a real offer, but we can't ignore it. It is indicative of a mental attitude. We may have to raise our price. We may have to raise and raise aggressively to win. We have to wait to see how serious the offer is. I don't think that the market will believe this offer. Bendix stock has only moved up a little. It won't move up a lot. You have a time advantage: you can buy first. Right now what you want to do is put the word out loud and clear that you are going to buy. The important thing is to keep our eye on the ball."

"How much is their offer worth?" asked Agee.

"Clearly the front end is worth $75 a share," said Higgins. "I don't know what the back end is worth. They say $55 a share, but that is based on the price of their stock yesterday, which is trading way up on our offer. If you take a more normal Martin Marietta stock price to value the swap, the back end is worth only $35. And I don't even know if that is meaningful. I can't guess what the stock will trade at if we both buy.

"Assuming that the $55 a share they are talking about is right, the average price is $65. They are offering us eight times what we earned in the past year. Our offer is ten times what they earned. The Martin Marietta offer for Bendix is less than the Bendix offer for Martin Marietta. Salomon Brothers believes that this offer is inadequate. I don't think that this is the time to sell the company, but if that is what you want to do, Salomon Brothers can find a company that will pay you a better price."

"If ever a bid was grossly inadequate, this is it," said Agee. "The price is too low in the first place. They know that as well as we do. But more important, only the professional traders will benefit from the front-loading. The small shareholders and our employees will get crumbs."

"I don't think that Marietta's claim about a time advantage is very meaningful," said Fleischer. "There is a Delaware statute that says that a subsidiary can't vote the shares of the parent against the parent. We can probably block Marietta from voting. There is a similar law in Maryland, but the wording is different. We have a better case."

Agee dismissed the bankers and lawyers. The directors took a vote. They rejected the Marietta bid.

After the board meeting, Higgins took Agee aside. "You are going to get calls from investment bankers eager to line up a buyer for Bendix," he said. "You might get some calls from companies. Don't take them. Refer them to us. We'll do the talking for you. That's our job. If you start talking to companies, people will believe that you aren't serious about your offer for Marietta. If no one believes you on that, they won't send in their stock and you won't be able to buy control.

"And besides, conversations about control sometimes wind up having a life of their own. Arbs hear a rumor that a bidder is about to come in and they start to gear up to tender to him, and more and more of our stock goes into their hands. Then if someone does make an offer for Bendix, we have to sell the company even if we don't want to."

"I understand," said Agee. "I won't talk."

"The company isn't for sale yet," said Higgins. "But you can't just find a buyer at the drop of a hat. I want to make a couple of calls to companies that are close to Salomon Brothers."

"No," said Agee, "No calls. I'm in control here and I'll decide when we start to call."

"I'm not going to say that we're for sale," said Higgins. "I want to give people some public information about Bendix so that we will be more than a name in the *Wall Street Journal.* That will help if we have to talk to them about selling the company later on."

"I repeat, Jay," said Agee, "no calls to anyone and no documents or public information to anyone. You're doing just great. Don't worry. We've got things under control."

"What about calling Kidder?" asked Higgins. "We can't

rely on the financial press as our sole communications link. I should be in touch with my counterpart."

"I don't want you calling anyone," said Agee. "It's a sign of weakness."

Higgins went back to his office and looked again at what the balance sheet of the merged company would look like if both Bendix and Martin Marietta bought. Ghastly. Wednesday morning, Higgins bought a carton of Kool-Aid packets and took it to his office. The Reverend Jim Jones had ordered his crazed cult followers to "defend" themselves against a congressional investigation by drinking purple Kool-Aid laced with cyanide. Higgins handed the envelopes out to his associates. "Marietta has just launched the Jonestown defense," he explained. "They are already preparing the Kool-Aid."

STERLING SILVER, WATERFORD CRYSTAL, AND BENDIX

•

4 Harry Jack Gray has spunk. He is tall, trim, and balding. He has craggy features and pale blue eyes. Gray swears under his breath whenever anyone mentions the success of his corporate archrival General Electric. He runs United Technologies as a one-man show. During the first seven years that Gray was at the helm, the company didn't have a president; Alexander Haig took the job for thirteen months before he became Reagan's first secretary of state in 1981. When Haig left, Gray, then sixty-one, didn't appoint a successor.

"High technology is the common denominator of all we do" is emblazoned on the back of the UTC annual report. Gray is proud of the slogan. When Gray came to United Aircraft in 1971, 75 percent of the company's sales came from the Pratt & Whitney engine division; P&W was having big problems designing an engine for the giant Boeing 747—and some of the other United companies were on what Gray calls the "going out of business curve." The answer was to control expenses in existing businesses and to diversify out of the engine business. Gray thought that the logical way to do that was to buy companies that could use the defense-developed technology in commercial markets. He set himself a goal of doubling revenues by 1980—United's sales were just over $2 billion in 1972—and formed a five-man acquisition team to help him put together a hit list. At the top: Bendix.

In 1973, Gray started to move. He bought Essex International, an Indiana-based wire and cable maker for $320 million. The next year, he made a run at ESB, the maker of Ray-O-Vac batteries. He lost that battle to Inco, a Canadian nickel producer; but in 1975, he was in the bidding ring again, this time for Otis Elevator. Otis resisted. Gray insisted. He eventually bought Otis for $398 million. Two years after that victory, Gray made a pass at Babcock & Wilcox, the maker of power plants. He sat down with George Zipf, the chairman of Babcock, to talk about a merger. Zipf wasn't interested. Gray called later to talk about the idea. Zipf still wasn't interested. Gray decided to go ahead anyhow. He called Zipf yet again.

"You are really pushy," snapped Zipf.

Gray did not buy Babcock. J. Ray McDermott, a Louisiana-based driller, bought the company for more than Gray thought it was worth. In 1979 the core of the Babcock-built nuclear reactor at Three Mile Island almost melted down. A few months after he lost the Babock battle, Gray made a second try. He bid for Carrier, the air conditioner-maker based in Syracuse, New York. Carrier didn't want to be taken over. The whole town rose against Gray. The local paper ran a cartoon of King Kong Gray atop the Carrier building. The Small Business Administration held hearings on the effect of a United takeover on Carrier's suppliers. The Justice Department sued for antitrust violations. Gray stood fast. He bought Carrier. He won his antitrust case the next year.

Then Gray bought Mostek, a pioneer maker of semiconductors. When Gould made a hostile offer for Mostek, Gray came to the rescue as a white knight. And Gray was not finished buying. He had by now changed the name of the company to United Technologies; when UTC sales neared $10 billion in 1979, Gray set himself a 1985 target of $20 billion. The only way Gray could ever hit that goal was by buying more companies, and so as soon as he saw the announcement of the Bendix bid for Martin Marietta, Gray called Stillman Brown, his chief financial officer and ordered up two studies: one on Martin Marietta and one on Bendix.

The acquisitions team quickly put together a top secret paper on each company. The team looked at how Martin Marietta would fit into the United Technologies family; they looked at how Bendix would fit. Then the acquisition team studied what buying each company would mean for the UTC balance sheet and what it would do to cash flow and earnings. Brown and Edward W. Large, the United Technologies executive vice-president for legal and corporate affairs, looked over the numbers. They brought the work to Harry Gray.

Gray was not enchanted with the idea of buying all of Martin Marietta. He liked the aerospace business, but a third of Martin Marietta's sales came from aluminum, cement, chemicals, and aggregates. Those were not the kinds of businesses that Gray wanted to be in—even in a good economy. Buying Marietta at the price Bendix had already bid would dilute UTC earnings $1.50 a share. That didn't appeal to Gray.

But Bendix was another matter. The company was a natural business fit for United Technologies. Bendix automotive was a match for UTC automotive. Bendix would catapult UTC into a leading position in a consumer electronics market. The Bendix industrial division would be a base for UTC to make the computer-controlled machine tools and robots that would be needed in the factory of the future. (Gray's vision of the factory of the future came complete with a Carrier air conditioner.) Bendix had some interesting aerospace contracts. At the right price, Bendix was an unbeatable buy.

There was a serious problem, however: antitrust. Bendix and UTC both made airplane fuel controls. Bendix sold 45 percent of all the fuel controls in the United States, UTC's Hamilton Standard division sold another third. And UTC's Pratt & Whitney division bought half of them. The Justice Department would never let the two companies merge. The overlap was a "showstopper." Gray had to think of a way to get rid of Bendix fuel controls.

Friday, just two days after Agee had called Pownall, Felix Rohatyn, a senior partner at Lazard Frères, came out to United Technologies headquarters in Hartford, Connecticut, for a long-standing lunch date with Stillman Brown. Rohatyn had made headlines in 1975 for engineering New York City's return from the brink of bankruptcy, but he was better known at United Technologies as the architect of the Otis and Carrier takeovers. That morning, Rohatyn had mergers on his mind. Rohatyn knew that Pownall and Gray were friends, and he thought that Gray might be looking for a way to help out. The standard way to do that was to bid as a white knight, but Rohatyn had a better idea. Bendix was on the UTC hit list. This might be the time to move.

Rohatyn, Gray, Brown, Large, and James Lyons, United Technologies' chief strategic planner, met for lunch in the elegant cherry-paneled private dining room just down the hall from Gray's office. The table was set with blue linen, sterling silver, and Waterford crystal. The plates were blue Spode.

"Bendix is vulnerable," said Rohatyn. "It has a cash pool of $500 million that we can use to pay for buying it. Bendix is about to do something that is going to reduce its own value. Bendix is worth more to United Technologies before it buys Martin Marietta."

.

.

Gray looked across the table at Rohatyn. "I'm interested in Bendix," he said. "But we've got an antitrust problem: fuel controls."

"We could sell the antitrust problems to Martin Marietta," said Rohatyn. Selling assets might be a way to get clearance from the Justice Department to do the deal. It would also give United Technologies more cash to pay for the purchase.

If it worked. Large's legal staff hadn't yet studied Bendix thoroughly, so he wasn't sure just how serious the problem was. No one at the table knew how the Justice Department would feel about a presale. It had never been done before.

The team finished their lunch about one o'clock. They left the dining room and walked to Gray's office. They sat at the round conference table. Gray talked. "I'm not bullish on the economy. I'm not bullish on Bendix automotive and industrial earnings. If we buy Bendix, we have to do it without diluting UTC earnings and without increasing UTC debt."

Monday morning, Ed Large flew to New York for a one o'clock luncheon with Marty Lipton of Wachtell, Lipton, United Technologies usual outside counsel. Large and his staff had by then pinpointed most of the antitrust overlaps with Bendix. Large wanted to know what Lipton thought about the idea of selling assets to Martin Marietta to solve those problems. Large said he didn't know yet how United Technologies would enter the battle, but it would probably be either as a bidder for Bendix or a buyer of assets from Martin Marietta. Lipton said that he thought the idea of a presale would work. A similar scheme had been proposed the year before, but since the company that made the proposal had been outbid, the idea had never been tested. Lipton felt confident that there wouldn't be a problem this time around.

Late that afternoon, Martin Marietta announced that it had rejected the Bendix bid and that it was making its own offer for Bendix. A little later, Bill Agee called Felix Rohatyn. Agee and Rohatyn had known each other for years and although Rohatyn had represented RCA in March, the two had always gotten on well. Rohatyn assumed that Agee wanted to talk about selling the RCA block. He agreed to see Agee at four the next afternoon, Tuesday, at the Helmsley suite.

Rohatyn and the United Technologies team kept working all day Tuesday on the idea of buying part of Bendix. That morning, Doug Brown, from Kidder, talked to Stillman Brown, from United Technologies, about the possibility of UTC buying Bendix automotive or industrial assets. Stillman Brown said he was interested. During the afternoon, Tom Pownall called his friend Harry Gray to find out more. Gray said maybe he'd buy all of Bendix.

At four o'clock, Rohatyn walked over to the Helmsley to keep his appointment with Agee. Agee didn't want to talk about the RCA stock, he wanted to get some advice on the Marietta bid for Bendix. He seemed concerned that Marietta had made a countertender. He said that Salomon Brothers had not discussed the possibility with him at any length before he made his own bid for Martin Marietta.

"How much is the Marietta bid worth?" asked Agee. "What does the back end of the offer mean?"

"I don't know," answered Rohatyn. "It is impossible to predict what Marietta stock is going to trade for if Marietta does buy Bendix. The back end of that offer is almost meaningless."

The two discussed the bid for a few minutes. Then Agee asked, "Is there any way that we can work together on this? Can you join the Bendix team as an adviser?"

Rohatyn answered carefully. "I have a very high regard for Salomon Brothers," he said. Ira Harris was one of

Rohatyn's closest friends. "I might be able to give you a different perspective, but I would be surprised if I could give you better advice. I would not have assigned a high probability to a Marietta counterbid for Bendix. That is a high-risk tactic. If I had been advising Marietta, I wouldn't have recommended it. And, at least for the time being, I have a conflict."

"What kind of conflict?"

"Lazard is representing a company that might be interested in making a bid for Bendix."

Rohatyn did not name his client. He assumed that Agee guessed that the Lazard client was United Technologies, since Lazard had represented UTC in the Carrier and Otis bids.

"I want to do what is best for the shareholders," said Agee. "If the price were right, I would be prepared to listen to a bid for Bendix."

"What kind of price would be right?" asked Rohatyn.

Agee didn't say. He talked about a range of $90 to $100 a share. Rohatyn had valued the company in the high $60's.

"If my client decides that he is interested and wants to talk to you before he goes public, I'll give you a call," said Rohatyn as he left.

Rohatyn walked down Park Avenue and across the street to the offices of Wachtell, Lipton. He and Marty Lipton called Harry Gray at six o'clock. Rohatyn told Gray that he had just met with Agee.

"Agee doesn't seem irrevocably wedded to that company," he said.

Gray, Lipton, and Rohatyn went over the pros and cons of a meeting with Agee before UTC launched a bid. Agee was talking about a price that was more than $20 above what Gray and Rohatyn thought the company was worth. Gray and Agee probably were not going to reach an agreement quickly if at all. The meeting would just lead to mis-

•

•

understandings and hurt feelings. Gray decided not to try.

Gray told Rohatyn to call Siegel and start negotiating a deal. Later that evening, Rohatyn did. He explained that he was representing United Technologies and that United Technologies was interested in Bendix. "All of Bendix," said Rohatyn, "not just a few assets. There is an antitrust problem. Would Marietta be interested in buying some Bendix assets from United Technologies?"

"What's the antitrust problem?" asked Siegel.

"Fuel controls," said Rohatyn.

Siegel called Pownall. "Are you interested in buying Bendix fuel controls from United Technologies?" asked Siegel.

"Work on it," said Pownall.

"This might be a good deal for us," said Siegel. "I like the idea of working with United Technologies. It is a lot easier to carve up Bendix with one buyer than to try to sell off assets one at a time. Gray has a reputation as a finisher and he has the financial muscle to make his offer credible."

Wednesday morning, Siegel called Rohatyn to set up a meeting for four thirty the next afternoon. The two bankers talked on and off all day Wednesday. By Thursday morning, United Technologies and Martin Marietta had settled on a framework for buying and breaking up Bendix. United Technologies would bid $75 a share for half of the company—just what Martin Marietta had bid. UTC would finesse the expiration dates on its offer so that no one had to choose whether to tender to United Technologies or Martin Marietta. UTC would buy the other half of Bendix by swapping UTC stock worth $50 a share. The "blended" price would be $62.50, but the price might have to be raised. It would take $900 million in cash to make that bid. Bendix had $500 million. Marietta would have to put up at least $400 million. Three hundred million would be the price of fuel controls. The Martin Marietta block that Bendix already owned was worth $69 million at the Bendix offering price of $43 a share.

•

Gray helicoptered from Hartford to New York in the middle of the afternoon Thursday. Tom Pownall was already waiting at Wachtell, Lipton when Gray arrived. The two friends sat down at the round table in Lipton's office and talked about Bendix. Pownall started by telling the story of the Agee phone call and the to-be-receipted letter. He explained the rationale behind the countertender. He said he was dismayed that the market didn't believe that Martin Marietta would buy Bendix.

"I thought from the moment I heard about the Marietta bid that Bill Agee would not believe it," said Gray. "That's why I'm interested in working with you. I think we can find some way to work together that will be a good deal for you and will be in the best interests of the UTC shareholders. And I don't think that he's going to lock his horns with United Technologies on the basis that he can outbluff us.

"Tom, we've got an antitrust problem," continued Gray. "And the only way that we can be of help is if you solve our Justice Department problem going in. You're going to have to buy fuel controls. And I'm going to need some money from you to make this attractive to my shareholders."

"How much money?" asked Pownall.

"Seven hundred million," said Gray.

"Four," said Pownall.

"That's not enough," said Gray. "We're going to give you value for it."

"What do you want for fuel controls?" asked Pownall.

"We've put a price of $300 million on it," said Gray.

Pownall had no idea how much fuel controls was worth.

•

•

Marietta wasn't in the jet engine business and Kidder hadn't been able to figure out much about the company from public documents. But Pownall knew that UTC was a major Bendix competitor and a major Bendix customer. He knew and trusted Gray. He was willing to consider the $300 million price tag.

Pownall and Gray negotiated for more than an hour. They considered a number of packages of assets that Marietta could buy from United Technologies and how much each package would cost. Gray suggested that Marietta take a $700 million package: fuel controls at $300 million, Warner & Swasey at $300 million, and a few other assets.

"No," said Pownall. Marietta had looked at Bendix machine tools twice now—once in putting together a hit list, once in countertendering—and had twice decided it didn't want Warner & Swasey. Besides, the company was worth less now than the $291 million Agee had paid for it because Agee had sold off some parts of the company since then. "We want more aerospace assets," said Pownall.

"I can't promise," said Gray.

Pownall and Gray came out of Lipton's office to caucus with their advisers; both teams had questions about the package Gray and Pownall were putting together. Gray and Pownall went back into Lipton's office to iron out the wrinkles. After another hour they had set up the basic mechanism. Martin Marietta would buy $600 million of assets. The package would consist of Bendix fuel controls at $300 million, the 4.5 percent Martin Marietta block, any other Bendix assets that UTC had to sell to get antitrust clearance, and enough aerospace assets to make up the balance. If Martin Marietta and UTC could not agree on which aerospace assets, Marietta would have the option of buying nonaerospace assets or the Elliott Turbomachinery company, a UTC subsidiary that makes oil compression equipment. Elliott had been for sale for months. It had almost

.

.

gone to Cooper Industries earlier in the year, but Cooper had backed down. The asking price was $200 million.

The teams sat down in the purple-walled conference room down the hall from Lipton's office. Siegel wanted to make sure that there really were $300 million of Bendix assets, in addition to fuel controls, that Martin Marietta wanted and UTC would sell. Otherwise it was pointless to start drafting papers: the deal wouldn't make sense. Siegel had drawn up a wish list of Bendix aerospace businesses that Marietta wanted. Gray took a look. He said he could not promise anything until he heard from Justice what had to be sold and until he saw the Bendix books. The two teams put together a list of "call" assets. Marietta would ask for those first. Then they made a second list of "put" assets. UTC could designate them to Marietta if there wasn't enough in the call basket to make $600 million. Siegel and Pownall studied the sheet. There was enough that Marietta wanted to go ahead.

Normally, both Gray and Pownall would have waited to have a draft document before taking a deal to the board. But this was a special case. There were already rumors that United Technologies was getting ready to enter the battle. Neither Gray nor Pownall wanted his board to hear about the handshake from a newscaster. Both decided to hold board meetings the next day, Friday, to get approval on the agreement in principle. The documents would be drafted Friday and Saturday; the wrinkles would be ironed out on Sunday; the agreement would be signed Monday; the deal would be announced Tuesday morning.

After the meeting, Gray headed back to Hartford on his helicopter. Pownall took his team across Forty-ninth Street to the Waldorf-Astoria. They were staying at the Towers. They went into Oscar's Restaurant on the ground floor to get some dinner before they went to bed. It was almost midnight. The negotiators sat down at the table and ordered. A few minutes later, their waiter came back with the restaurant manager. The waiter looked embarrassed. He said that the kitchen had just closed. The manager said that the Bull & Bear Restaurant across the lobby was still open. The team walked across the lobby and ordered again.

"I'm not sure about the advisability of spending $600 million for assets we don't know much about," said Leithauser.

"Gray and I are good friends," said Pownall. "We are doing this in good faith."

"I think this deal with United Technologies may be a strategic mistake," said Adams. "If UTC makes an offer for Bendix that says that UTC will proceed only if Bendix does not buy Martin Marietta, then Bendix is going to buy Martin Marietta. Buying Martin Marietta is going to be Agee's best defense against United Technologies. This deal is supposed to strengthen our bid, but it may backfire."

"That's a possibility we have to consider," said Menaker. "But we also have to bring credibility to our offer."

"Larry, you've spoiled my evening," said Pownall to Adams. "I was going to go upstairs and get a good night's sleep, knowing that I'd finally solved our problem. Now I won't."

"United Technologies isn't putting any pressure on Agee to buy our stock," said Leithauser. "Agee is going to buy our stock anyway. The new offer might scare him into bargaining."

"We don't have a lot of leverage with Gray," said Adams.

"It's an all-or-nothing deal," said Menaker. "Either we sign the contract with Gray to firm up our offer, or we don't. I'm agreeing that there's a risk that the deal might backfire, but as you just said, we aren't in a position to dictate terms. If we want credibility, we have to take what Gray will give us."

•

•

The five Marietta strategists kept talking about the deal and what would happen. "There could be a three-way peace agreement," said Menaker. "Gray is coming in partly to help us. He might be willing to drop his offer if he thought that his dropping would make Agee drop the Bendix offer for us. And there's a possibility that Agee will want to sell his company. Gray is clearly convinced that he can negotiate a deal."

Gray had not told Pownall about the meeting between Agee and Rohatyn, but Agee had made no secret of his willingness to sell Bendix at the right price. When *Fortune* magazine had asked Agee in January 1982 how he would react to a takeover bid, Agee had said: "I have only one rule. To protect the interests of the shareholders."

The Bull & Bear Restaurant was empty. Every ten minutes the waiter came up to the Martin Marietta table to hint that it was time to leave. Finally, at two in the morning, the waiters wanted to go. "The restaurant is closed," said the maitre d'.

Menaker looked at his watch. "It's only two o'clock."

"We all want to go home," said the maitre d'.

"We'll go," said Pownall. He paid the bill. The waiter took his tip and left for the night. The Marietta team kept talking. The cleanup crew started to work. Finally, Pownall and his team headed upstairs to bed.

•

The *Wall Street Journal* had gotten wind of the meeting at Wachtell, Lipton. Felix Rohatyn was extra careful about keeping the secret. So he didn't tell even his secretary where he was going when he left his office to catch the helicopter to United Technologies for the board meeting. Rohatyn usually caught a helicopter out to Southhampton on Fridays with a group of business friends. Today he couldn't do that; he called to cancel. When Rohatyn got to the Eastside

Heliport to catch the UTC Sikorsky to Hartford, his friends were already waiting for their helicopter.

"Oh, you're coming with us after all," said an investment banker in the group.

"No," said Rohatyn. "I'm going somewhere on business."

The United Technologies helicopter landed on the pad outside. The pilot came into the waiting room. "Mr. Rohatyn," he announced, "the United Technologies helicopter is waiting to take you to Hartford."

"United Technologies is a client?" asked the banker.

"Oh, no," said Rohatyn. "I'm just going up for lunch."

•

The Martin Marietta board meeting was scheduled for ten o'clock at the Dewey, Ballantine uptown offices.

Pownall outlined the terms of the deal to the directors.

"Three hundred million is a lot to pay for a business we don't know much about," said Leithauser. "But based on the information we have, the price seems fair. United Technologies estimates that the division has a book value of $200 million, a replacement value of $300 to $400 million, sales of $200 million, and a pretax profit margin of 25 percent."

"The price is twelve times earnings," said Siegel. "That's a fair multiple for aerospace assets."

"We aren't talking about a book-value deal," said Leithauser. "The price of fuel controls is fixed at $300 million."

Peter Wood made a presentation on the fuel controls business. "I haven't had a lot of time to work on this," he said. "I have some information from United Technologies." Wood read from a sheet of yellow legal paper "Fuel controls are devices that monitor the gasoline input into an engine. They are complicated hydromechanical devices that must function correctly at extremes of temperature and are a key to takeoff and landing.

"Each engine has one fuel control," he continued. "A plane with three engines, like the Boeing 727, has got three. A fuel control costs between $120,000 and $140,000. Fuel controls need to be refurbished—taken apart and put back together—every three years. There is a substantial spare parts market. The United States sales totaled $350 million last year; Bendix sold 45 percent of the total; United Technologies' Hamilton Standard division sold 35 percent. Only three companies buy fuel controls—United Technologies' Pratt & Whitney division, General Electric, and Rolls Royce—Pratt & Whitney is Bendix's biggest customer."

"How well do we know what we're getting," asked Bradley.

"We'll get good value," said Pownall. "Gray will keep his word."

"We don't have a lot of options," said another director.

"Even if we had other options, this would be a good deal for us," said Siegel. "The market doesn't believe our bid. We can afford $600 million. Gray has a reputation as a finisher."

"I know Gray," said Jack Byrne. "I knew him when I was up at Travelers insurance in Hartford. I have a lot of confidence in him. We have to do something. My friends on Wall Street say that confidence in our offer is flagging."

The directors endorsed the agreement in principle.

"What do you think will happen when this goes public?" asked a director.

"Agee will call," said Siegel.

•

The United Technologies board met by telephone at one o'clock that afternoon. Gray, Brown, Large, Lipton, and Rohatyn sat around the table in the United Technologies boardroom. Pehr G. Gyllenhammar, managing director of Volvo, called in from Gothenburg, Sweden; Robert J. Carlson, the UTC executive vice-president in charge of Pratt & Whitney, called in from his hotel in London.

Gray explained how the deal with Martin Marietta worked. United Technologies would bid for Bendix. Martin Marietta will buy $600 million of assets, including all antitrust problems. "That's the basic transaction," he said. "Let Stillman fill you in on all the important details."

"He's done given you all the details along with the structure." Brown laughed. "There's not much more I can say except that it's a good financial deal for the corporation."

The directors laughed too.

"Lipton and I feel that the Justice Department will accept the transaction," said Large.

The directors approved the deal. The meeting had lasted twenty-five minutes.

•

Harry Gray and Stillman Brown flew up to Nantucket on Friday afternoon. Brown had two cottages on the island, and he had weeks ago invited Gray to use one over the Labor Day weekend. Gray didn't see a need to change his plans. Gray played tennis on Nantucket. He went boating. He talked to his team in New York. On Sunday afternoon, he was strolling down Main Street when William M. Kearns Jr., a Lehman Brothers corporate finance partner, waved to him from in front of The Sweet Shoppe ice cream parlor. Kearns had on an old shirt and a pair of Marine Corps pants. He looked as if he hadn't shaved in days. He was eating an ice cream cone. Gray hadn't talked to Kearns since July. He walked over to say hello.

"Holy cow," said Gray. "I can't believe you're a Lehman Brothers partner."

"I'm on vacation, Harry," said Kearns.

"So am I," said Gray. Gray had on a crisp sports shirt, pressed pants, and a pair of shiny loafers. "I've been playing tennis. I just beat a couple of guys who are much younger than I am."

"How come you don't do more corporate finance work with us?" asked Kearns.

Gray didn't answer. He smiled mischievously. "Watch the papers," he said.

Gray walked into The Sweet Shoppe and bought his own cone. He talked to Kearns for a few minutes and then sauntered down the cobblestone street to his cottage.

•

The lawyers at Wachtell, Lipton had drafted the documents Friday night. Ed Large flew into New York from Hartford on Saturday morning to take a look. Large and Lipton tinkered with the wording that afternoon. Then the Martin Marietta people got to see how the draft was coming. They were not pleased; this was not the agreement they thought they had made on Thursday night. Leithauser got out a pad and made a list of "tall poles" in the contract that would have to be negotiated:

- The $300 million price for fuel controls was absolutely fixed. It would not be adjustable for errors in UTC assumptions.
- United Technologies would sell aerospace call assets to Martin Marietta at "agreed to" prices, not book.
- United Technologies would "put" Bendix businesses to Martin Marietta at book. Also: the put assets could include some United Technologies securities at below market rates.
- The $600 million would be a prepayment, not a payment on the transfer of assets.

•

•

- Marietta would buy the 4.5% block of Martin Marietta stock that Bendix owned at $43 a share, the price Bendix was offering for the company, not the $27 a share that Bendix had bought it for.
- Martin Marietta would pay United Technologies $2.5 million if the deal fell through.

Of all the tall poles, the tallest was the price of fuel controls. Martin Marietta just didn't know how much fuel controls was worth: it might be more than $300 million, it might be less. Pownall couldn't endorse a deal that meant paying $600 million for a package of assets one half of which he couldn't identify, the other half of which he couldn't say much about. He couldn't recommend it simply because he was a close friend of Harry Gray. If he could nail down the value of the $300 million fuel controls purchase, though, he would know enough to stand behind the deal.

There wasn't a lot to go on. The official Bendix filings with the SEC were pretty oblique. The sales numbers were broken down by plant not product. There weren't official numbers on fuel control profits. The newspaper and magazine clippings in the Kidder files filled in a few of the gaps. Bendix fuel controls were made in South Bend, Indiana; San Diego, California; and Quebec. The South Bend factory was part of a huge Bendix complex that manufactured parts for three different divisions. One union bargained for all the employees. There were cross-seniority clauses in the contract. Bendix was considering moving a portion of the plant to North Carolina, where labor costs were lower.

Martin Marietta needed more information on the numbers. Sunday morning, Gray ordered a team of engineers from Hamilton Standard and Pratt & Whitney to help out. The UTC team met in Hartford for a series of conference calls with the Marietta financial staff. They told Marietta what they knew about Bendix fuel controls. Hamilton

Standard was Bendix's main competitor, and so Hamilton kept close watch on Bendix's business. Hamilton knew which planes had Bendix fuel controls, how much each fuel control cost, what kinds of service contracts Bendix had and what kind of future those contracts had. Pratt & Whitney was Bendix's largest customer. Pratt & Whitney's most popular engine—the F-100 that powers both the F-15 Eagle and the F-16 Fighting Falcon fighter planes—used a fuel control made partly by Bendix and partly by Hamilton Standard. Pratt & Whitney had to do procurement studies for the government on the cost of the engine, and so it had to get information from Bendix on the cost of the Bendix part of the fuel control. The government doesn't let one contractor have a much larger profit margin than another. UTC knew how much it made on the F-100. It could guess how much Bendix made on the fuel control part.

Martin Marietta had some Deep Throat sources of its own. During the week, half a dozen former Bendix executives had called Kidder to volunteer information about Bendix. One had thought the matter so important that he had called from a fishing lodge where he was vacationing. Information came in on the plant square footage, the number of employees, the volume of back orders. Martin Marietta had estimates of sales, earnings, and profit margins. They even had some internal Bendix projections on future business volume.

But Martin Marietta still did not have enough information to go ahead with the deal when the teams sat down to talk about the tall poles on Sunday afternoon. UTC made some concessions. The Marietta stock would be valued at Bendix cost, $27 a share. UTC would not put UTC securities to Martin Marietta. The price of Elliott would be $175 million. Large called Gray. Gray refused to bargain on the $300 million fixed price.

The negotiations almost collapsed. No one at Martin

Marietta could understand why Gray was being so inflexible.

"Go back and work on the price point with Gray," Menaker told Ed Large. "He is being unreasonable."

Large called Gray again. Gray would not budge.

"Harry won't yield," Large told Pownall.

Martin Marietta kept gathering information on fuel controls. Early in the afternoon, Pownall held a telephonic meeting of the Martin Marietta steering committee. He explained that the terms of the deal had changed since it was presented to the board on Friday morning. He detailed the new terms. "We just can't justify the price for fuel controls," he said. "Three hundred million may be right, but I don't know. There is more information coming in. I want to recess the meeting until this evening. Maybe we will have enough by then to evaluate the price. We can't wait much longer."

The Martin Marietta team made another attempt to negotiate the fixed price point. Large called Gray. Gray and Brown were on a boat. An hour later, Large got through. Gray would not concede.

By four o'clock, Martin Marietta still seemed miles from signing a deal. UTC had to put its plan to bid for Bendix the next morning on hold. One of the advertising people called the *Wall Street Journal* to cancel the tombstone announcement that UTC had reserved to announce its offer.

One of Siegel's Deep Throats called back late in the afternoon. The Deep Throat had driven a hundred miles to find a former Bendix employee who had just moved and didn't have a telephone but did have information. The Deep Throat gave Siegel the detailed numbers Siegel had asked for.

That did it. Martin Marietta still didn't know for sure what fuel controls was worth, but it looked like it was at least $300 million, and maybe $400 million. When the steering committee met by telephone again at dinnertime, Pownall said that the new information had finally come in.

"I want to bring the proposal to the whole board," he said. "I will recommend that it be accepted."

The steering committee agreed. The full board would meet at ten o'clock the next day, Tuesday, September 7.

The Martin Marietta directors sat around the conference table at Dewey, Ballantine. Pownall explained the changes that had been made in the agreement since the last session. The $300 million price for fuel controls was fixed, but on the basis of the information that the Deep Throats had called in, the price seemed right.

"This is a really good deal," said Siegel. "It is certainly fair. It could be a great deal. The fuel controls business is worth $300 million to $400 million. We only have to pay $300 million."

The directors had a lot of questions. The meeting dragged on.

"You had better wind up pretty soon," said Zuckert over the speaker phone. "It's the last day of the season up here in Maine, and my hotel is going to close."

The directors laughed.

Pownall summed up the package. "Obviously, Gray's bid for Bendix is an attention-getter," he said. "It is lower than ours. Gray has left himself some room for modification. There is a clear opportunity that Gray will raise and that he will come back to us to ask us to help by buying more assets."

The directors approved the revised package.

●

The day after the board meeting to reject the Marietta offer, Jay Higgins and his arbitrageur, Marty Weinstein, had called Al McDonald, president of Bendix, with a market report. The stock exchange had just closed at four o'clock,

●

●

and Higgins summed up the activity. "It looks good, Al," he said. "It is exactly what we said would happen. Marietta is up. Bendix hasn't moved. There is no volume in our stock. There are lots of rumors: United Technologies, Combustion Engineering, Rockwell. But there's nothing solid. You hear these rumors whenever there is a bid. We've heard that UTC is going to make a bid for Martin Marietta, that it is going to make a bid for Bendix, and that it is going to make a bid for both."

Higgins was ready to sign off, when Weinstein's assistant buzzed from the trading room. "I've got an arb on the phone who says it's urgent," she said.

"Put him through," said Weinstein.

Weinstein took the call on the other line. The arb was so excited that he could hardly get the words out. "Lazard Frères was just restricted in Martin Marietta and Bendix," he told Weinstein.

Weinstein passed the word to Higgins and Higgins explained to McDonald what it meant. Abitrageurs made their money by buying the stock of takeover target companies at market and selling it to the raider for a premium. Investment banking houses don't let their arbs make money on deals the houses are involved in. When a banker's arb is restricted it means that the banker is representing a company that is thinking about making a bid. Lazard must be ready to enter the brawl. And Lazard traditionally represents United Technologies.

Higgins made some calls around to check out the rumor. He knew that Gray and Pownall were buddies. He knew that Gray was interested in aerospace. He knew that Gray was company hungry and that Bendix was an attractive target. At first, Higgins couldn't pin anything down. Then an arb called Weinstein to say that he had posted a photographer in the lobby of the Wachtell, Lipton building every night for three nights running.

.

.

"He took a picture of everyone who went in," said the other arb. "We didn't get Gray, but we got Siegel and Rohatyn. Something is cooking."

Higgins knew that Wachtell, Lipton was Gray's outside law firm. He had the Salomon Brothers advertising man call his sources at the *Wall Street Journal* to find out if United Technologies had any advertising plans. The Salomon flack reported back that UTC had reserved a "tombstone" ad for Tuesday morning. Tombstones are used to announce deals.

At the Bendix eight o'clock strategy meeting on Friday, Higgins brought up the possibility of United Technologies entering the battle. "There are a lot of rumors about UTC," he said. "They're getting stronger. We should start thinking about our immediate reaction to that."

"Gray's been interested in Bendix for quite a while," said Agee. "Gray can't buy us. His antitrust problems are too great."

Fleischer suggested that Hughes Hubbard, Bendix's usual outside law firm, look at antitrust over the weekend, just in case UTC made a bid. Agee agreed that that was a good idea.

"Martin Marietta's team is planning a blockbuster announcement on Tuesday," said Higgins. "That's what my sources say. According to the *Wall Street Journal* this morning, the Marietta people met at Wachtell, Lipton until late last night. My arb says he's heard the term 'defense pact.' Why don't we have the directors meeting on Saturday or Sunday to make a decision on what to do about proration. Then we can get out a blockbuster announcement of our own on Tuesday. Maybe we can be out first."

"I want to see their blockbuster before I do anything," said Agee. "I don't want to show my hand unless I have to. The Bendix directors are already working hard to get into New York for all these board meetings. I don't want to make them ruin their Labor Day weekend on short notice."

"I don't see the point in having the board meeting over the weekend," said Fleischer. "Let's understand where we are on United Technologies before we do anything."

The advisers discussed how Martin Marietta might structure a joint bid with United Technologies. Then they talked about the options that Bendix had when the Bendix proration pool closed at midnight Saturday. Weinstein had predicted that Bendix would get 60 percent of the Marietta stock, but even if Bendix did get that 60 percent, the war was far from over. Shareholders could pull their stock out of the pool until the withdrawal deadline the next week. Bendix had to make sure that the stock that was now tendered stayed tendered. That was the only way to win.

"We will have a board meeting Tuesday afternoon. There will be a meeting of advisers at my suite at four on Labor Day," Agee stated.

Later in the morning, McDonald called Higgins. That meeting we are having on Monday is a very important meeting," he said. "We will be displeased if we don't see the most senior Salomon Brothers talent there."

Higgins knew that meant Gutfreund, the chairman of Salomon Brothers, and Harris, the famous deal-maker based in Chicago. Higgins called Harris. He said that Agee was having a Bendix strategy meeting on Monday in New York and that Agee wanted Harris at it.

"I don't know anything about this deal," said Harris. "Why do I have to come? You run the M&A department and you have been running it for four years."

"Agee only likes to hear things from great men, and he wants to hear our strategy from you," said Higgins.

"Okay," said Harris.

"Agee also hates big meetings," said Higgins. "Meetings with Agee don't last long. I think we need to have a meeting of our own first so that you are totally up to speed when you walk into Agee's strategy meeting."

"Fine," said Harris. "Come to my suite at the Regency first."

The Bendix prorate pool closed at midnight Saturday with 58 percent of the Martin Marietta stock tendered. McDonald called Higgins on Sunday morning.

"Let's run a blockbuster ad on that total in the *Washington Post*," he said. "I want to have it on the desk of every congressman and senator and lobbyist. We want to say that the referendum Bendix has received from Martin Marietta shareholders is twice the highest voter participation in any of the last five presidential campaigns."

Higgins was stunned. "Fifty-eight is good, but it's not great. It's just what we expected. You can't run an ad like that. Besides, they've got a tender out for us. What if they get more stock than we did?"

"Impossible," said McDonald. "Our employees own 23 percent."

●

Monday afternoon at three, the team of Bendix lawyers and bankers met in Harris's suite at the Regency. Everyone had on sports clothes, except Fleischer. He had on a coat and tie.

"Well, counselor," said Harris to Fleischer. "The prorate pool has closed. We have to make sure the stock stays in. What are the options? I'm told that Agee wants the brass at the meeting. Gutfreund and I will be there, but as you know, he and I haven't been doing the deal. You had better bring me up to speed."

"There are basically four things that we can do," said Fleischer. "We can do nothing. We can raise the number of shares that we buy. We can waive some conditions. We can raise our price. Let's go through the pros and cons of each option one by one."

The advisers talked for almost an hour. Finally the team

agreed that the best step was to raise the cash price that Bendix was offering for the Martin Marietta stock.

"I think we should make a conditional raise for all the shares with a split of $7 a share," volunteered Weinstein. "Make an offer with a forty-eight-hour fuse. Say that we'll pay $54 a share if management endorses the idea and $47 if not. The $7-a-share difference is a quarter of a billion. We can send out 'dear fellow shareholder' letters—we're a shareholder—saying 'don't let management screw you out of a quarter of a billion. Write, call, make management accept this great deal.' That ought to put pressure on Martin Marietta to accept."

"That's not my first choice," said Fleischer. "I don't think conditional raises are very effective. First, I have never felt pressure when I was advising a target client considering a conditional raise. If Martin Marietta doesn't accept the conditional offer, we will just end up where we started. We will have set a floor for our next raise. There is no evidence that conditional offers work."

"I think that the chances that Marietta will accept a conditional raise are less than 5 percent," said one of the lawyers.

"I really think that we should go with a straight raise," said Fleischer.

"All right, so we just raise," said Weinstein. "The minimum that the market is going to take is $50 a share. Anything else is going to look skimpy."

"I think I'm up to speed," said Harris after an hour. "Let's go."

Agee's meeting began at four in the Helmsley suite. Most of the team at the Regency meeting weren't invited. Agee wanted only two lawyers at his meeting—Fleischer and Fontaine—and three bankers. Four of the Salomon Brothers team came, though; Higgins and Tanner, who were working on the battle, and Harris and Gutfreund, who weren't. Higgins had wanted Weinstein to come along too, in case Agee asked a very technical arbitrage question that Higgins couldn't answer. Weinstein wasn't allowed into Agee's suite. He waited in McDonald's suite with Kayser and Rowny and did the Sunday *Times* crossword puzzle.

Agee, Cunningham, McDonald, and Fontaine were waiting in the suite when the team from the Regency arrived. Agee knew that the Bendix pool had closed with 58 percent of the Marietta stock, almost exactly what Weinstein had predicted at the early strategy meeting.

"Now what?" asked Agee.

Fleischer explained that Bendix had to keep the stock in the pool and went down the ways to do it that the bankers and lawyers had just talked through. First Bendix could do nothing. There was no competing bid out for Martin Marietta. There wasn't really a reason for an arbitrageur to pull his stock: he couldn't get more money for it from someone else. But if Bendix wanted to make a show of strength, then it couldn't just do nothing. There were several options. Bendix could waive the conditions to its offer. There were two full pages of excuses to withdraw the bid in the Bendix offering circular. Most of them were legal boilerplate. Some of them were important. Bendix could pull the tender if the litigation went badly. Bendix could pull its offer if Congress declared war. Dropping some of the conditions didn't cost anything, but it did show a determination to buy.

"There's a risk," said Fleischer. "We might have to buy even if we don't want to, depending on which conditions we waive and what happens. If we just say we won't drop because Martin Marietta has made an offer for us, we're on the safest ground. If we waive all the conditions, we are committed if something unpredictable happens, like Martin Marietta burning down.

"We can raise the numbers of shares that we buy. If we

•

•

say we will buy all the shares that have been tendered, we're essentially making an any-and-all bid. There is less reason to pull out. Buying more shares might give us some extra leverage in the courts. We can go to a judge and say 'your honor, we own 60 percent.' There are cons to that. Raising the number of shares won't preempt a new bidder from coming in, and if a new bidder comes in, we can't buy for ten days. Raising is expensive.

"That leaves the fourth option: raising our price. Raising the offer means that a new bidder for Marietta has to come in at a higher price. It will be more difficult for Marietta to find a white knight. We are clearly committed to the deal. And raising our price for them increases their cost to buy us, since we will have less cash.

"There are two ways to raise: conditionally and unconditionally. The advisers have talked this through. We are recommending an unconditional raise."

Agee asked some questions. Cunningham sat right next to him and listened.

"I think this has been very useful," said Agee. "I'll think about these options. I'll tell you what I've decided at the board meeting."

•

Higgins was leaving his office downtown for the board meeting at the General Motors Building at half past twelve Tuesday, when the UTC blockbuster announcement came over the tape. Higgins called McDonald. He read the clip over the phone. "It isn't very complete," he said. "It sounds like they're chopping us up to solve their antitrust problem and offering less for us than Martin Marietta did."

"What do you think?" asked McDonald.

"It looks like the whole aerospace industry is lining up against Bendix and Bill Agee," said Higgins. "It's us against them."

•

•

Higgins wanted to talk to Agee. Earlier that morning, Agee had asked Higgins whether Higgins thought it was a good idea for Bendix to raise both the offering price and the number of shares that it would buy. At the time, Higgins had said yes. He had changed his mind. Higgins walked to the head of the table.

"I've been thinking about raising the number of shares to 65 percent," he whispered. "I've chatted with Fleischer about it. Salomon Brothers doesn't think it's a good idea right now. Let's go with just raising the price."

"Why?" asked Agee.

"It takes a lot of cash to raise both the price and the number of shares," said Higgins. "We lose flexibility. It hurts the balance sheet. If we want to do more than raise to $48, let's raise the back-end swap. In any event, let's not give away that flexibility right now."

"Okay," said Agee.

Higgins walked to the back of the room and sat down. Agee began the meeting.

"When Marietta rejected our offer, their board gave salary guarantees to twenty-seven people," said Agee. "I think we ought to give our executives the same kind of protection. I'd like the board to consider golden parachutes for our people."

Agee and the other Bendix executives and advisers left the boardroom. John Cooke, head of Bendix human resources, and John Fontaine had drawn up draft contracts. The outside directors spent an hour discussing them. There was no question that the directors wanted to give out the contracts, but they had to decide just who would get them: would it be only a small circle of top executives or a larger pool of officers? The directors finally settled on sixteen key members of the management team. Agee's staff had put together a sheet listing the provisions of each proposed parachute. The directors talked through them one at a time.

They decided that Agee's contract needed to have a longer life than the others, because he was going to have the most trouble finding a similar job at another company. Agee would get his salary for five years. The others were down for three. The directors fiddled with the terms in the draft. Then they called Agee and the others back into the boardroom.

"Just before the meeting began, United Technologies made a tender for Bendix," said Agee. He passed out copies of the Dow wire on the bid. Fleischer started to explain what it meant.

"Is this official?" asked Rumsfeld.

"It came off the Dow," said Fleischer. "We don't have the offer to purchase, if that's what you mean."

"It isn't very complete," said Rumsfeld.

"Well, no," said Fleischer. "As far as I can tell, United Technologies plans to buy Bendix, and sell some Bendix assets to Martin Marietta to solve its antitrust problems. If that is really what they have in mind, it probably won't work. The concept just doesn't make sense. We're going to buy control of Martin Marietta before United Technologies can possibly buy control of Bendix. United Technologies can't solve its antitrust problems by selling Bendix assets to a Bendix subsidiary."

The directors were irked by Gray's bid. It was lower than the Marietta bid that they had already rejected as "grossly inadequate." It was just about book value, and Gray seemed to be selling assets to Marietta for more than book. Gray was intending to get a $600 million cash payment from Marietta and another $500 million out of Bendix. UTC would make money on the deal, and UTC was proposing to break up Bendix even before it owned the company.

"Harry Gray gets the greatest deal of the century," said Fleischer. "Buying Bendix this way costs him nothing. Our cash, plus what Marietta is paying him, more than covers what he expects to pay for the company."

Agee wanted to move on to the Bendix bid for Marietta. The bankers and lawyers hadn't yet had a chance to analyze the UTC proposal. It would be discussed at the next meeting, when there was more information.

"The Bendix proration pool closed on Saturday night with 58 percent of the Marietta shares," said Agee. "I want to do something to keep the stock in the pool. I suggest that we raise our cash offering price."

"Salomon Brothers thinks that raising the cash offer is the right thing to do at this point," said Higgins. "Raising your offer is a real show of strength. It tells the market and the boys at Marietta that you're deadly serious. It puts pressure on them to do a friendly merger. And this new United Technologies offer makes a raise extremely important. We don't want it to look like we've been blown apart by the UTC offer. The best defense against United Technologies is a strong offense on Martin Marietta."

"Raising unilaterally is bidding against ourselves," said Tavoulareas of Mobil. "We've got a pile of stock in the pool. It isn't going to leave. We are just wasting money."

"I think Tav is right," said Fontaine of Hughes Hubbard. "A raise now is bidding against ourselves. We ought to save that option until we really need it."

"Raising unilaterally is a strong signal to the arbs," said Higgins. "They are expecting us to raise to $50 a share. We need their stock."

"There is no reason to tip our hand so soon," said Tavoulareas. "We need to keep our options open."

Agee sat silent at the head of the table. Higgins and Tavoulareas argued through the pros and cons of the raise.

"Raising might preempt a white knight from coming into the bidding. We might raise the price of Marietta over someone else's range."

"We don't need to raise the offer a penny to win. We should save our money in case we need to put it on the table later on."

"We have to signal resolve. Doing nothing is not only saving options for later, but it is also showing a lack of resolve right now."

"I think a cash raise would be appropriate at this point," ventured Fleischer.

The directors talked about it. They decided to try.

"I suggest that we go to $48 a share," said Agee.

That increase would cost $80 million. The directors talked it over. They voted to raise.

"CITIBANK CAN'T
DO NOTHING"

On the wall behind Ed Hennessy's desk is a print of a Philippine eagle. Hennessy calls it his $20 million eagle. It cost him $20 million. Before Hennessy came to Allied Chemical Corporation in 1979, Allied and Armco Steel had been haggling over how to settle a long-term fixed-price coal contract. The chairmen of the two companies were hardly on speaking terms. A few days after Hennessy moved into the Allied president's office in Morris Township, New Jersey, he called Harry Holiday, chief executive officer of Armco.

"I am coming out to Armco headquarters," said Hennessy. "I'm not leaving until this suit is settled." Hennessy found a solution after one trip and a few phone calls: Allied gave Armco $20 million and a money-losing coal mine. Once the papers on the settlement were signed, the Armco team threw a party for Hennessy at the 21 Club in New York City. Hennessy had admired the set of bird prints on the wall at Armco headquarters. C. William Verity, chairman of Armco, presented the eagle to Hennessy that evening.

When Edward L. Hennessy, Jr., became president of Allied Chemical Corporation in May 1979, the Armco suit was only one of the company's big problems: there were other lawsuits; there were regulatory problems. Allied's earnings were lackluster. It had too much debt. The name Allied Chemical notwithstanding—Hennessy later changed it to Allied Corporation—the company made its money selling oil. More than three quarters of earnings came from the energy division, and much of that income was generated and taxed overseas. Allied did sell an array of chemicals, but the business was highly cyclical and only marginally profitable. Allied didn't have a stake in a fast-growing high-technology market. Hennessy's number-one assignment was to bang the balance sheet back into shape—and that meant paying down debt, dumping unprofitable divisions, and diversifying.

Hennessy seemed cut out for the job. The trim, tough son of a Boston lumber salesman, Hennessy doesn't take nonsense. His manner is gruff New England. He is a finance man; he calls himself a "return-on-assets nut." Hennessy had been a controller at International Telephone and Telegraph when ITT was run by the legendary Harold Geneen. A hop, skip, and jump later, Hennessy became chief financial officer and senior executive vice-president at United Technologies. For eight years, Hennessy had helped Harry Gray orchestrate UTC's takeovers. He was Gray's right-hand man, but Gray was reluctant to name Hennessy president of the company. When an Allied headhunter called, Hennessy jumped ship. Six months later, he was chairman of Allied Chemical.

There had been nothing hesitant about Hennessy's moves once he arrived. The week he took office, Hennessy set up a team to study corporate strategy; his orders were to find high-technology companies for Allied to buy. Two months later, Hennessy bought Eltra Corporation, maker of Prestolite batteries and the world's largest supplier of typesetting equipment. In July 1981, Hennessy bought Bunker

Ramo Corporation, a computer components maker. Three months after that, he bought Fischer Scientific, a leading supplier of instruments to hospitals and laboratories. He bought two dozen small companies. All the while, Hennessy attacked Allied's operating problems. In forty months, sales had doubled; earnings had tripled.

Hennessy was still thinking about another big acquisition when the battle between Bendix and Martin Marietta erupted. Allied had studied Bendix, and Hennessy knew that Bendix would fit right into Allied's new strategy. Buying Bendix would be a quantum leap toward making Allied the kind of company that Hennessy wanted it to be. But Hennessy didn't believe in hostile takeovers and he didn't think that Bill Agee would be receptive to a merger proposal. Hennessy made no moves. When the announcement that Bendix was bidding for Martin Marietta came over the wire, Hennessy thought that the time might be right. He watched carefully. But he waited two weeks before he asked the financial staff to work up some numbers on a possible buy; he didn't want anyone to know that Allied was interested.

Soon the vultures started to circle. Hennessy got calls from several investment bankers who wanted to help him buy Bendix. First Boston, a particularly aggressive banking house, had called several times. Peggy Hanratty, First Boston's assistant creative director, had even called Hennessy on the Sunday of Labor Day weekend, while he was boating off Nantucket Island. Hennessy didn't commit himself. He wanted to stay flexible.

The day after Labor Day, United Technologies bid for Bendix. Bendix was in play. A few minutes after the announcement came over the tape, Hennessy called his old friend John Gutfreund. Hennessy did business with Salomon Brothers. He wanted to find out about Bendix.

Gutfreund's secretary said that he wasn't in the New York office that day. She took a message. Gutfreund had not called back, and Hennessy called him again early Wednesday morning. This time, Gutfreund was in Canada. Hennessy told the secretary to switch him to Jay Higgins.

"Does your boy Agee know how much trouble he's in?" asked Hennessy. "Harry Gray doesn't play around. Does Agee want another bidder?"

"I think he understands the situation," said Higgins. "I've been telling him. But don't do anything yet. Agee may want a white knight, but he doesn't need something out of the blue from right field. That will only make the situation worse."

"Well, if he wants me to come in, I can help." said Hennessy. "I know Gray's bid is inadequate, but the point is that Agee is in real trouble now. I'll give him a better bid and I won't strip the company when I'm finished. Agee's got some very good businesses. It's a good fit with us."

"I know that," said Higgins. "If we start calling around for a white knight, you're my hometown favorite. I'll make sure you get the first call."

Later that morning, Hennessy got a call from Bruce Wasserstein, co-director of mergers and acquisitions at First Boston.

"You saw the announcement," said Wasserstein. He meant the UTC bid. "If you're interested, you've got to get your oar in the water. The Bendix situation is pretty fluid, but it looks like there may be a chance for you to do something."

"I'm not sure I want to buy Bendix," said Hennessy. He didn't say that he had already called Salomon Brothers. "I like some of the businesses. I like especially the technology and defense sectors. I might want to buy those."

●

After Tom Pownall signed the agreement with United Technologies early Tuesday afternoon, he took his team to

Dewey, Ballantine's downtown offices to tie up some legal loose ends. Late in the afternoon, Roy Calvin left for Newark Airport to catch the Martin Marietta jet back to Bethesda. Pownall planned to follow him in an hour or so. At a little after five, Pownall was talking to Fullem when a messenger arrived with an envelope from Bendix. Inside was the letter from Bill Agee raising his cash price to $48 a share.

"What should I do?" asked Pownall. "Should I call a board meeting right away?"

"I would," said Siegel. "You don't want to leave any doubt in Agee's mind. If you give Agee an answer tonight, he'll know you mean business." The *Wall Street Journal* weekday deadline is nine o'clock. Martin Marietta had to get a press release out by then.

"We'll have a meeting by telephone," said Pownall. "We'll do it as soon as the phone company can get it together."

Pownall called his secretary in Bethesda and asked her to arrange a board meeting. Menaker called Newark Airport. The Marietta plane was still on the runway. Calvin was on board having a drink. Menaker asked him to come back to Dewey.

Siegel called his office and asked his assistant to run the numbers on Agee's latest bid through the computer. He needed to know what the $48 a share front-end meant in terms of value. The assistant called back when the numbers were ready. Siegel scribbled down some notes.

The board meeting began at seven thirty. The Marietta executives sat around the table in the Dewey conference room. Menaker read Agee's letter out loud.

Dear Mr. Pownall:

As you are by now well aware, approximately 58 percent of the shares of common stock of Martin Marietta Corporation were tendered to Bendix through last Saturday in addition to the 4.5 percent of your shares that Bendix already owns. We believe that this result represents decisive approval of our proposal by the stockholders of your company.

In the spirit of seeking to effect a harmonious, commercially viable solution, Bendix' Board of Directors has authorized me to raise our price to $48.00 per share for the cash tender offer. Other elements of our initial offer remain intact. I would welcome the opportunity to meet with you in order to discuss our proposal and deal with any questions you or your Board may have.

Martin Marietta's Board is distinguished and experienced. I am certain that they are all well aware of their fiduciary responsibilities to all of your stockholders, including the decisive majority who have demonstrated their desire that our proposal be effected.

Your offer contends that it is probable that, for legal reasons, Martin Marietta will be able to exercise control over Bendix before Bendix can exercise control over Martin Marietta. I trust that your Board is not relying on this sentiment as a basis for continuing your offer. We believe that the analysis underlying this contention is faulty. Apart from legal reasons for our view, we find it unrealistic, once we have purchased control over Martin Marietta, that your Board would continue in its efforts to purchase Bendix shares against the opposition of the company's dominant stockholder and in the face of potential substantial liability of its members for their actions.

The combination of our two companies on the basis we have proposed will result in an enterprise of very strong financial capacity, diversified in important segments of the economy and committed to being one of the preeminent competitors in the defense arena. This prospect is obviously preferable to that of a company stripped of substantial assets and left in a debilitated financial condition which your analysis acknowledges would result from the continued pursuit of your counteroffer.

We have just had the opportunity to note the proposed offer by United Technologies Corporation for Bendix. We have requested our financial and legal advisors to carefully review the offer from all aspects. From the published reports, however, it is immediately apparent that the financial consideration proposed by United Technologies is even less than that proposed by Martin Marietta which our Board, after consultation with Salomon Brothers, determined was grossly inadequate. I also have noted that the United Technologies offer appears subject to a variety of conditions which raise questions about its commitment to the transaction. Finally, the entrance of United Technologies, with the concurrence of your company, confirms the judgment of our Board that Martin Marietta did not have the financial capacity to acquire Bendix and its offer was diversionary in nature.

Our Board's business decision to seek a combination with Martin Marietta was made after a long and thorough study. We do not think that recent events challenge the wisdom of our conclusion.

For all of the above reasons, I think it important that you and I meet promptly to discuss our revised proposal in a spirit of understanding and with a view to achieving a sensible, business-like solution in the best interests of shareholders of both companies.

> Very truly yours,
> William M. Agee

"Who is Bill Agee to tell us what our duty to shareholders is?" asked a director.

•

•

Siegel talked about the financials. He pointed out that the raise was even less than the $50 a share that the arbs had bet was the minimum. Zuckert could not believe that Martin Marietta had been lowballed twice.

"I recommend that we reject the offer," said Siegel. "With the UTC offer on the table, Martin Marietta has more attractive alternatives."

The board agreed.

Siegel ordered a takeout pizza and sat down in an empty office with Menaker and Calvin to draft a response. Pownall decided that this letter would also be released to the press. Two could play at that game.

Dear Mr. Agee:

We have taken note of your most recent revision in The Bendix Corporation's cash tender offer for Martin Marietta Corporation's common shares.

Our board of directors, who are well aware of their responsibilities, are indeed distinguished and experienced, as you correctly observed in your letter to me of this date. Upon consideration of your revised offer, that Board has voted unanimously tonight to reject it on grounds of inadequacy and as being distinctly contrary to the best interests of Martin Marietta shareholders.

I can find no useful purpose to be served by a prompt meeting with you on the basis that you requested.

It has been, and it remains, our conclusion that if these two companies are to be combined, it is in the best interests of shareholders that the combined enterprise be on the terms of our offer of Aug. 31 to purchase a majority of The Bendix Corporation for $75.00 per share.

In this connection, we find it curious that Bendix is persisting in its attempt to deny the Bendix shareholders the opportunity to participate in the very generous tender offer we have made for Bendix. We also find it puzzling that Bendix is pursuing its attempt to alter Bendix's charter in order to prevent the Bendix shareholders from deciding for themselves what is in their own best interests.

You should be aware that our legal advisers have reiterated their view that there is no present legal impediment precluding us from exercising control over Bendix once we purchase a majority of the Bendix shares pursuant to our offer.

You should by now clearly understand that we intend to achieve the objectives which we have established, either through our acquisition of Bendix or our agreement with United Technologies.

Very truly yours,
Thomas G. Pownall

•

After the board meeting Tuesday afternoon when the directors had approved the raise to $48, Agee and McDonald sat down at the round table in Agee's office to talk about Salomon Brothers.

"Salomon Brothers' advice has been ad hoc and largely reactive," said McDonald.

"I think we should broaden our circle of advisers," said Agee. "We need more input."

Late Tuesday afternoon, Michael Rowny, the Bendix vice-president whom Agee had assigned to the merger, called Bruce Wasserstein at First Boston. Ever since he launched his bid for Martin Marietta, Agee had been deluged with phone calls from investment bankers trying to solicit Bendix's business. First Boston had called the day that Bendix bid for Martin Marietta, to find out if there was anything First Boston could do. First Boston had called the day that Martin Marietta had bid for Bendix to suggest that

•

•

Bendix add First Boston to the Bendix team. First Boston had called the day that United Technologies had bid for Bendix to suggest that Bendix add First Boston to the team. When Agee decided to go ahead and hire a second banker earlier that day, he put First Boston on the list of people to call.

Wasserstein met with Rowny and Don Kayser, Bendix's chief financial officer, at nine on Wednesday morning. Wasserstein gave his standard sales pitch. He produced a copy of his full-color brochure. He handed Rowny a package of xeroxes of stories about the big deals that he had worked on. Rowny called Wasserstein back later in the afternoon to set up a meeting with Agee for eleven o'clock at the Helmsley Palace.

When Cunningham let Wasserstein and his partner Tony Grassi in the door, she smiled and turned to Agee. "You remember, Bill," she said, "I told you about Tony. He interviewed me during business school." Grassi had talked to Cunningham about working for First Boston when she had graduated from Harvard.

"That's right," said Grassi.

"Mary is one of my best advisers," said Agee. "She used to be an investment banker." Cunningham had in fact worked for Salomon Brothers as an intern one summer.

The four sat down in the living room. Cunningham brought a tray of oatmeal cookies and a bottle of Seagram's champagne. The oatmeal cookies were good. The champagne was awful.

"I'm thinking of adding you to the team to focus on the defense against United Technologies," said Agee. "I feel responsible for making sure we focus on that while we stay on course on Martin Marietta. The worst thing that could happen would be to sell the company for $63 a share. I'm not against selling the company, but I'm not going to do it at that price."

"What do you see as your options?" asked Wasserstein.

"Bruce," said Agee, "what I want to hear from you is your very best thinking."

"Well, what have you done?" asked Wasserstein. "What kind of analysis do you have of Martin Marietta?"

"I carry that around in my head," said Agee.

"What?" said Wasserstein. "What about contingency planning? Have you thought about options? There are lots of possibilities. You could make a conditional raise. You could look for a white knight. I have talked to companies that might be interested in either the whole company or in some Bendix assets."

If a new company made a bid for Bendix, all of the other companies that had already bid had to wait through a ten-day holding period. Old bidders couldn't buy any Bendix stock until ten days after the announcement. The delay was supposed to give shareholders a chance to consider the latest offer, but it would also flip the time advantage in Bendix's favor. The United Technologies bid had already postponed Martin Marietta's buy-date by one day: originally Marietta had been clear to buy on September 22, fifteen business days after it bid for Bendix; United Technologies had made a bid for Bendix six days later so the buy day was now the 23rd. The new bidder didn't have to bid for all of Bendix to trigger an extension. A bid for Bendix stock from someone who wanted to swap it for Bendix assets or hold it as an investment was just as good.

Agee and Wasserstein talked for an hour. Agee didn't say much about his views. He wanted to get Wasserstein's. Wasserstein didn't say much about his views. He wanted to keep his options open so that he could work for one of the other companies he had talked to if Agee didn't hire him. McDonald walked in and out.

"The board will make an official decision on Friday," said Agee, "but I think you will be asked to join the team.

.

.

Why don't you start working tomorrow."

"Well, we haven't done a lot of work on Martin Marietta yet," said Wasserstein.

"You do that," said Agee. "We'll talk about it over the weekend."

"I can't offer any panaceas," said Wasserstein as he left. "It's late in the game. I don't work miracles."

Higgins had heard rumors that Agee was looking around for a new investment banker. Late Wednesday afternoon, John Gutfreund had called to say that Agee was going to add another adviser to the team. First thing Thursday morning, Higgins stopped at Agee's office to talk about it.

"I think hiring First Boston is a bad idea," said Higgins. "It will look like a rout for Bendix. It will be an inspiration for the other side."

Agee shook his head. "I don't want to be accused of not using all the talent on Wall Street," he said.

"You shouldn't hire another banker in the middle of a deal," said Higgins. "Companies don't do that. Your team will appear to be divided. It will be terrible public relations. The bankers will be fighting each other, playing games and not working together."

"Don't worry, Jay," said Agee. "You've done super. I'm just adding some extra horsepower. I'll do everything I can to help the public relations problem."

•

By the week after Labor Day, the public relations efforts at both Bendix and Martin Marietta were going strong. The day that Bendix had announced its offer, the lobbying team had sent out the prestuffed packages of information to every Washington politico on their list. The New York staff sent similar information kits to reporters. A Bendix executive called the governor of every state that had a Martin Marietta facility and the mayor of the town where the plant was. Then Bendix released an exchange of letters between Bill Agee and Frank Carlucci, the deputy Secretary of Defense. The Defense Department did not oppose the merger. Agee wrote that the merger would create a stronger national defense.

Thursday morning, Martin Marietta released a letter that Tom Pownall had written to "congressional leaders most intimately acquainted with national security matters":

> The media has been filled in recent days with reports on Martin Marietta Corporation's battle against the unwanted tender offer launched against us by The Bendix Corporation. The attack against us involves much more than just another raid on valuable corporate assets, although it is that, too. It also raises serious questions that may affect programs vital to national and international security plans.
>
> Martin Marietta, as a prime system contractor, is engaged in a significant group of critical major projects, many of which are highly visible (i.e., Pershing and MX).
>
> What happens to this work in the hands of a management with no credentials in prime systems? Bendix does participate in the aerospace business at present, but its contracts are mainly in the category of subsystems and components. Its management's reputation, as you can determine from reference to current reports, reflects expertise concentrated on financial aspects of management, not on operations. Indeed, a recent major journal (*Business Week*, August 13, 1982) noted that the Bendix chairman, Mr. Agee "sees himself as a wily financier."
>
> There are enormous differences in handling major

prime systems and in being a "sub" or a component maker. Throughout its entire history, Martin Marietta has concentrated on the prime systems business. The professional careers of all our top management have been devoted to it. Executive insights and executive management philosophies are vital matters. As you have observed from your vantage, these insights by top management are frequently the essential difference between success and failure on major, complex defense systems.

The skilled professional and technical work force that Martin Marietta has developed is a national asset that must be preserved, intact. Under the control of a corporate management with a different commitment, a different philosophy, there would be unacceptable risk. The background, the experience, the dedication, the personal involvement of top executive management are crucial elements in the creation and the maintenance of the business environment in which this vital work is carried forward. So, the question is not whether an inexperienced management would intentionally dismantle the assets or disperse the critical talents, but whether it could or would sustain it, absent the depth of insights required to create it in the first place.

For these reasons, among others, we are resisting the forcible attempt by Bendix to take over Martin Marietta on grounds that it is clearly against the best interests of Martin Marietta and its shareholders. It also is not in the national interest.

The Martin Marietta lawyers had had trouble getting a copy of the Bendix SESSOP rules. When they finally got their hands on the document, the day after Martin Marietta launched its countertender for Bendix, they discovered that the Bendix employees could only withdraw shares from the plan on the first of every month. The Martin Marietta offer expired on the twenty-eighth of September. It was logistically impossible for the employees to sell their shares to Martin Marietta. And it looked like Citibank, the plan trustee, couldn't sell the shares either. The Bendix rules said that Citibank could only sell on the orders of the plan members.

Then Doris Rush, a Martin Marietta pension lawyer, started to think about a solution. The Employee Retirement Income Security Act, ERISA, said that the trustee of a retirement plan had to follow the plan rules as long as the rules let the trustee do what a "prudent" investor would do. Rush thought that ERISA meant that Citibank had to evaluate the Martin Marietta offer. Citibank could decide not to tender, but it couldn't not tender just because the plan rules said so. The Dewey, Ballantine lawyers didn't think that Rush would get anywhere with her argument, but Rush tracked down an ERISA expert at the Labor Department who agreed with her. That was encouraging. Just after the contract with United Technologies was signed, Rush called Arthur Sporn, a pension expert at the New York law firm Barrett, Smith, Schapiro, Simon & Armstrong for a word of advice. Sporn is one of the top pension lawyers in the country.

"Could you write an opinion saying that Citibank has to consider the offer?" Rush asked Sporn.

"Yes," said Sporn. "I agree with you. But this is a complicated and delicate subject. It is not the sort of thing that can be done in twenty-four hours."

"Twenty-four hours?" asked Rush. "Who is talking about twenty-four hours? I'll be there in two. Start drafting."

First thing Wednesday morning, Sporn finished up his opinion. Martin Marietta sent a copy of it to Citibank. Then

Carol Trencher, a Dewey, Ballantine ERISA lawyer, called the Labor Department in Washington to see if she could get the federal government to put a little pressure on Citibank. Trencher talked to a government ERISA lawyer. She told him what the plan rules said and what was happening. She asked him what the official policy was on a plan that did not give the trustee the authority to tender shares: could Citibank sit back and do nothing?

The official considered the question. "Citibank can't do nothing," he said.

Trencher called Fullem. Fullem called Menaker. The team began to discuss the position that the Labor Department had taken. Early that evening, Fullem called the Citibank lawyer handling the SESSOP.

"Is it true that Citibank is not going to tender the SESSOP shares?" asked Fullem.

"Yes, it is," said the lawyer.

"Are you aware that the loss to employees if we take control and you didn't tender will be over $100 million?" asked Fullem. The employees would have to accept the lower back end of the Marietta offer.

"We have reviewed the situation with our counsel," replied the lawyer. "We do not have the power to tender."

"Are you aware that the Labor Department disagrees with you?" asked Fullem.

The man was silent. "You say the Labor Department disagrees?"

"Yes," said Fullem. "We have discussed the matter with them. They said to us, and I quote 'Citibank can't do nothing.' "

"You told them what kind of plan we have? That we don't have the authority to sell the shares?"

"We did indeed."

"But what can we do? It is seven o'clock. The pool closes

tomorrow at midnight. There is no way that we can call all of the plan members in twenty-four hours and find out what they want to do."

"You can tender," said Fullem. "You can then spend a whole two weeks talking to them to find out if they want to withdraw."

The man thought for a minute. "That's a good idea," he said. "That's a very good idea. I'll talk to you tomorrow."

By the middle of Thursday afternoon, Fullem had still not heard back from Citibank. There were so few Bendix shares in the Marietta prorate pool that Fullem was afraid that the offer would be a disaster. The strategists had already written a press release explaining that the reason Marietta had pooled only 25 percent of the Bendix shares was that Bendix had mailed out the Marietta material to shareholders late. Labor Day weekend had come smack in the middle of the solicitation period. Fullem called Citibank. The lawyer he had talked to the day before was at a meeting.

Larry Adams came into Fullem's office. Fullem said that he thought he was making progress toward getting the SESSOP shares tendered.

"I'll bet you five dollars Citibank doesn't tender," said Adams.

"It's a deal," said Fullem.

Fullem called Citibank again. The lawyer was still unavailable. An hour later, Fullem placed another call. The lawyer was at a meeting. Fullem said he had to talk to the man. The lawyer came to the phone.

"We haven't made a decision yet," said the Citibank lawyer.

"Well," said Fullem. "I just wanted you to know that if you don't decide to tender by five o'clock, Martin Marietta intends to sue you. And I happen to know that there is also a Bendix employee, a plan member, who will sue you as well."

At five o'clock, Fullem called to find out how many shares had been sent into the Marietta tender pool. The total was only 3 million. Marietta had bid for 12. It was going to be embarrassing.

Fullem called for an update on shares in the pool: 3.4 million.

At eight, Fullem called again. The total was almost 7 million. Dick Katcher of Wachtell, Lipton called in from the U.S. Tennis Open about ten o'clock to find out how it was coming. There were 9 million shares in the pool.

George Davidson, a Hughes Hubbard litigator, was working on a lawsuit in Conference Room C when a man from Citibank called. He said his name was Bissett. It was after ten o'clock, and Davidson knew that something must be seriously wrong. Otherwise Citibank would have let the matter go till morning.

"Is Mr. Agee there?" asked Bisset.

Davidson was surprised. Bill Agee did not spend his nights in conference rooms at Hughes Hubbard. "No, of course not," he said. "Maybe I can find him for you."

Bisset said that Citibank had an important letter for Mr. Agee. Davidson got in touch with Hal Barron, Bendix's general counsel. Barron called Citibank. A staff lawyer read the letter to him over the phone. Then Barron called Agee.

Bill Agee was holding a strategy session in his suite when the call came. He knew that Citibank had drafted a letter to SESSOP members saying that the bank did not have the authority to tender and that the letter had been delivered to the printer at six o'clock that night. Now Barron told Agee that Citibank had decided to tender after all.

"You're kidding," said Agee. Agee knew that Harry Gray was on the Citibank board. He thought that maybe that explained the Citibank tender.

.

.

At eleven o'clock Fullem called to find out how many shares had been tendered: 10 million. At seven minutes before midnight, one of the Dewey, Ballantine lawyers watching the shares come in called Fullem. Citibank had tendered the SESSOP shares. Marietta had collected three quarters of all the Bendix stock.

It was an emotional victory. Bill Agee was a SESSOP member. Even some of his stock had been tendered.

RAISING THE ANTE

•

When Bendix rejected the Martin Marietta bid, it opened a new battlefront by proposing shark repellents to be approved by its shareholders. Martin Marietta immediately launched its counterattack. Most shareholders don't come to special shareholder meetings; instead they send in absentee ballots called proxies. To convince shareholders to vote their proxies, both Bendix and Martin Marietta planned to deluge shareholders with letters, mailgrams, and telephone calls explaining just why the Bendix shark repellents were such a good or bad idea. The traditional Wall Street wisdom is that you can't pass shark repellents in the middle of a takeover war, but since 23 percent of the Bendix stock was owned by Bendix employees, Martin Marietta was worried that the amendments just might get through.

Bendix had an edge: Bendix knew what the shark repellent amendments said. Marietta didn't. The Martin Marietta lawyers couldn't even figure out how many there were. Bendix wrote a letter to shareholders explaining why the proposed amendments were a good thing; Martin Marietta wrote a much more general letter saying that all shark re-

•

•

pellents were a bad idea. Bendix sent out its letter as soon as it was drafted. Marietta couldn't mail its letter until the lawyers saw the Bendix letter and knew that their answer made sense.

The Bendix proxy statement finally came out on Wednesday, the day before the Martin Marietta proration pool closed. The Marietta lawyers got a copy hot off the press, read it through, and rushed their own statement to the printer. As the printer was setting up the machines for the run, a Dewey, Ballantine lawyer called from his office to say that Marietta had to change the color of its proxy card: they couldn't use the same shade as Bendix. The printer suggested red.

"You can't use red proxy cards," said the proxy solicitor. "No one sends red cards. Voters won't send them back."

The printer didn't have another color. The lawyers scampered through the stock. They uncovered some gray cards with the wrong kind of corners. They would do. The presses started to roll.

All that Martin Marietta needed now was a list of the addresses and telephone numbers of the Bendix stockholders. Bendix had said that would be waiting in Southfield Friday morning, September 10.

Early Friday morning, a Dewey, Ballantine lawyer named Barry Biggar flew out to Michigan to get the Bendix shareholder list. He was expecting Bendix to do everything it could to make it difficult for Marietta to copy the list, and so he had asked Marietta to send out a team of technicians and some equipment. When Biggar got to the airport, the team was waiting. They had just what he had asked for: a microfilming machine in case Bendix didn't provide xeroxing equipment; a battery pack in case the room the list was in had no electrical outlet; a set of spotlights so that the team could see if the room had no lights;

and enough film to copy six thousand pages, three times what Dewey, Ballantine estimated it would take if Bendix ran off the list with only twelve names on a page.

The team arrived at Bendix about noon. Biggar reported to the building with a proxy solicitor and a technician. He left the equipment in the parking lot. He didn't want the equipment confiscated before he saw the list. A cordon of guards and a Bendix lawyer met Biggar at the front entrance of the building and escorted him to a small room next to the employee cafeteria. There was both an electrical outlet and an overhead light. The list was on the table in four large cardboard cartons. Bendix had run it out of the computer with only three names on a page.

Biggar could hardly believe his eyes. The superlist was at least twelve thousand pages long. He could photograph only six thousand. Biggar brought in the technicians and the equipment.

"This is going to take twelve hours," said one of the technicians when he saw the list.

"Get started," said Biggar. "The sooner we start, the sooner we will finish."

By four o'clock, the technicians had finished copying only one box. Biggar started to worry. Bendix might kick him out at five o'clock. He told the technicians to get a drink to brace up for the long night. Then he called the Martin Marietta lawyer in Delaware, where Bendix had said that morning they would produce a list.

"Bendix told the judge that they would *give* us a list," said the lawyer. "I'd just take that one."

Biggar called the Bendix lawyer who had been working with him.

"We have been promised a list," he said.

The Bendix lawyer didn't know anything about that, but said he'd find out. An hour later he came back. "It's yours," he said, pointing to the list. "I have a second copy for United Technologies and I will have a computer tape of the list for you tomorrow."

•

Harry Gray had flown out west on Wednesday afternoon. Conquistadores del Cielo was holding its annual ranch convocation at the A-Bar-A Ranch in Wyoming that week. And Gray didn't want to miss it. Conquistadores was founded by Jack Frye and John Walker of TWA in 1937. It is the aerospace industry's equivalent of the Bohemian Club. Once a year the members meet to compete at knife throwing, pistol shooting, and horseshoe tossing. They hold secret meetings. They don't tell outsiders what they talk about. Everyone who is anyone in aerospace is there.

On Wednesday night, Clark MacGregor, the United Technologies senior vice-president for external affairs, went to a reception in Washington of the Business Coalition to Support a Balanced Budget. Gray had been invited, but since Gray was in Wyoming, MacGregor went in Gray's place. During the reception, Agee walked over to MacGregor.

"Hi, Clark," he said. "No disrespect to you, Clark, but I was hopeful of being able to see Harry. I would have enjoyed talking to him."

MacGregor thought that Agee sounded worried. "I can and will call him," said MacGregor. "Give me your phone number."

Agee gave MacGregor two numbers, one at the Helmsley, one at his office.

MacGregor called Gray in Wyoming. He explained that he had just spoken to Agee and that Agee had expressed disappointment that Gray hadn't been at the Washington meeting. "He wants you to call him as soon as possible," said MacGregor. "He seemed very anxious to talk to you."

•

•

MacGregor read off the two phone numbers Agee had given him. Gray wrote them down. He marked the message urgent.

First thing Thursday morning, Gray called Bill Agee's office number. A secretary answered. "Mr. Agee is not available," she said.

"Well, I was told that he wanted to talk to me and that it was very urgent," said Gray. "So let him know that I called. If I were doing your job, I guess I'd get in touch with him and tell him, because unless somebody has been misquoted, he said it was very urgent."

By late Thursday afternoon, Agee still hadn't called Gray. The business day was winding to a close on the East Coast. Gray was starting to get worried. He called Agee's office number again. The same secretary answered.

"There must be some misunderstanding," she said. "I did get hold of Mr. Agee and he said he really isn't all that interested in talking to you. Whenever you get back here is fine."

"Okay," said Gray. He asked the woman for her name. She said it was Barbara. Gray wrote that down next to Agee's office number.

Tom Pownall flew out to Wyoming for the Conquistadores meeting on Thursday night. Pownall was president of the club and, although he had missed the first three days of the outing at the A-Bar-A Ranch because of the Bendix battle, he felt an obligation to act as the master of ceremonies for the closing sessions. Pownall had asked the ranch manager to put a direct line to Martin Marietta headquarters in his suite. The phone service at the ranch was rather primitive. The rooms didn't have their own phones; the switchboard was an old plug-in model.

Friday morning, Pownall went to breakfast with Harry Gray. The two were sitting at the table with several other aerospace executives when the cook came out of the kitchen.

"There's a man on the phone in the kitchen for you," said the cook. "He says he's got to talk to you. It's a Mr. Agee."

Gray was a little surprised that Agee had chosen breakfast time to call. As he stood up to go into the kitchen to talk, the waiter arrived with breakfast. He set a steaming plate of scrambled eggs and bacon at Gray's place. Gray followed the cook into the kitchen. Gray could hardly hear himself think over the clatter of the pots and pans.

"Is there somewhere in here that's quieter?" he asked. "Is there a room where you sit down and make up menus and those things?"

The cook led Gray into a tiny office with a tiny desk. There was an antique phone on the desk. Gray picked up the receiver.

"How soon can we get together and talk?" asked Agee.

"Well, Bill," said Gray, "I'm happy to talk to you, but I'm in Wyoming right now and I was told that you weren't necessarily in any hurry to talk to me."

"There must be some misunderstanding," said Agee. "I do want to talk to you."

Gray pulled the slip of paper with the phone number written on it out of his pocket. He read off Barbara's name.

"This is the person who told me that," said Gray.

"Well, that's my secretary all right," said Agee.

"Bill," said Gray. "I'm not going to fly back from here just to talk to you. We could have had a meeting before I came out, but you said you couldn't do that." Rohatyn had called Agee just before the offer was announced. Agee had told Rohatyn that he didn't need to meet with Gray then. "I will come back on Sunday. I'll be happy to meet with you in New York on Monday or Tuesday."

"How about Saturday?" he asked.

"No," said Gray.

"How about Sunday?"

.

1   2   2

.

"No. I've got a commitment to carry people back on our airplane. Look, I offered to talk to you before I came out here. I'll meet with you on Tuesday. It will take a certain amount of extra effort, but I'll get there."

Agee agreed to meet on Tuesday.

"Let's meet in New York City at ten o'clock," suggested Gray. He had to be in New York for the Citibank board meeting that afternoon.

"Fine," said Agee. "Why don't you come up to my suite here at the Helmsley."

"I don't think that's an appropriate place for us to meet," said Gray.

"Well, Mary and I are here and we can talk," said Agee.

"I'd be happy to meet you at your New York office," said Gray.

Agee then suggested a law office. Gray agreed to meet him there.

•

After he called Gray, Agee went to the Bendix board meeting. He was just walking into the boardroom, when Higgins pulled him aside.

"Bill, we've got to meet with Hennessy," said Higgins. "Hennessy has been calling us. He wants to sit down and talk with you. He wants to be a white knight. It is critical that we talk to him."

"I'm going to see Harry Gray next week," said Agee. "Have John set something up with Hennessy for Monday or Tuesday."

Agee went into the boardroom. Higgins called Gutfreund to ask him to set up a meeting.

The first item on the Bendix agenda was the SESSOP. Citibank had tendered the shares the night before. Richard Pogue, the lawyer from Jones, Day, Reavis & Pogue hired to study the situation, gave a status report. The tender was unauthorized. The company had drafted amendments to the plan rules. Employees would be allowed to withdraw their shares a couple of days early so that they could sell them to Martin Marietta. Taking the shares out of the plan to sell to Martin Marietta would trigger all the usual tax and benefit penalties. The income would be taxable, not tax deferred. "Nonvested" shares that had been contributed by Bendix in the past two years would be forfeited. An employee who withdrew some shares couldn't participate in the SESSOP for the next six months. Under the new rules, Citibank would sell shares only if the owner told the bank to sell. Undesignated shares would stay in the SESSOP.

Next, Agee asked Fleischer to talk about the United Technologies offer.

"The antitrust lawyers tell me that they have a good case against UTC," said Fleischer. "They don't think that the deal with Marietta will solve the antitrust problem."

Two antitrust lawyers stood up to explain just why. There were three parts to the case. First: the laundry list of products overlaps, many of which UTC conceded. Bendix claimed that it might not be possible physically to separate the product lines that UTC would have to sell to Martin Marietta; to sell the product lines in bigger separable chunks would cost much more than $600 million. Second: the scheme just didn't make sense. Bendix would control Martin Marietta before United Technologies could buy Bendix and begin to sell parts of Bendix to Marietta. UTC could not solve antitrust overlaps with Bendix by selling parts of Bendix to a Bendix subsidiary. Third: potential competition. According to senior Bendix engineers, the next revolution in airplane engineering would be the integration of fuel and flight control systems. Already, a prototype system had been developed for the Harrier jump jet that makes an almost vertical takeoff from the landing strip. To keep the plane from somersaulting when it noses up, the up-and-down steering gear is connected to the throttle by computer: the fuel mix is based on the angle of the nose of the plane to the ground. Someday that kind of sophisticated engine system would be used in all commercial planes and there are only three companies that make both parts of the system: Bendix, United Technologies, and General Electric. If UTC sold Bendix fuel controls to Martin Marietta, there would be only two.

The directors talked about Gray's bid. Agee thought that the transaction that Gray had negotiated with Martin Marietta was terribly favorable to him. "At virtually no cost Gray had an opportunity to buy some very valuable assets of Bendix. Agee was against the proposal for three reasons. One: the combined offer was very low. Two: it requires significant dismembering of Bendix. Three: most important, the shareholders who would receive the lowest value under Gray's offer were the Bendix employees." Agee assumed that the SESSOP members wouldn't sell; that meant they would get stock, not cash, if UTC won. The directors rejected the UTC offer.

"We've got to make a strong move in connection with rejecting the United Technologies offer," said Higgins. "The market thinks that Harry Gray only makes a bid when he is serious. Bendix stock is moving up. Marietta's proration pool is full. You have to do something. You can't just wait around and give the impression that you're disorganized and that you've been taken by surprise."

"As I see it," said Agee. "There are three options. We can increase the number of shares that we buy. We can waive some conditions. Or we can increase the cash price."

"We've raised once," said Rumsfeld. "Now you're talking about raising again. How much do you think this company is worth?"

"A lot more than $48," said Agee. "I'd prefer not to say."

"Maybe you had better," said Rumsfeld. "You may be counting on board support that is not there. We need to talk about how much we are willing to pay."

Agee asked the bankers and lawyers to leave. The directors talked about price. Agee reminded them that they had okayed $50 to $52 a share at the first board meeting, but he didn't want to be pinned down. He wanted to keep his flexibility.

The advisers came back into the boardroom. Agee asked Fleischer to explain the strategic options. "Gentlemen," said Fleischer. "There are two things you can do now to make the offer stronger. You can waive conditions or you can increase the number of shares that you are going to buy. The conditions that are now in the offer say that we can walk away right now. There has been a lot of litigation. Martin Marietta has bid for us. Those are both outs under our offer. If we say we won't withdraw because Marietta has bid, we strengthen our commitment."

"We want to signal resolve to the market," said Higgins. "The arbitrageurs are playing a game of probability. They look at two things: how many cents they get on the dollar of stock tendered if we buy and how likely we are to buy. An offer that gives them only fifty cents on the dollar, but is sure to happen because there are no conditions, may be 'stronger' than an offer of one hundred cents on the dollar that has holes like swiss cheese. The number of cents on the dollar depends on two things: how much more stock was tendered than we asked for and how much we are going to pay for the shares we buy. If we raise the number of shares we buy, we raise the number of cents on the dollar, because we buy more of everyone's stock. If we waive conditions, we are making the offer more certain. Raising the number of shares that we buy is important, but waiving conditions is a stronger move."

"Which are you recommending," asked a director, "raising or waiving?"

"The strongest step is to do both," said Higgins. "No one has ever waived all the conditions and I am going to stop short of recommending that. You can certainly consider it. I am recommending that you waive the litigation and the Marietta tender as conditions. I am also recommending that you raise the number of shares."

Agee polled around the table to find out what the directors thought about the two options.

"This isn't the time to waive conditions," said Tavoulareas of Mobil. "We don't want to put all our cards on the table until the end of the battle. We don't need to do anything now. We should save our ammunition." Tavoulareas had been an active player in the merger game. The year before he had lost two headline battles: Conoco and Marathon Oil.

"I think it's important to do something," said Higgins. "The market believes in Gray. Bendix stock is moving up."

"We need to save our strength," said Tavoulareas. "There is no point in doing anything now."

"With all due respect to Mr. Tavoulareas, I just don't agree," said Higgins. "If Gray raises his bid now, he is going to get all our stock. The arbs are going to forget our offer for Marietta and tender to Gray, and by the time we find a white knight and announce a new offer for Bendix, no one is going to tender to our white knight because Gray will be able to buy the next day. We have got to act now. We have got to signal strength."

Higgins and Tavoulareas discussed the merits of waiving for about ten minutes.

"I want Bendix to take the strongest step possible," said Higgins. "I think we should waive as many conditions as possible. I know that there has never been an unconditional offer, but that is the strongest thing that we could do. That is what I would do if I were on the other side."

Making an unconditional offer was pretty risky. The directors chose the safer route of just giving up the right to pull the offer, because of the legal skirmishes to date and the Martin Marietta bid for Bendix.

Agee suggested that Bendix raise the number of shares it was going to buy to 55 percent of the Marietta stock. The directors had talked about doing that on Tuesday, and they knew that it was a strong step. It was also expensive. They approved the raise.

As soon as the board meeting was over, Higgins hurried to Salomon Brothers. When he got to his office at seven-thirty, he had a note that Gutfreund had already left to catch the *Concorde* to London. The pink slip said that Gutfreund had tried to reach Hennessy, but Gutfreund hadn't been able to get through. Gutfreund had left a message for Hennessy to call Higgins about Bendix. Higgins waited for half an hour, but Hennessy didn't call. Higgins went home for the night.

Later in the evening, Higgins called Agee.

"Gutfreund left a message for Hennessy, but didn't get to speak to him," Higgins said. "I've called Hennessy's number myself, but no one answers. I'll keep trying."

"Jay, to close the loop on this subject," said Agee, "you don't need to call Hennessy. Hennessy and I spoke this evening. His intentions are honorable, and he's there if I need him."

"That's great, but we've got to meet with him and his group to make sure they're there," said Higgins.

"We'll talk about it next week," said Agee.

Hennessy called Higgins at home on Sunday night.

"When I got back to my office on Friday, I tried to call you," he said, "I haven't been able to get through."

"I've been on my boat this weekend," said Hennessy.

"I spoke to Agee late Friday. I told him that Allied is there if he needs us. Beyond that we didn't get very far. What does Agee want to do?"

"Ed, I don't know," said Higgins. "I want him to sit down and meet you. Before the board meeting on Friday, he told me to go ahead and set up a meeting. Then he tells me on Friday night that he has talked to you and knows you're there and that he doesn't need to meet with you. I keep telling him time is running out."

"Tell him that I am ready to meet with him anytime, anywhere," said Hennessy.

"Ed, believe me," said Higgins, "if we decide to do a deal, you're my hometown favorite. I'll do everything I can to get Agee to meet with you as soon as possible. He hasn't been very cooperative, but if I make any progress, I'll let you know. Agee is very independent."

DECISION TREES

 Saturday was a lovely, sunny day in New York. Agee and Cunningham went to the semifinal match of the U.S. Tennis Open in Flushing Meadow with Fleischer and his wife and Warren Phillips, chairman of Dow Jones, and his wife. The first match was Jimmy Conners versus Guillermo Vilas. Connors won. During the intermission, Fleischer and Agee walked out of their box to talk.

Agee had told Fleischer on Friday afternoon that he and Gray were going to meet in New York on Tuesday. Fleischer didn't think there was any point in meeting; he didn't think Agee would be able to make Gray pay a higher price for Bendix. Fleischer had called his antitrust expert and the lawyer had told him that there was a chance that a meeting between Agee and Gray could compromise the Bendix antitrust suit.

"I don't think it's a good idea to meet with Harry Gray," said Fleischer. "The meeting could hurt our case. The only time to talk to Gray is when you are in a position of strength."

"I'll think about it," said Agee.

Agee and Fleischer walked back to the box. The second match was Ivan Lendl against John McEnroe. Lendl upset McEnroe. Agee left early.

●

It rained all day Saturday in Wyoming. The rodeo had to be canceled. Pownall wanted to ride: he had won the rodeo twice before, and anyone who wins a Conquistadores event three times gets to retire the trophy. Instead, Pownall went to the Conquistadores board meeting, the membership meeting, and the awards ceremony.

Then Pownall sat down to play some poker with Harry Gray. Gray asked Pownall about the possibility of a joint raise: United Technologies would raise its cash offer for Bendix to $85 a share; Martin Marietta would buy $100 million more in Bendix assets from United Technologies.

"I'll think about it," said Pownall. "Raising the ante isn't going to be easy."

Gray said that he was willing to sell Martin Marietta another United Technologies company instead of more Bendix assets if UTC and Martin Marietta couldn't come up with a big enough package of Bendix businesses. The price of the company was $400 million. Pownall asked some questions about the UTC company. Gray answered them. He offered to have his people meet with the Marietta financial staff the next day.

"I'll think about it," said Pownall.

Pownall called Siegel at his home in Green Farms, Connecticut.

"I'm out in Wyoming playing poker," he said. "Gray wants to raise his offer and he wants us to raise our ante. Can you get together a meeting in Bethesda tomorrow to talk about that?"

"How much does Gray want us to raise?" asked Siegel. He wasn't sure he liked the idea.

●

●

"A hundred million," said Pownall. "He's offering to sell us another UTC company for $400 million, and, of course, fuel controls for $300 million."

"We'll talk about it," said Siegel. "And we've got to talk about something else. We have to strengthen our bid. Agee thinks he can beat UTC on antitrust and he thinks that once he buys our stock, we won't buy his. He is rationalizing that no target has ever kept resisting after the raider bought a majority of his stock. But we have an advantage: we can kick out his board by written consent before he can do anything to ours. I think the best way to convince him that we are serious is to announce that we are going to buy unless either Bendix drops its offer for us or the shark repellent amendments pass."

Siegel didn't say so, but he had another reason for the suggestions. He knew that Gray liked the Martin Marietta aerospace business and sensed that Gray wanted to buy the whole company. If Martin Marietta's offer for Bendix were more credible than United Technologies', Marietta might be able to keep its independence.

"I'll think about the idea," said Pownall.

Siegel called the advisers for a meeting in Bethesda Sunday afternoon. Gray left for Connecticut Sunday morning. Pownall flew back to Maryland.

•

At three o'clock Sunday afternoon, Pownall and his team sat down with Siegel and his team in Pownall's office.

"I don't think that Martin Marietta should be thinking about increasing the ante at all," said Siegel. "If Gray wants to raise his bid, let him pay for it."

"The company he wants to sell you just isn't worth $400 million," said Wood. "I followed the industry when I was at McKinsey & Company, and I've made some guesstimates

•

•

at earnings. It doesn't fit with your businesses. It's not a good deal."

"United Technologies thinks it is worth the $400 million," said Pownall. "They know the company better than we do. I feel very comfortable working with Harry. I have every reason to believe we will be treated fairly."

"Raising the ante is more certain than going on by ourselves," said Leithauser.

"I am going to recommend the raise to the board tomorrow," said Pownall.

"What about strengthening our offer?" asked Siegel. "I want to propose to the board that we make a formal statement that if Bendix buys, Martin Marietta will buy. If we do that, then Bendix makes both decisions. Rationally, Bendix will withdraw."

"What if Bendix doesn't?" asked Pownall. "Won't that be a disaster?"

"No," said Siegel. "If both companies buy, Marietta will have a difficult year. We'll have to sell some assets, maybe issue some stock. But that's doable. We've already talked to some buyers. We've got one that wants to buy the truck brake shoe business. Another wants to buy Warner & Swasey. A. G. Becker, the investment banker, says that it has a consortium that wants to buy the industrial division. There have been two calls on Marietta chemicals, two on cement, one on aluminum."

•

Wasserstein met with Agee and Cunningham in the Helmsley suite at ten on Sunday night. He had suggested that Tony Grassi come along, but Agee had said he wanted to see Wasserstein alone. The three strategists sat at the dining room table.

"Bill, this is a mess," said Wasserstein. "As long as Marietta is committed to buy, the timing difference puts you behind the eightball. Once they buy your stock, they will throw you out. There is no solution to that problem. You are in bad trouble here, just like the papers say."

"I can buy first," said Agee. "I can't believe that I can get thrown out first."

"Marietta can take control first," said Wasserstein. "If you don't do something soon, your company is going to get sold for $62 a share.

"Bill, I don't have a stake in what has happened so far, so I'm going to be perfectly candid with you. First, before you propose a deal, your team is supposed to do its homework. As far as I can see, that wasn't done. We don't know of any qualitative work on Marietta. We have done some for you over the past few days. Marietta is worth $51 to $60 a share.

"Second, before you propose a deal, your team is supposed to do some contingency planning. As far as I know, there wasn't any here. You have lined up no extenders, no asset deals, no additional financing, no white knight. You have to have a second or third defense line."

Wasserstein had brought the First Boston qualitative study of Martin Marietta with him. He pulled out the slender, dark blue binder and set it on the table. He worked through the pages with Agee. When he had finished, Wasserstein got out a hand-drawn decision tree that he had put together and a calendar of important dates. He handed copies of both to Agee and Cunningham.

"Bill, you have to understand that there is a serious risk here that whatever the lawyers are saying about voting, you can lose even if you buy first," said Wasserstein.

"But if they can't vote, doesn't that mean we can win?" asked Agee.

"Do you want to bet your company on their not being able to vote?" asked Wasserstein. "You won't find out whether or not they can vote until it's too late. If they can, you will have sold your company for a bargain-basement price. If they can't, but they have already bought, then you 'win,' but it's a Pyrrhic victory because you may be a target anyhow. Fleischer says that Marietta might be able to sell any nonvoting shares that it owns to someone else who will be able to vote them."

"There's always the chance that the shark repellents will pass," said Agee.

"That's a long shot," said Wasserstein. He pointed to the decision tree. He guided Agee through the branches. That was tricky, since some of them didn't connect to anything. "You have to think about what you can do and what Marietta will do in response," said Wasserstein. "No matter what you do, they can make a move to beat you. The bottom line is that there are real problems here and you have three options: bribery, war, and peace.

"Bribery means you go down and seduce them. You make a conditional raise with a long fuse. You say that you will increase your bid if they will do a merger friendly. You leave that offer on the table until you buy. The tactic has worked before: just last summer American General made a conditional raise on its offer for NLT and NLT accepted, even though NLT had made a Pac Man and could buy first."

"Now wait a minute," said Agee. "We just raised from $43 to $48."

"You mispriced the company," said Wasserstein.

"We've made a raise," said Agee. "We've given the money away. We don't want to bid against ourselves again."

"You ought to make a conditional raise," said Wasserstein.

"We aren't going to do that," said Agee.

Wasserstein pointed to the dark blue binder on the table. "The company is worth $51 to $60 a share," he said.

"What are the other alternatives?" asked Agee.

"There's war," said Wasserstein. "We can keep fighting. There are some aggressive options. You can find an ex-tender bidder. You can make an asset deal. You can look for a white knight. You can make a self-tender."

Wasserstein put two lists on the table in front of Agee. "We have put together some names of companies that might be interested in bidding for all or part of Bendix," he said.

"Maybe we should be thinking about investors," said Agee.

"I've got a list of investors," said Wasserstein. "I've talked to some potential asset buyers." First Boston had contacted Allied over Labor Day weekend. They had talked to a group of private investors that wanted to buy any Bendix assets at a discount. They had spoken with a company that liked one of the auto parts businesses.

"Bill, you need a safety net in case things go wrong," said Wasserstein. "We have to pursue all the options. Later we can choose, but we have to get ready now. I'll need some information about Bendix, internal information, so I can have my people make up a brochure. You can't go around selling a company or an investment without some infor-mation."

"What's the third option?" asked Agee.

"Peace," said Wasserstein. "You can negotiate a with-drawal. It will have to be a three-way withdrawal; it will have to involve selling back the 4.5 percent block of Martin Marietta that you already own, and you will have to get a good price for that block or you are going to be a target. You can't accept a peace without honor."

"I know that," said Agee. "I don't want to sell the com-pany for $62 a share."

"There ought to be a line of communication between the two sides," said Wasserstein. "I'd like to call Marty Sie-gel to get a sense of where Marietta stands."

"Isn't that a sign of weakness?" asked Agee.

"It is useful to talk," said Wasserstein.

"Maybe you should call," said Agee. "I'm going to meet with Gray on Tuesday. He wants to talk about my role at United Technologies."

"I'd cancel," said Wasserstein. "Unless he tells you he wants to talk about raising his price for Bendix, it isn't a good idea to meet with him."

"I'll think about it," said Agee.

•

The Martin Marietta board meeting was scheduled for ten o'clock on Monday morning at the Bethesda headquarters. Just before the session began, Pownall called Gray in Hartford. "The board is going to consider announcing that we will buy Bendix unless they drop their offer or their shark repellent amendments pass," said Pownall. "I'm going to recommend it."

"Why are you going to do that?" asked Gray.

Pownall didn't have time to explain. "I'll come up to Hartford to talk to you about it." he said.

"This afternoon?" asked Gray.

"Yes," said Pownall.

Pownall walked into the boardroom. After Menaker had given a quick legal wrap-up, Siegel stood up.

"Agee believes that he can beat United Technologies on antitrust and he doesn't believe that we will buy his shares once he buys ours," said Siegel. "We have to make our offer more credible than United Technologies'. We have to make it clear that we will buy. There are a lot of outs on the offer right now—excuses we can use not to buy. If we waive those outs, if we say we will buy unless Bendix backs down or the shark repellents pass, we are putting the decision into Agee's hands. Making that announcement will increase the probability that Agee will either do a deal with Gray or agree to a three-way lay-down or talk about a merger on our terms. If we are going to do this, we have to do it today, because Agee is meeting with Gray tomorrow.

"This is a very strong step," continued Siegel. "It's a risk. There is a chance that Bendix will keep ignoring us and buy. We talked about the possibility of a double buy at the first board meeting. I said that if both sides bought, we'd have to sell $1 billion in assets and that if we sold Bendix industrial and Marietta cement, we'd end up having swapped Bendix aerospace for Marietta cement. I want to go over that again."

Siegel took out a set of spread sheets that his staff had worked up for him over the weekend. "This is what the balance sheet looks like under nine different asset sale scenarios at a couple of different prices each. We believe that we can sell automotive for $500 million, industrial for $250 to $300 million, and cement for $300 million to $350 million. Even under the worst case, with no recovery next year, it is livable. Kidder has seen companies emerge in worse shape from leveraged buyouts."

"It can be done," said Byrne. "My company worked through some tough times," Geico had been nearly bankrupt when Byrne was brought in because Geico's auto insurance was underpriced. "This is going to be difficult."

"Geico is a good example," said Siegel.

Pownall asked Fullem to list the conditions that Marietta could now use as an excuse to withdraw its offer. Fullem ticked them off: Marietta could withdraw if someone sued it or if the suit seemed to be going badly. It could withdraw if the New York Stock Exchange stopped trading completely; if Bendix issued new stock or sold a division; Marietta could drop its offer if Bendix dropped its offer for Marietta or if Bendix passed any changes in the charter or bylaws. Martin Marietta was about to waive all but the last two.

"Isn't that putting the company in too tight a box?" asked Bradley. "Shouldn't there be a condition that says that Martin Marietta will withdraw if Bendix meets our price?"

"That is implicit in the condition that says that we will withdraw if they do," said Fullem. "If Bendix meets our price, the two companies will sign a merger agreement. They will withdraw their offer for us. We will withdraw our offer for them."

"You don't put something like that in writing," said Siegel. "That would leave a hole a mile high in the waiver. It wouldn't mean anything if we put that condition in."

"Are there any outs left if Bendix does buy?" asked a director.

"Just the shark repellents," said Fullem. "This is the last decision that the board will make if Bendix buys. But the only rational decision for Bendix to make is not to buy. If Bendix does buy, Kidder says that we will be financially viable if we then buy their shares. Legally we could still have an edge because of the difference in the corporate statutes that I keep talking about. There is a chance that both sides will be able to vote the shares that they buy. If that happens, we have won. But the most likely outcome is a Mexican standoff. The possibility that they will be able to vote our stock but we can't vote their stock is zero."

The directors voted to waive the conditions to the offer.

"Agee will call," said Siegel. "He will finally start to be rational. We're a defense contractor and we're going to call this Assured Second-Strike Capability, acronym ASCAP."

"Harry wants to raise his cash offer to $85 a share if Bendix will agree to merge," said Pownall. "He wants us to help by putting up another $100 million. We could do that, but what Harry really wants is to sell us a UTC division for $400 million. We would also get fuel controls for $300 million. That would be the total $700 million package."

Peter Wood of Kidder made a presentation on the company Gray had offered. "This isn't a purchase that should interest Martin Marietta," he said. "It isn't a company that you can sell to anyone else in this economy. It isn't a company whose earnings justify Gray's price. By my guesstimates, what Gray wants is 30 percent too high."

"I don't think that putting up extra money is a good idea," said Siegel. "I think $600 million is enough. We shouldn't be increasing the ante at all. We just waived the conditions on the offer. Why don't we wait and see if Agee responds, before we do anything with Gray?"

The directors agreed that that was the best idea. They voted Pownall the authority to negotiate with Gray. The steering committee would have to approve any new deal.

•

As soon as the board meeting was over, Pownall, Menaker, and Leithauser drove to Dulles Airport to catch the Martin Marietta jet to Hartford. When they landed at the UTC airport at three o'clock, a van was waiting to take them to the UTC gold glass headquarters building.

Gray was on the phone in his office when Pownall and his team arrived. The three walked through the UTC boardroom to the president's office. The office had been unused since Al Haig left United Technologies more than a year before.

"Well Tom," said Menaker. "Maybe this will be your office someday."

Ten minutes later, Gray was ready to talk. The three Martin Marietta men sat at the conference table in Gray's office with Gray, Brown, and Ed Large.

"Why did you waive the conditions?" asked Gray. He was troubled that Marietta had taken such a drastic step and that Marietta had done so without consulting him.

"We had to do something," explained Pownall. "Bendix will be able to buy us on Thursday. We needed another attention getter."

•

•

Pownall pointed out that United Technologies and Martin Marietta were in rather different positions. United Technologies was simply bidding for Bendix. Gray didn't have to worry about being bought. Pownall did. Waiving conditions had seemed like a good way to get Agee to sit down and negotiate.

Gray explained that the waiving of conditions limited his options. Although Gray had not mentioned the idea to Pownall over the weekend, UTC had been considering launching a new double-pronged attack. UTC would raise the cash price for Bendix, if Bendix would agree to merge. UTC would continue to try to buy Bendix even if Bendix bought Martin Marietta—but at a cash price of $20 a share less. Now Gray couldn't do that. Marietta had announced that it would buy half of Bendix in cash at $75 a share even if Bendix bought Marietta. UTC could not compete for Bendix at $55 a share.

The phone rang. It was Bill Agee. Gray walked over to his desk to take the call.

"We can't meet," said Agee. "The meeting might have an adverse impact on our antitrust case."

"*What* antitrust case?" asked Gray. "We don't have an antitrust case. United Technologies has already said what we're going to do as far as fuel controls are concerned, and we believe that the Justice Department will give us clearance on the basis of what we've already negotiated."

"Well, that's what my lawyers are telling me," said Agee.

"I'll tell you, Bill," said Gray, "I'm not a lawyer, but if I were you, I think that I would sit down and talk to me because you do have a personal stake in this thing and United Technologies just might be successful in this venture."

"Well, there's nothing personal in this," said Agee. "But I would just like to follow the lawyers' advice."

Gray walked back to the table. "Agee just canceled our meeting on the advice of his counsel."

"That sounds to me more like a change of heart," said Menaker. "I doubt his counsel would give such advice."

The strategists talked about the fact that Agee had canceled the meeting. There wasn't much to say. They talked some more about the Martin Marietta decision to waive conditions. Gray said that Bendix would be worth less after it spent its cash and that he didn't think it was worth the $75 a share that Martin Marietta would have to pay. He didn't think that the timing of the announcement was the best.

Gray wanted to go ahead with a friendly raise. He talked about that. Pownall explained that while he was interested, the board was really interested in buying more aerospace assets. They liked the Bendix oceanics division. They weren't keen on the UTC company. It didn't fit with Martin Marietta.

About six o'clock, Pownall, Leithauser, and Menaker headed for New York. Gray said that he was going to call a UTC board meeting to approve the raise. Pownall said that he would take the idea back to the Marietta steering committee.

●

When Siegel got back to his office from the Martin Marietta board meeting late Monday afternoon, there was a stack of telephone messages on his desk. Beside them was a copy of the Dow Jones wire report of the Martin Marietta announcement. The time on the bottom was twelve thirty. Siegel read through the phone slips. Wasserstein had called at twelve thirty-five. Siegel called Wasserstein.

"Of course, I saw your announcement," said Wasserstein. "Let's open up a line of communication like we have on all the other deals we've worked on."

●

●

"That's okay with me," said Siegel. "I've been waiting for Bendix to call."

Wasserstein said that Bendix had three options: bribery, war, and peace. Bendix could raise its price and do a friendly deal; Bendix could continue with its hostile offer; Bendix could negotiate a peace settlement and sell Martin Marietta back the 4.5 percent block of stock that Bendix already owned.

"Well, the only ones within my control are one and three," said Siegel.

"I'll call you back," said Wasserstein.

At seven o'clock Tuesday morning, Pownall, Menaker, Leithauser, and Siegel met for breakfast at the Martin Marietta suite in the Waldorf Towers. Pownall talked about the meeting with Gray in Hartford the day before. Siegel said that Agee, in the person of Bruce Wasserstein, had finally called.

"Bendix is willing to come to terms," said Siegel. "Wasserstein called me five minutes after the announcement went across the tape. He gave an indication that he might settle. I think we can get a peace. That's the best alternative."

"It is the best alternative," said Pownall. "I hope we can get it."

"If we negotiate a peace, it will have to be a three-way peace," said Siegel. "Do you think that Gray will be willing to back down?"

"One of the reasons that Gray got into this is the personal relationship between us," said Pownall. "I think he will back down if we tell him that this is the best thing for us."

"You had better be sure," said Siegel. "You had better start thinking about calling Gray."

IN SEARCH OF THE GREAT EXTENDER

Agee had called a strategy meeting for four o'clock Monday afternoon. As Higgins walked into Agee's office, he pulled Fleischer aside.

"Is Agee really meeting with Gray?" he asked.

"That's off," said Fleischer. "Don't worry."

Agee came in. The advisers sat in the big, white chairs at the round table and talked through the alternatives. Agee liked the idea of a great extender who would bid for 5 percent, 10 percent, 15 percent of Bendix as an investment. Agee wasn't keen on selling Bendix assets. He wasn't eager to sell the whole of Bendix cheap. But he did want names. The bankers gave some. Higgins had brought some annual reports. He took them out of his briefcase. Agee didn't want to look. Among them: Esmark, Penn Central, and Allied. Early in the battle, Harris of Salomon Brothers had met with some executives from Penn Central on another matter. Harris had asked if Penn Central was interested in buying Bendix. The answer was maybe. Higgins had passed that on to Agee, but Agee didn't want to pursue it. Agee asked the two teams of investment bankers to put together a shorter sublist of the best potential white knights.

"We ought to be talking to Allied," said Higgins. "You know they want to talk. I don't think anyone is going to be interested in this 5-10-15 percent minority investment just to trigger an extension of Marietta's withdrawal date."

"Jay, I don't want you to be talking to anyone on our behalf," said Agee. "Don't make any calls."

The Marietta announcement about buying Bendix stock unless Bendix withdrew had come over the wire early in the afternoon. Fleischer thought there might be a loophole: the language of the announcement could be read like a chinese puzzle. It said that Marietta could drop its offer for Bendix if Bendix passed a charter or bylaw change. Maybe any bylaw change would do.

"This speculation is just great," said Higgins. "Maybe they have strapped themselves to the masts and won't back down for anything. How do we know? We've got to talk to them. We can't communicate with them solely through the *New York Times*."

"No," said Agee. "Don't you make any calls."

Wasserstein met with Agee and Cunningham at the Helmsley suite at eleven o'clock Monday night to talk about the list again. This time, Wasserstein had a new copy of his decision tree. The updated version had been drawn by his art department: it had thirty-two different branches. It was a little complicated to read. Wasserstein explained it to Agee.

"We ought to start making some calls," said Wasserstein. "The clock is ticking."

"I'm not sure I want to make any contacts at all," said Agee. "I'm not sure I like the idea of selling all or part of Bendix. What about investors? Who are the top two?"

"Allied and Esmark," said Wasserstein. "This deal is going to be complicated. Those guys are sophisticated. They will understand quickly."

·

·

"Call them," said Agee.

"You should be aware that Salomon Brothers is very close to Esmark," said Wasserstein. "They have been Esmark's bankers for years. Ira Harris is a friend of Don Kelly, the chairman of Esmark. I know Kelly and I can make the call, but maybe Salomon Brothers should be involved."

"No," said Agee. "You call."

"What about selling some assets?" said Wasserstein. "Can I make some calls on that?"

"Call the two best asset-buyers too," said Agee.

First thing the next morning, Tuesday, September 14, Wasserstein called Ed Hennessy at Allied.

"Ed, as you know we're working for Bendix now," said Wasserstein. "You told me last week that you might be interested in buying some Bendix assets. Are you still interested? This is a mess."

"No kidding," said Hennessy. "What are those guys at Bendix doing? This fight is bad for American business. Why don't you try to straighten things out?"

"We're trying to straighten things out," said Wasserstein. "We talked about assets before, but how do you feel about making a minority investment in Bendix? An investment may flip into buying some assets. It may flip into buying the company. It's conceivable that you'd just like to make the investment."

"Not to me it isn't," growled Hennessy. "I buy companies and assets. I don't understand how this happened. How did Agee get into this mess? How does he work?"

"I want you to meet Agee," said Wasserstein. "He is worried about being taken over by United Technologies. You might as well find out about the situation."

Hennessy agreed.

Next Wasserstein called Donald Kelly, chairman of Esmark. Esmark is a Chicago-based holding company that sells industrial products, chemicals, food, high fidelity, and personal products; it owns Estech, STP, Swift, Jensen, Playtex, Danskin, and Jhirmack. Esmark is always on the lookout for acquisition. Lately it had been thinking about a minority investment.

"Remember the investment we talked about?" said Wasserstein. He had proposed an investment scheme that didn't fly. "Well, I've got another one: Bendix. Are you interested?"

"I might be," said Kelly. Kelly was always willing to look at another company. "But I'd like to speak to Agee directly. I've heard a lot of unusual things about him."

Wasserstein called Agee and told Agee to call Kelly. "Esmark might be interested," he said.

Agee called Kelly.

"Let's talk," said Kelly. "Esmark doesn't usually do this kind of deal, but maybe we can work something out. How soon can we get together?"

"I'm tied up until eight o'clock tonight," said Agee.

"We at Esmark are available any time. We work around the clock," laughed Kelly. He told Agee that he and Roger Briggs, the vice-chairman of Esmark, would be at the Helmsley at eight that night.

"We'll need to have some investment bankers and lawyers there to explain what's going on," said Kelly. "You bring your team from First Boston. We'll bring Salomon Brothers."

"No," said Agee. "No bankers and no lawyers. This is just a meeting of principals."

"Whatever you say," said Kelly, "but I don't see how we can discuss a deal without investment bankers. I don't know much about the situation. I don't know much about Bendix and this looks pretty complicated."

"I don't want bankers," said Agee. "I just want to talk."

In the middle of the afternoon, Harry Gray called Bill Agee. The United Technologies board had just met by telephone and approved a friendly raise for Bendix. Gray was waiting for an answer from Martin Marietta on the financing before going public, but he wanted to set up a meeting with Agee to talk about it. Agee agreed that it might be a good idea for the two to meet.

"I want a little time to think over the idea," he said. "How late can I call you?"

"Well, I'll probably be at the office here until seven thirty or eight," said Gray. "And then after that I'll be at the house."

"How late can I call you at home?" asked Agee.

"Well, if I get home by eight, eight thirty, I should be finished eating dinner by nine, nine thirty, and I guess I'd like a call before ten."

Agee promised he would call back that night.

At a little after eight, Kelly and Briggs arrived at the Helmsley. Cunningham let them into the suite and offered them champagne.

"We'll have beer," said Kelly.

The three men walked into the living room. Kelly settled on the brown couch. Agee pulled up a chair from the dining-room table. Cunningham brought in beer and champagne. Agee reviewed what had happened. He explained that he was looking for an extender bidder to block the Marietta purchase.

"A bid like that will probably get you your delay," said Kelly. "How much of Bendix are we talking about?"

"We don't need to pin down the details," said Agee. "I'm just exploring my options. I want to find out if you're interested. I can't promise that we'll even want you to make a bid if you decide you want to do it."

"Let's talk about Bendix," said Kelly.

Agee didn't want to say much about Bendix either. He was general. He talked briefly about Martin Marietta. Kelly

•

•

and Briggs asked some questions. Agee said he would get them information.

"I'll call you tomorrow if I'm interested in an investment," said Kelly.

At twenty to ten, Harry Gray and his wife had just finished dinner and were chatting at the table, when the phone rang. It was Bill Agee.

"I've been thinking about this a great deal," he said. "I don't think that a meeting with you would serve any useful purpose. I guess we'll both go ahead with the way we've been going."

Gray was amused. "I think the way you're going is going to be rather destructive to Bendix," he said. "I think if I were you, I would reconsider."

"My principal job is to serve the interests of the shareholders of Bendix," said Agee. "Even if the antitrust problems with a United Technologies merger could be solved, your price is totally inadequate."

"Look, Bill," said Gray. "My offer is out there on the table. I've just had a glass of wine with my wife. I'm kind of laid-back on the situation."

Agee was caught off-guard. "If you want to raise your price substantially, I would be interested in talking," he said. "The plan you have devised to carve up Bendix does not serve the interest of the Bendix employees."

Gray thought he heard a voice in the background. "You've got to make up your own mind, but my advice to you is that you ought to talk about this, because it could go a way that you don't want it to go," said Gray.

"Well, that's kind of interesting," said Agee. "Mary and I have just had a bottle of champagne and we're going out to dinner and we're kind of relaxed too."

"Bill," said Gray. "Enjoy your champagne, if you have another bottle, and enjoy your dinner."

.

.

Roger Briggs, vice-chairman of Esmark, called Jay Higgins first thing on Wednesday morning. Briggs was a close friend of Higgins, and Briggs's son worked in the Salomon Brothers mergers and acquisitions department.

"Do you think that an investment of 5 percent, 10 percent, 15 percent in a combined Bendix–Martin Marietta makes sense for Esmark," asked Briggs.

"Rog, I can't believe this," said Higgins. "I suppose we can make the numbers work, but I just don't believe I'm hearing this. Agee has been talking about that kind of deal, and I keep telling him that no one is going to be interested. I have used your name with him as recently as yesterday, but he says he doesn't want to talk."

"That's funny," said Briggs. "He wasn't at a loss for words in his hotel room last night with Mary."

"What?" asked Higgins.

"Don and I were in New York yesterday," said Briggs. He and Don Kelly. "Sorry I didn't stop to see you, but it was a quick in and out, a last minute thing. Wasserstein called Kelly yesterday morning and then Agee called and we came into New York. We met with them at their suite last night. We wanted you to come, but Agee said no. Agee was vague about what they wanted, and it was clear that they weren't working with us exclusively. Anyway, tell Agee that Esmark isn't interested in an investment in Bendix. A white knight bid or some assets, maybe, but not an investment."

•

Harry Gray's Hartford office is paneled in cherry. On the wall there is a painting of a clipper ship called Spirit of the South. In one corner is a Williamsburg print couch and a red Essex chair. Across the room is a seven-legged semicircular antique desk. Gray sometimes works there, but he prefers the drumtop conference table in the far corner. He was sitting at that table with Alexander Haig, when Tom Pownall called late Wednesday morning, the 15th of September. After Haig had stepped down as Secretary of State in June, he had come back to United Technologies as a consultant. One of his new jobs was to head a new UTC advisory committee on international policy. Haig had come to Hartford that day to discuss the committee with Harry Gray.

Pownall said that the Martin Marietta steering committee had approved the $100 million raise. Gray called Brown and Large. He explained to Haig what was happening. A few minutes later, the members of the UTC acquisitions staff started to parade through the office with updated studies. One of the public relations people came in with a letter and a press release. Gray signed the letter and initialed the release. Then he called Bill Agee.

"I want to read you my letter," said Gray.

Dear Bill,

Upon Bendix entering into a merger agreement with United Technologies, United Technologies will revise its cash tender offer for 11,900,000 shares of Bendix common stock to increase the price per share from $75 to $85. The merger agreement would provide that following the tender offer the balance of the Bendix common stock would be exchanged for United Technologies common stock on the basis of one share of United Technologies common stock for each share of Bendix common stock.

We believe that the present competing tender offers by Bendix and Martin Marietta create an intolerable situation for both companies, their shareholders and employees. Our offer is an alternative that will resolve the situation. The Bendix shareholders will receive a greater premium for their shares than under the Mar-

tin Marietta tender offer and the merger agreement between United Technologies and Bendix could be structured so that the Bendix shareholders have an
opportunity to participate equally in the cash and stock
portions of the transactions. Martin Marietta will
achieve its objective of remaining an independent company. With the cooperation of all three companies, there
will be no antitrust issues and we will be able to complete the merger of Bendix and United Technologies in
a short period of time.

We believe the merger will benefit both Bendix and
United Technologies shareholders since the comple-
mentary skills and talents of the two companies offer
real advantages.

The time for action is now. We are today prepared to
enter into a merger agreement on our revised terms.

Sincerely,
Harry J. Gray

"Let's get together and talk about it," said Gray.

"Well, that's kind of interesting," said Agee. "We'll take
it into consideration. The board will review it."

"Let's get together and talk about it," repeated Gray.

•

The Bendix strategists sat at the round table in Agee's office for their four o'clock strategy meeting Wednesday
afternoon. Fleischer got out a spiral notebook and gave a
summary of all the legal activity. Martin Marietta was having trouble. It had filed a standard motion to have the
Michigan state takeover law declared unconstitutional so
that Bendix couldn't use it. The federal court had refused.
The Michigan State Bureau of Corporations had then tried
to enforce the law by issuing a cease and desist order against
Marietta.

•

•

Fleischer said that he had drafted a letter to Pownall that said that Bendix would raise its price conditional on Martin Marietta accepting. The two companies would sign a merger agreement. Bendix would withdraw its offer for Martin Marietta. Martin Marietta would withdraw its offer for Bendix. Agee wasn't interested.

"What's new with you, Jay?" asked Agee.

"Not too much," said Higgins. "Esmark isn't interested."

"Not interested in what?" asked Agee.

"I'm not sure, because I wasn't there last night," said Higgins. "But I gather a stake in a combined Bendix–Martin Marietta."

"That's very interesting," said Agee.

"Bill," said Higgins. "You haven't been interested in listening, but I've talked to you about Esmark for two weeks. They are our oldest banking client. Briggs's son works for me. That's family to Salomon Brothers and family to me. Personalities aside, these are the people we should be talking to. More people on the team than you should be talking to them, to be sure that they and we are ready if we need them. If we do need them, we're going to need them in a heartbeat."

Agee leaned back in his chair. "Jay, it is true that you have identified the central issues," he said. "But every deal has to have a quarterback and I gotta tell you, on this one, it ain't you. There is only one quarterback here and it's me. I don't want you making any calls. Do I make myself clear?"

"Okay, Bill," said Higgins. "You're the client. But I've got to tell you that I think that's a mistake. I think you also ought to be talking to Allied, Penn Central, and a couple of others."

"Fine," said Agee. "I hear you. Thanks."

At eleven o'clock Wednesday night, Wasserstein met with Agee and Cunningham at the Helmsley for a strategy session. Wasserstein wanted to set up a meeting with the investor group that he had been talking to. The president of the group had told Wasserstein that the group needed early confirmation of the sale because it had to line up the credit to pay.

"No," said Agee. "I don't want a meeting."

"Bill, you need a safety net," said Wasserstein. "You should pursue this."

"I've got a company that I can't identify that will make an extender bid in any event," said Agee. "I don't like the idea of selling assets."

Wasserstein had found out earlier in the evening that Martin Marietta had been negotiating with LTV, the aerospace and steel conglomerate based in Dallas. Siegel had told Wasserstein on Tuesday that Marietta wasn't soliciting a white knight or an extender bidder. Wasserstein had repeated that to Agee. Now Agee and Wasserstein discussed the fact that Marietta was talking to potential bidders. Wasserstein said that he would find out more about the negotiations on Thursday morning.

Agee and Wasserstein talked over Wasserstein's latest version of the decision tree.

"What about a conditional raise?" suggested Wasserstein. "What about suing the banks that are financing the offer? We want to put maximum pressure on Martin Marietta to settle."

●

The Martin Marietta steering committee met in Bethesda at ten o'clock on Wednesday morning. First they decided to go ahead with the $100 million raise to United Technologies. Agee had canceled his meeting with Gray. Bendix would be able to buy at midnight Thursday. Raising the ante with Gray now seemed like a no-lose option: either Agee accepted Gray's higher offer and withdrew its bid for

Marietta or he didn't. If Agee did, Marietta got more assets; if Agee didn't, raising didn't cost Martin Marietta anything.

Pownall explained that Martin Marietta was talking to "partial" white knights who wanted to buy Martin Marietta assets and had offered to do it by buying Marietta stock and swapping it. If Marietta could get a new bid for its stock filed and mailed by five the next day, a partial white knight might be able to block Bendix from buying its stock. Pownall named the options:

(1) Holderbank, a Swiss cement company was thinking about buying Martin Marietta cement. Holderbank's investment banker had been talking to Kidder for almost two weeks. There were some problems because of differences in the U.S. and foreign laws. Holderbank hadn't made a formal offer—but Kidder sensed that the company was thinking too low.

(2) W. R. Grace, a New York–based chemicals giant, liked the look of the Martin Marietta Master Builders division that made sealants for concrete. Grace had been working on a deal for a couple of days. The Grace lawyers were worried that they couldn't finish up the papers in time. Martin Marietta didn't like the price that Grace was offering, but six top Grace executives were at Kidder that morning trying to strike a deal.

(3) LTV was taking a look at the Baltimore aerospace division. W. Paul Thayer, the chairman of LTV, was a close friend of Pownall. The negotiations had begun the night before and Pownall didn't know what kind of price LTV was going to offer. Thayer's team of engineers was still in Baltimore inspecting the plant.

"If Holderbank or Grace or LTV announces an offer for Marietta stock, there is a fifty-fifty chance that Bendix won't be able to buy tomorrow night," said Menaker. "Bendix will challenge any new offer for part of Martin Marietta as a sham transaction, but if we have a legitimate bidder, the

•

•

courts might hold that the deal is valid and trigger the ten-day extension."

The steering committee liked the idea of an extender bid for part of the company. They agreed that the committee would meet again if Pownall could negotiate a deal. They wanted to give it their final approval.

After lunch, Brown and Wood arrived in Bethesda. They met in the war room with Leithauser and Pownall to talk about how much the Baltimore aerospace division was worth. Kidder had run some numbers; so had Leithauser; they agreed that the price tag for the plant was $160 million, and that it might sell for as much as $200 million.

While the Martin Marietta strategists talked, the LTV team arrived. James Paulos, LTV's chief financial officer had flown in from LTV headquarters in Dallas. The LTV staffers met in a conference room upstairs in Marietta aerospace divisional headquarters to talk about how much they thought the plant was worth. They settled on $125 million.

Paulos walked downstairs and made his offer: LTV would bid for 5 percent of Martin Marietta at $50 a share; then LTV would swap that stock plus a lump of extra cash for the Baltimore plant; LTV would get a guarantee that it can buy the plant in cash if the tender scheme didn't work.

"That sounds low," said Pownall. "But we'll struggle with it."

Pownall sat down in his office to think. He called Leithauser in. "Is the $125 million enough?" he asked.

"I can't recommend that we accept it on financial grounds," said Leithauser. "The plant is worth more than that. I don't know the value of independence."

Pownall called Siegel in New York.

"The price isn't right," said Siegel. "Your people agreed with Kidder that the plant is worth $160 million. Doing this deal might not trigger an extension. Marty Lipton says it is only an even bet legally. You are going to lose some tax credits. And if we find a partial white knight so will Bendix. Time is more critical to them. If they can get a few more days they might be able to push those charter amendments through—and in that case our offer won't work. If you accept the LTV offer, you might win this battle and lose the war."

Pownall called Paul Thayer. By then the LTV board had met by telephone to approve the offer. Pownall explained that the bid just wasn't high enough. Thayer offered to raise and the two negotiated a $10 million price hike. Pownall called Menaker into his office.

"Is this guaranteed to give us ten more days?" he asked.

"No," said Menaker. "The best I can give you is fifty-fifty."

It was almost eight o'clock. The *Wall Street Journal* ad closing time was eight. LTV had to know by then if it had a deal. Pownall decided: the bid was too low. He called Thayer once again.

"Paul," he said. "I'm sorry, but I can't let it go for that."

"Well, we tried, didn't we," said Thayer.

"Yes," said Pownall. "We tried, and we didn't make it. Thanks for the effort."

WAITING FOR
MIDNIGHT

•

 Jay Higgins had tried to call Ed Hennessy on Wednesday, the 15th to tell him that he wasn't getting anywhere setting up a meeting with Agee. Hennessy was on an offshore drilling rig in the Gulf of Mexico and couldn't be reached. Thursday morning, Hennessy called Higgins.

"I'm in the middle of this debt-equity swap with Salomon Brothers," said Hennessy. "What do you think about my disclosure?"

"I'm the wrong person to ask," Higgins said. "I don't know anything about debt-equities."

"I'm talking about my disclosure on the Bendix deal," said Hennessy.

"What?" asked Higgins.

"Bendix," said Hennessy. "Don't you know I've been talking to Bendix?"

"Ed," said Higgins. "You called me Sunday night to say that you'd talked to Agee and he didn't want to meet with you. I have tried to set up a meeting for you, but he says no."

"Well, Agee and Wasserstein have been on me the last

•

•

couple of days to come in with a complicated investment scheme," said Hennessy. "I don't think that we want to be a partner. We don't want 15 percent. We want all of Bendix."

"I don't know what to tell you," said Higgins. "I don't know anything about your talks with Bendix. Agee is absolutely impossible. I can't understand what he's doing."

After he hung up on Hennessy, Higgins put in a call to Siegel. Agee had told Higgins not to do that. He asked for a home phone number in case Agee decided later that night that he wanted to negotiate a deal after all. Siegel gave Higgins the number.

"You know I've been talking to Wasserstein all week," said Siegel. "An hour ago he told me he was calling from Agee's office. I'll tell you what I told Bruce. If Bendix buys, Martin Marietta will buy. If you want to walk away from us, go right ahead, but I think I can negotiate a three-way peace treaty."

Thursday morning, Agee met with Wasserstein and Grassi in his office. Bendix would be able to buy the Martin Marietta stock at midnight. Wasserstein had had the First Boston staff working with Kayser, the Bendix chief financial officer, for several days to put together what Wasserstein called the "Kidder Sheets," his best guess at the financial analysis that Kidder would present to the Martin Marietta board. The First Boston team had computed numbers on what the balance sheet of the joint company would look like if Marietta bought after Bendix bought, and then looked at how the balance sheet could be restructured with asset sales or debt and equity issues. Kayser and his team had adjusted the numbers for Bendix taxes and pension liabilities. Wasserstein reviewed the sheets with Agee.

"Marietta might buy," said Wasserstein. "It is certainly conceivable. The joint company is going to have to sell a lot of assets if that happens, but I'm sure that Kidder will tell them that that is doable. That is what these numbers say."

Then Wasserstein talked about the Bendix options. "We have the three scenarios that we've been discussing since Sunday," he said. "Bribery, war, and peace. Marty Siegel and I have been doing a lot of talking. We have made some progress. We're going to keep talking all night. I want to find out what their selling price is. I want to know what their best peace offer is. I think maybe we can work something out, but you need to have authority to try any of the three. You need the board to give you the power to raise your offer, to buy the shares at $48, or to make a peace."

"Siegel told you that he wasn't talking to extenders and we know that last night Marietta was negotiating with LTV," said McDonald. "Do you still trust him?"

"Yes," said Wasserstein. He had talked to Siegel about the LTV negotiations that morning. Siegel had said that Martin Marietta was just responding to an approach. Siegel didn't believe that partial white knights worked anyhow. "I think we can trust him on this."

Then Wasserstein talked about the meeting he had scheduled with Hennessy for five that afternoon. Agee and Wasserstein discussed what Agee should say. "Hennessy is tough," said Wasserstein. "He doesn't take any nonsense."

Agee's secretary buzzed. Jay Higgins was on the line.

"I just talked to our good friend Ed Hennessy," said Higgins. "He tells me that he's not wild about a 5 percent, 10 percent, or 15 percent investment in Bendix, but that he might have a much greater appetite for all of Bendix or for some assets."

"That's interesting," said Agee. He was going to meet with Hennessy at five.

"I also just got off the phone with Siegel," said Higgins. "He tells me that a three-way lay-down is probably available."

"Bruce has correctly relayed to me the substance of Siegel's peace offer," said Agee.

"Bill, there is obviously a lot going on here that I don't know about," said Higgins. "But from what I do know, if it were my company, I would take a lay-down."

"Are you coming to the board meeting?" asked Agee.

•

Thursday had begun with good news for Bendix on the legal front. In Baltimore, Judge Young had turned down a motion by Martin Marietta to stop Bendix from buying at midnight. In New York, Martin Marietta had sued Bendix and Citibank late Wednesday afternoon to try to get the new SESSOP rules modified. As soon as he got the case, Judge Edelstein had suggested that the lawyers give him twenty-four hours to review the papers. Neither side wanted to wait. The next morning, the lawyers reported that they hadn't reached an agreement. Edelstein was clearly annoyed at being asked to make a decision on the case by midnight. "Even the process of osmosis wouldn't have helped me much in learning what these papers contain."

At the end of the Thursday morning hearing, Edelstein threatened to put the case on hold for twenty-four hours while he figured out what the two sides were arguing. The Bendix lawyer objected; he didn't think that it was fair to stop Bendix from buying that night just because Marietta didn't like the Bendix rule that said that Citibank would withdraw uninstructed shares from the Marietta pool. Then the Marietta attorney handed Edelstein a copy of the four-page letter that Agee had sent to Bendix employees explaining that they would be subject to a number of penalties if they decided to sell their stock to Martin Marietta. The letter suggested that SESSOP members consult a tax lawyer before making a decision.

•

•

"If your honor were disposed to call Judge Young," suggested the Bendix lawyer.

Edelstein said that he would be available later in the day.

During the break the Bendix lawyer in New York called Marc Cherno, the chief Bendix litigator, who was in Baltimore. He explained that Edelstein was thinking about blocking Bendix from buying that night; he suggested that Cherno have a Baltimore lawyer call Judge Young to find out if Young would be available to consider the SESSOP case that evening. Young had already cleared Bendix to buy that morning. Maybe he would take the SESSOP case into his own hands. A Baltimore lawyer made the call. Young said that he would be available. A little later that afternoon, Young called the Baltimore lawyer back to say that there would be a meeting in his chambers at three o'clock. The Baltimore lawyer couldn't imagine what the meeting was for, since there wasn't a motion before Young. When the lawyers from Bendix, Martin Marietta, and United Technologies sat down at the table in Judge Young's chambers, Young said that he had decided to issue a ten-day restraining order. None of the companies could officially do anything relating to buying one of the others until the order expired. The lawyers from Martin Marietta and United Technologies grinned. Cherno from Bendix turned white. He said that he was appealing the order. He didn't think that it had any basis in law.

•

Just before the Bendix board meeting began, Agee called Don Kelly of Esmark. "We're having a board meeting today to go over some major issues," said Agee. "Let's get together afterward for a cocktail."

"Bill, I've sent one message that Esmark isn't interested," said Kelly. "I guess that you didn't get it. I'm not interested, but I wish you good luck."

Agee walked into the boardroom. He read the letter from Harry Gray out loud. The directors turned down the new offer.

Then Fleischer gave a legal update. He had talked to all of the key attorneys working on the Bendix lawsuits across the country to put together a progress sheet. Bendix was winning in Michigan, but that was a sideshow. The important cases were in Maryland and Delaware.

"We are going to sue in Maryland to block Marietta from buying," said Fleischer. "There is a one-in-three chance that it will work. The outcome on voting is very uncertain, but it is more likely that we'll win in Delaware than that they'll win in Maryland."

Fleischer talked about what it meant legally if Bendix bought that night. Marietta had said that it had waived the conditions on its offer and that if Bendix bought, so would Marietta. "They pulled all but two of the conditions," said Fleischer. "They said they would withdraw if we withdraw or if we passed charter or bylaw changes. They didn't limit themselves to the amendments that our shareholders are voting on. We can take advantage of the broader language of the waiver and pass some other amendments. Unless they don't want to do a deal, that will give them justification for dropping their offer. If our reading of the waiver is wrong— if a court decides that using another charter or bylaw change to trigger withdrawal is improper—then Marietta and Bendix, which owns Marietta, will be liable for the difference between Marietta's offering price and whatever the Bendix stock sells for. That's probably about $300 million."

"The withdrawal right on our offer for Marietta expires at midnight," said Agee. "Let's talk about what to do. How do you see Martin Marietta, Bruce?"

"It's a great company," said Wasserstein. "I'm going to defer to my corporate finance expert."

Tony Grassi talked through the First Boston qualitative work. "Aerospace: defense business excellent. Excellent research and technological base. Aluminum: industry has been depressed and will remain weak until 1984–1986. Invested $200 million in plant and expansion and modernization during 1981. Cement: business is hurt by poor economic conditions. Two new efficient dry plants in Utah and Iowa position the company in energy belt areas." He looked up. "Martin Marietta is a good company. It is in a good position to take advantage of a recovery."

"How do you see things, Jay?" asked Agee.

"Well, Martin Marietta's crown jewels are great," said Higgins. "That's how this whole thing got started. But the aluminum and cement businesses are in a real slump and I don't know that they are great even when the economy is good. It seems to me that Martin Marietta has made a lot of investments where it shouldn't have. Its aluminum plant uses hydro power, which has become expensive. That business is the pits. But yes, on balance, Martin Marietta is a fine company."

"That's fine," said a director. "But what about buying the stock?"

Agee turned to Higgins. "What does Salomon Brothers think about buying the stock?"

"Salomon Brothers does not have a recommendation on whether you should or shouldn't buy. That is a uniquely personal corporate decision. I can tell you what we think about the alternative scenarios."

Higgins held up one finger. "If you negotiate a friendly deal tonight at any of the prices that Salomon Brothers has heard discussed, then you've got yourself a very fine acquisition." Higgins lifted a second finger. "If you buy tonight in the absence of a negotiated deal with Martin Marietta and you put all your chips on the legal strategies and do prevent them from buying, you've been a gamesman supreme, you've won." Higgins lifted a third finger. "If you buy tonight and you fail to keep them from buying, you take the balance sheet numbers from here into the next room. The debt-equity ratio goes to 70 percent, 80 percent. Could you live with that? It is theoretically possible. But just to get back to a balance sheet that isn't technically in default on your loan agreements, you have got to make a debt reduction of $1 billion and issue $500 million in new stock. You will have a hard time selling much of Martin Marietta in today's market. The most aggressive equity guy we have—the one who's always way off in right field—thinks you might be able to float $150 million in new stock, not $500, so you're $350 million short there. Could you do it? I guess so. It is not something I like to contemplate."

"What is different now than when we started, when you told us to go ahead?" asked a director.

"You have to look at things when they happen," said Higgins.

"How do you see things, Bruce?" asked Agee.

"Two companies buying each other is a difficult thing," said Wasserstein. "You get what I call the black hole syndrome: all the equity vanishes." The directors laughed. Wasserstein looked straight at Agee. "The opportunity, however, is to snatch the economic rewards that Martin Marietta has earned through its position in the marketplace." Wasserstein made a sweeping upward gesture with his hands. "Sure there is the risk that they'll buy—indeed, we pointed out that Kidder will tell Marietta that it can be done—but you have to calibrate the business risk against the opportunity."

Then Kayser talked through several possible ways to

restructure the balance sheet of the joint company if both sides bought. He said that a double buy would be financially possible.

"Okay," said Agee. "So what happens if we buy and then Marietta buys is that we get a lot of debt. It will be difficult. It is not desirable. It is not what we started out to do. But it is livable."

The directors talked about whether Marietta really would buy if Bendix did. Agee polled around the table to get a sense of what the directors wanted to do. They wanted to buy.

"The situation is changing pretty rapidly," said Agee. "What I want to do is appoint a committee of three directors to reconvene when we have more information. Then we can make our decision."

The directors agreed.

"I want the committee to have the authority to buy, the authority to raise the price, and the authority to approve a three-way peace," said Agee.

The directors voted the committee the authority to go ahead with each of the options. Wasserstein grinned at Agee. He jerked both thumbs up.

"I want you all to know how I feel about this," said Agee. "I am for buying up here." He raised his hand above his head. "For raising here," he waved his hand at eye level. "And for quitting down here." He dropped his hand toward the floor. "If they make an offer that makes financial sense, who knows?" Agee paused. "Art just explained that Marietta might be able to withdraw if we pass some bylaw changes," said Agee. "We should do that."

Fleischer read the text of two innocuous changes that he had drafted. One set the number of board members at fourteen. The other prevented anyone who had violated his fiduciary responsibility to Bendix or a Bendix subsidiary from sitting on the board. The directors approved both amendments.

Agee adjourned the meeting. He talked briefly to the members of the committee of directors as he left the board-room. Then he talked to Fleischer.

"Judge Young just issued a ten-day order blocking us from buying," said Fleischer. "I don't understand why he issued it. There wasn't a motion in front of him. I don't think that there is any legal basis for it. We have appealed. I think we will be able to buy tonight."

Higgins tapped Agee on the shoulder. "Good luck," he said.

"Thanks, Jay," said Agee.

Agee turned to McDonald. "See you in the suite at ten." Then Agee and Wasserstein left the General Motors Building for the Helmsley Palace to meet Hennessy.

Ed Hennessy had been in New York that afternoon for the monthly board meeting of the New York Federal Reserve Bank. He was going on to a $1000-a-plate fund-raising dinner for Senator Strom Thurmond of South Carolina at the Union League Club that evening. Allied had some plants in South Carolina, and Hennessy and Thurmond were personal friends. Thurmond had asked Hennessy to co-chair the fund-raising committee in New York.

Agee and Wasserstein were waiting at the elevator bank when Hennessy came into the lobby of the Helmsley Palace. Wasserstein did the introductions. Agee and Hennessy got on the elevator.

"I'll be talking with Marty Siegel about our options," said Wasserstein as he left.

Agee and Hennessy sat down in the suite to talk about how an Allied investment in Bendix might work. Hennessy had already talked to Wasserstein about the idea, but he needed to know more about Bendix and more about what had happened during the merger battle. Agee explained that he wasn't yet prepared to sell Bendix. He wanted Hennessy to buy a 10 percent stake. Hennessy said that was possible; Allied would swap the stock for assets. Agee would not talk about assets.

"Well, frankly," said Hennessy. "I want to buy the whole company, but I'm flexible. If I can participate in a friendly way, I want to do it."

"My preference at this stage is to get the Martin Marietta transaction accomplished and at the same time be in a position to move forward," said Agee. "I would welcome you as a shareholder."

Agee and Hennessy shook hands. Hennessy left for the Strom Thurmond party.

When Hennessy got to the Union League Club, he charged up the stairs to the library where cocktails were being served. He had invited his friend and neighbor Bill Kearns, the Lehman Brothers partner in charge of the Allied corporate account. Hennessy wanted to talk to him. Hennessy spotted Kearns in a circle of executives.

"Where have you been the last couple of weeks?" Hennessy asked Kearns. "I haven't seen you around."

"I was on vacation in Nantucket," said Kearns. "I was there over Labor Day weekend."

"*I* was there over Labor Day weekend," said Hennessy. "I took my boat up. I wish I had known you were there," Hennessy paused. "You'll never guess who I saw playing tennis on Nantucket."

"Sure I can," said Kearns.

"I dare you," said Hennessy.

"Harry Gray," said Kearns.

"Oh," said Hennessy. "That's right. He was playing tennis and taking phone calls. He didn't see me."

"I had an ice cream cone with Harry Gray at The Sweet

Shoppe on Nantucket Island last Sunday," said Kearns. "I just bumped into him."

"What do you think about Gray and United Technologies joining the battle with Martin Marietta?" asked Hennessy.

Kearns started to say something when Harry Gray came into the library. Gray was also on the Strom Thurmond fund-raising committee. Hennessy had his back to the door so he didn't see Gray. Gray started for the bar and then he saw Kearns. He grinned. He walked over to the group of businessmen and stood beside Hennessy. He stuck out his hand. "Hi, Bill," said Gray. "Boy, you sure cleaned up your act since I saw you last. Now you look like a Lehman Brothers partner."

Hennessy stiffened.

"You look pretty good yourself," said Kearns as he shook Gray's hand.

Gray turned to Hennessy. They shook hands. "Hi, Ed," he said.

"Hi, Harry," said Hennessy.

Gray went to the bar to get a drink. He came back to talk to Kearns. Kearns suggested that Lehman Brothers set up a business lunch for Gray. Gray was called to the phone. It was Tom Pownall. Pownall said that Agee seemed to be willing to negotiate, provided that United Technologies would agree to a three-way peace.

"Is that what you really want?" asked Gray.

"Yes," said Pownall.

"I'm willing to lay down," said Gray.

Gray called Marty Lipton. He called Ed Large in Hartford and told him to come down to New York that night. The three would meet with Rohatyn at Wachtell, Lipton.

Tom Pownall had spent most of the day Thursday trying to catch up on the running of Martin Marietta. Then, at a little after four thirty, the Baltimore counsel had called Menaker to say that Young had unexpectedly issued a ten-day restraining order putting all three offers on hold. The decision had been appealed almost immediately by Bendix; Judge Winter on the appeals court would hear the case that night. Pownall and Menaker discussed the case with their Baltimore attorney. The hold order gave them leverage. It meant that Bendix couldn't buy until after the shareholder meeting on Tuesday. If Agee lost in Southfield, he would, in effect, have been turned down by his shareholders on buying Martin Marietta. And the Marietta proxy solicitors thought that Agee would lose.

At five o'clock, Pownall and Menaker walked down the hall to Rauth's office. Martin Marietta had always had the option of amending its bylaws to force Bendix to wait more than ten days to call a shareholder meeting to install a new board. Menaker had told the directors at the very first board meeting that they should make the change as late as they could to give Bendix as little time as possible to attack the change in court. Now, just seven hours before Bendix could buy, the board met by telephone to consider the change.

Rauth, Pownall, Adams, Leithauser, Menaker, and Calvin sat on the couch and chairs in Rauth's office and talked into the speaker phone. Menaker explained that the Maryland corporate statutes set the legal notice limits at ten to ninety days. The New York Stock Exchange and the SEC both recommended a thirty-day notice period to call a meeting. Marietta had never called one with less than that. Extending the notice period to thirty days seemed legally unassailable. The directors unanimously approved the modification.

After the board meeting, Menaker drove to Baltimore for the Judge Winter hearing. Pownall went back to his office. Siegel called to say that negotiations with Wasserstein were about to begin.

After he had introduced Agee to Hennessy, Wasserstein had walked the two blocks up Madison Avenue to his office on Fifty-second Street. He had called Siegel as soon as the board meeting ended, but Siegel wasn't in the office. At a few minutes after five, Siegel returned Wasserstein's call. Siegel had just heard about the temporary restraining order. "Another ten days," he joked.

"I'm going to call you every hour on the hour," said Wasserstein.

"What are we going to talk about?" asked Siegel.

"The three options that we've been talking about all week," said Wasserstein. "Bribery, war, and peace."

"The only thing I want to talk about is peace," said Siegel.

"There are three parties in this," said Wasserstein. "If you want peace, you have to guarantee that United Technologies wants peace too."

"I think I can negotiate a three-way lay-down," said Siegel.

"I'll call you at six," said Wasserstein.

Wasserstein assembled the First Boston team in his office. "What do you think of this idea of peace?" he asked. "Do you think it is good for Bendix. Do you think it is good for First Boston?"

The bankers agreed that a settlement was good for First Boston: it cast them in the role of peacemaker. And the First Boston bankers agreed that a settlement might also be good for Bendix. It had to be an honorable peace; a humiliating withdrawal would leave Bendix vulnerable to a raid at a low price.

Wasserstein called Siegel again at six. "I think I can work a three-way deal," said Siegel. "But I'll need twenty-four hours to do the mechanics." Siegel didn't need the time.

He was sure that Gray would agree, but he wanted to stop Bendix from buying if the Young decision was reversed.

"How much does Marietta want for a friendly merger?" asked Wasserstein.

"I thought that the purpose of this discussion was to talk peace," said Siegel, "but if you make me an offer, I'll take it to the board."

"We've been authorized to go to $52," said Wasserstein.

"If you make me an offer, I'll take it to the board," repeated Siegel.

"Give me a feel for what you need," said Wasserstein. "How about a number with a six in front of it? How much lower can we go?"

"Make me an offer and I'll take it to the board," said Siegel. "How much do you want for the block of Marietta stock you own?"

"I'll call you back at seven," said Wasserstein.

Wasserstein left his office to meet Fleischer for dinner at the Tse Yang chinese restaurant next door to the Helmsley Palace. It was convenient to Agee's suite and the food was good. At seven o'clock, Wasserstein left the table to call Siegel.

"We'll sell you the block for $48 a share," said Wasserstein.

"We'll pay you the $27 a share that you bought it for," said Siegel. "I don't see how we can pay more than cost, but we'll consider looking at expenses."

Siegel called Lipton to find out what Gray's expenses were. Lipton said $5 million.

Wasserstein called Siegel back an hour later. "Bendix will be willing to sell for $43 a share," he said, "the original offering price, plus expenses."

"I said I was willing to consider cost plus expenses," said Siegel. "I think $33 or $34 is a more appropriate price.

You know you are going to have to pay Gray's expenses. That will be $5 million."

"You've got to be kidding about paying Gray's expenses," said Wasserstein. "I'll call you back at nine."

By nine o'clock Wasserstein had figured out his own costs. "Bendix owes its investment bankers $2 million each," he said. "That's a total of $4 million. Bendix owes its lawyers about $3.6 million."

"Okay," said Siegel. "Your expenses are $7.6 million. Plus Gray's $5 million makes a total of $13 million I'll pay that. It will be $35 a share."

"You'll have to be thinking higher," said Wasserstein. "Can you go to $37.50, half way between cost and our original bid? Think about it. I'll call you at ten o'clock."

Siegel called Pownall. "We're only $2.50 apart on price," he said. "I think we're close to a settlement. If Bendix won't sell the block back for less than $37.50 a share, I advise that you accept."

Pownall was optimistic that things were going to work out. He was sure now that Agee would make an agreement. He envisioned going to New York the next morning for a meeting with Agee to shake hands on the lay-down. He started to psyche himself up for the press conference he would have to announce the settlement.

At a little after nine, Judge Winter reversed Judge Young. The leverage between Bendix and Martin Marietta suddenly shifted to Bendix. Now Bendix could buy before it held the meeting. Bendix could own a majority of Martin Marietta in less than three hours.

Siegel had gone home from his office earlier in the evening. He waited in his study for Wasserstein to call back with his next offer. Ten o'clock. No call. Siegel kept waiting. The call didn't come. When Wasserstein still had not called by ten thirty, Siegel started to worry. He called Wasserstein's office. Tony Grassi answered.

·

·

"I need to talk to Bruce as soon as possible," said Siegel, "and certainly before midnight."

Then Siegel called Pownall. "Wasserstein didn't make the ten o'clock call," he said. "I don't know what's going on."

Pownall called Gray in New York. Menaker came back from the hearing in Baltimore, and he and Leithauser waited in Pownall's office for Wasserstein to call.

Wasserstein still hadn't called Siegel by eleven. Siegel called Wasserstein's office again. Grassi answered.

"I've got to talk to Wasserstein before midnight," he repeated.

"I've talked to Bruce," said Grassi. "He can't call right now. He'll get to you when he can."

Siegel assumed that that meant soon. He called Pownall. He said that the negotiating line was about to open. Then Siegel called Lipton at Wachtell, Lipton. "Wasserstein is going to call me back," he said. "I think we may see peace yet."

"I don't know," said Lipton. "We got word that Bendix has told the press to stand by for an important announcement tonight. I think they are going to buy."

"I just can't believe that they would be that foolish," said Siegel.

Wasserstein didn't call. Back in Bethesda, Menaker and Leithauser got ready to leave.

"They aren't crazy enough to buy that stock," said Leithauser. "No one is that crazy."

"I think Agee is crazy enough," said Menaker. "I think he is going to buy."

•

Wasserstein and Fleischer had finished their dinner at nine thirty. Wasserstein had walked to the Helmsley Palace to wait in Agee's suite and Fleischer had gone to the General

•

•

Motors Building to pick up his briefcase and meet Mc-Donald. There was a message for Fleischer: Bob Fullem had called. Fleischer called back.

"We just passed a bylaw ammendment," said Fullem. "The notice period for a Martin Marietta shareholder meeting is now thirty days. If you buy you can't take control for thirty days, not ten."

When Wasserstein arrived at the suite, Agee and Cunningham were talking about the situation. They were drinking Seagram's champagne and eating oatmeal cookies. Wasserstein reported on his discussion with Siegel.

"They seem to want in the high fifties for the company," he said. "I think they will shade the price a bit. They are willing to pay $35 a share for the 4.5 percent block. That is the $27 a share you paid for it, plus expenses."

"That is not what we would call a peace settlement," said Agee. "And if you're going to come back with a peace settlement, it had better be substantially better than that."

McDonald and Fleischer arrived from the General Motors Building. McDonald had heard that Winter had reversed Young. He and Fleischer had discussed the decision on the walk to the Helmsley. In the suite they talked it over with Wasserstein and Agee. The question was whether Bendix should continue to negotiate and try to use the threat of buying as a lever to force Martin Marietta to pay more for the block or agree to a friendly merger. Wasserstein wanted to try. McDonald didn't.

"They haven't negotiated with us since the day we began," he said. "We offered to negotiate. We were ready to negotiate."

"I want to find out their last offer," said Wasserstein.

"They aren't bargaining in good faith," said McDonald. "Yesterday Siegel told you he wasn't looking for an extender. Then it turned out they were talking to LTV. Do you still trust him?"

•

•

Agee sat on the couch next to Cunningham and listened.

"I've heard those guys are trying to wake up Warren Burger to get him to block us from buying," said McDonald. The Bendix team at the General Motors Building had picked up that rumor. "They will do anything to keep us from buying."

"Al, I think it's unlikely that Marietta is looking for Burger at this time of night," ventured Fleischer. "The chief justice isn't interested in preliminary restraining orders with no judicial implications. I think we might call Marietta."

"The terms they are offering are unacceptable," said McDonald. "Siegel is jerking you around. I can tell you, we will have more leverage after we buy."

"Once we buy, the dynamics have changed," said Wasserstein. "As I said at the board meeting, you can't go home again. We are going to have to negotiate with them sometime. I said I would call. I want to call."

"There is nothing to talk about at this late hour," said McDonald. "You are just trying to preserve your friendship with that banker. Now is the time to buy."

"I'm not saying that we shouldn't buy," said Wasserstein. "I just want to get their last offer. And if you don't want to negotiate with them in any regard, I want to tell them that the negotiations are over. That is common courtesy."

"Courtesy!" yelled McDonald. "Courtesy! You should be less concerned about courtesy and more concerned about strategy and your client's interests. It's a privilege for you to be sitting in this room. We've eliminated one set of bankers. We may have to do it again."

"Courtesy is important to me," said Wasserstein.

"Courtesy may be important to you," yelled McDonald.

"But you should care more about the deal. We're your client."

Agee spoke. "I have decided to buy," he said quietly. "I see what you are saying Bruce, but Marietta just isn't in the ball park. We are going to buy at midnight, and we will buy as many shares as we can. I have checked with our people and we only have the money to buy 70 percent. The more shares we buy, the worse it looks for them to buy our shares as a subsidiary. We will negotiate in the morning."

McDonald looked at Wasserstein. "You are sequestered and impounded," he said. "You can't call out. You can tell your friends that tomorrow."

A little after eleven, Grassi called Wasserstein. "What are you doing?" he asked.

"I'm drinking Mary's champagne," said Wasserstein. He and Grassi thought that Seagram's champagne was terrible.

McDonald heard Wasserstein. "Don't tell them that," he said.

"It's Tony Grassi," said Wasserstein.

"How do you know what he is going to relay to Marietta?" asked McDonald.

"Siegel called again," said Grassi.

"I can't call out," said Wasserstein. "They've got me sequestered."

One of the public relations people called from the General Motors Building and read the press release over the phone. Agee and McDonald spent half an hour rewriting it. Fleischer contributed the headline: "Bendix Buys Control of Martin Marietta."

Then the team got ready to buy. McDonald had told his staff at the General Motors Building to pick up the phone on the second ring when he called at midnight. He tested the number several times to make sure that they picked up on the second ring and not the third. A few minutes before midnight, Agee called the General Motors Building. Kayser, Rowny, and Fontaine were standing by. Agee left the line open. At midnight Agee told Kayser to buy. Kayser called the bank that was waiting to issue the checks. "Buy," he said. "And keep buying until we own 70 percent of Martin Marietta."

Agee listened for a few minutes. Then he hung up. Bendix owned the majority of the shares of Martin Marietta.

Wasserstein finally called Siegel at half past twelve. "As you gathered, I couldn't call," he said. "I'm sorry. I wasn't allowed to call. I just wanted to explain that." Wasserstein thought that Siegel knew that Bendix had bought. "Of course, we'll have to set up a meeting between Pownall and Agee," he said.

Siegel still didn't know that Bendix had bought. "I'll have to check with my client to see what arrangement can be made," he said. "I'll call you back."

"Just a minute," said Wasserstein. He realized that Siegel didn't know. "We bought the shares."

There was a long silence from Siegel. "He's a fool."

The die had been cast. Martin Marietta was committed to buy.

A CONDITIONAL
WHITE KNIGHT

10 First thing Friday morning, Bill Agee got a call from Jay Higgins.

"Bill, Al McDonald called me at two thirty this morning and I see from the *New York Times* and the *Wall Street Journal* that you've bought the shares."

"Yes," said Agee.

"How do you feel?" asked Higgins.

"I feel great," said Agee.

"Well, Bill, please listen to me," said Higgins. "Please pick up the phone and call Martin Marietta and when they won't talk to you, go down to Bethesda and give them $5 a share more on the front end and on the back end and give the man some dignity with which to walk off the field. This game is not over yet. We have got to do something right this minute. I'm begging you."

"Jay, thanks," said Agee. "I'm not going to call anybody. I'm not going to Bethesda. Mary and I are going to Michigan and we're going to have a nice weekend and I hope you do too. I know you've been working awfully hard. Go on home. There aren't going to be any meetings or discussions with anybody. We'll be in touch."

About eleven fifteen, Agee called Jack Byrne. Byrne was in Chicago giving a lecture at the University of Chicago Business School. Agee told the professor who took the call that he needed to talk to Byrne right away, and Byrne left the podium to come to the phone.

"The principals ought to sit down and talk about this. We have got to avoid this collision course," said Agee. "Will you help me set up a meeting?"

"I'll try," said Byrne. "But you should understand that we intend to buy the stock."

"It is irresponsible to buy the stock," said Agee.

"We are going to buy the stock," said Byrne.

"Why won't Marietta management talk to me?" asked Agee. "I have said in every one of my letters that I wanted to talk."

"Have you ever picked up the phone and called Mr. Pownall?" asked Byrne. He cut the call short.

During the afternoon, each of the Martin Marietta directors received three hand-delivered copies of a letter from Bill Agee that Art Fleischer had drafted the night before. One went to the home, one to the office, one was sent in care of Martin Marietta.

Be advised that The Bendix Corporation has today, through its wholly-owned subsidiary, Bendix Acquisition Corporation, purchased approximately 19,300,000 shares of common stock, par value $1 per share ("Shares"), of Martin Marietta Corporation. . . .

As the controlling stockholder of Martin Marietta, Bendix hereby demands the following of you:

1. Attached to this letter as Schedule I is a list of the fourteen persons whom Bendix proposes be elected to the Board of Directors of Martin Marietta. The Bendix designees are all of the members of the Bendix Board of Directors. . . . Bendix requests that a meeting of the

Board of Directors of Martin Marietta be convened promptly at which all the present Martin Marietta Board members would resign seriatim and the fourteen Bendix designees would be elected to the Board. . . .

In anticipation of the Martin Marietta Board's declining to call such a Board meeting, however, Bendix is today requesting the Secretary of Martin Marietta to call a special meeting of stockholders for the purpose of removing all of the members of the Martin Marietta Board of Directors and electing new directors in their place. In addition, Bendix is commencing litigation to assure that the Secretary will call the special meeting.

2. Bendix hereby demands that the Martin Marietta Board immediately take all action necessary or appropriate to cause the immediate termination of (1) Martin Marietta's offer to purchase up to 11,900,000 shares of Bendix common stock and (2) the agreement, dated September 7, 1982, between Martin Marietta and United Technologies Corporation. Be advised that Bendix is seeking a court order enjoining the Martin Marietta Board from proceeding with the offer and agreement under the circumstances of Bendix' position as the controlling stockholder of Martin Marietta.

3. Bendix hereby demands that the Martin Marietta Board resolve that Martin Marietta will not attempt to vote any shares of Bendix common stock which Martin Marietta may own or may hereafter acquire. . . . Any attempt by Martin Marietta to vote any Bendix shares will be treated by Bendix as unauthorized, unlawful and ineffective.

Bendix believes that each member of the Martin Marietta Board owes a fiduciary duty to Bendix as majority stockholder of Martin Marietta which precludes any action by the Board or any director which could injure Bendix or its investment in Martin Marietta in any way. Bendix will seek in its litigation to hold each member of the Board fully and personally responsible for all damages which Bendix, Martin Marietta and their respective stockholders may sustain as a result of the Board's failure to comply with Bendix' demands in this letter.

I, and other members of the Bendix organization would be pleased to meet with the members of the Board of Directors of Martin Marietta at the earliest time to discuss the foregoing matters.

The Bendix Corporation
By: William M. Agee

When Gene Zuckert got his copy of the letter, he called Frank Menaker. "Did you see the letter that Agee sent me?" he asked.

"I'm sorry about that," said Menaker. "It's unprecedented. I don't know what to say to you. Try to ignore it."

Griffin Bell just laughed when he got his letter. "Mr. Agee is giving me advice on my duties as a director," he told his wife. "I am deeply appreciative of Mr. Agee."

●

Ed Hennessy called Bruce Wasserstein on Friday morning. He wanted to talk about the investment deal. He explained that he wanted an option on Bendix. "I'm possibly interested in Bendix as a whole," he said. "I want to be able to buy some Bendix assets."

Wasserstein repeated that what Agee wanted was time; Agee wasn't eager to sell parts of Bendix. "This is a deal that seems to fit your needs and Bill's. You two have met. Let's work out the terms."

Agee had talked about a 10 percent investment. But Hennessy wanted to do something bigger—he was thinking of more like 30 percent. Hennessy and Wasserstein discussed how that kind of investment could be structured. Wasserstein made notes on a pad. Allied would make a tender offer for 10 percent of Bendix. That would trigger the extension. Allied would buy a block of Bendix preferred stock that could be converted into 10 percent of Bendix common. Allied would have the right to buy between 5 percent and 10 percent of Bendix on the open market. Allied would sign a three-year standstill agreement with Bendix—the expiration date would be Agee's birthday in 1985—and Allied would elect two directors to the Bendix board. Allied would welcome a Bendix investment in Allied, although Bendix had no present plans to make one.

"What's the price going to be?" asked Hennessy.

"Eighty a share," said Wasserstein.

"Why?" asked Hennessy.

"That's the right price for the whole company," said Wasserstein. "This investment just triggers the Martin Marietta extension date. It doesn't stop United Technologies from buying Bendix. You are a conditional white knight."

As soon as he had left his meeting with Agee the night before, Hennessy had been thinking about getting an investment banker on the Bendix deal. He had given his neighbor Bill Kearns of Lehman Brothers a ride home from the Strom Thurmond dinner on the Allied helicopter and hinted to him that he might want to sign Lehman on.

"Ed," Kearns had said, "why don't you do more business with me?"

"Allied does do business with you," Hennessy had replied.

"All you give me are the crumbs off the table," Kearns had said. "You've done three major acquisitions at Allied and I haven't been involved in any of them. I have a good acquisitions guy, an ex-marine named Eric Gleacher. I think you two could work very well together."

"I may need a tough acquisitions guy next week," Hennessy had told Kearns.

"Great," Kearns had said. "I'll have Gleacher meet you tomorrow morning at eight o'clock sharp."

"Let's wait," Hennessy had said. "Let's talk Monday or Tuesday."

Now things were moving quickly. Wasserstein had called back to schedule a meeting at First Boston that afternoon, the 17th of September. Hennessy called Jay Higgins at Salomon Brothers.

"Are you going to the meeting?" he asked.

"What meeting?" said Higgins.

"There's a meeting at First Boston to talk about an Allied-Bendix deal," said Hennessy.

"No, Ed," said Higgins. "I don't know about any such meeting. Agee told me half an hour ago there weren't going to be any more meetings. But good luck and keep your eyes open."

"I'm going to need a banker," said Hennessy. "Virtually everyone in town is tied up. Who do you suggest?"

"Try Lehman Brothers," said Higgins. "And try to get Gleacher. He's a good guy."

"That's what I've heard," said Hennessy.

Wasserstein called Hennessy again. Fleischer had drafted the official language of the term sheet and Wasserstein wanted to read it to Hennessy over the phone. It was general. When Wasserstein had finished, Hennessy asked him about bankers.

"Try Lehman Brothers," said Wasserstein. "Try Eric Gleacher."

"Is he good?" asked Hennessy.

"He's good," said Wasserstein. "I'll line him up for you. I'll line up a lawyer for you too."

"Fine," said Hennessy. "I'll handle Kearns."

•

•

Hennessy called Kearns. "Things are moving more rapidly than I had expected," he said. "Meet me with your merger guy at First Boston at two. You had better be sure that this guy is good. If he is good, Lehman Brothers will be very happy. This deal is going to have high visibility. But if you let me down, I don't ever want you to set foot on Allied property again."

When Eric Gleacher got to his office on Friday morning, there was a message for him to call Wasserstein.

"I've personally arranged for you to be hired by Allied in a deal that Allied is thinking of doing with Bendix," said Wasserstein. "Allied is going to buy Bendix stock through a tender offer. Can you get up here soon so we can talk about it before the Allied people come at two?"

"I'll be there soon," said Gleacher.

Wasserstein's office was full of lawyers by the time Gleacher arrived. Fleischer was there. So was Morris Kramer from Skadden, Arps, Slate, Meagher & Flom who had just been hired by Allied. Wasserstein gave Gleacher a typed copy of the term sheet that he had read to Hennessy over the phone.

Hennessy and the Allied team got to First Boston at two. Kearns and his partner J. Tomlinson Hill came in about the same time. They all sat down in a conference room together to talk about the deal. Gleacher pointed to some holes he saw in the agreement. Allied needed outs in case things didn't happen the way that Bendix wanted them to. Allied had to be able to drop its offer if Martin Marietta bought. Allied had to be able to drop its offer if United Technologies bought. If Allied did make an investment in Bendix and United Technologies later raided the company, Allied would be able to sell its shares at a premium.

Hennessy called Agee to say that he had agreed to the general term sheet. He tried to pin Agee down on assets to swap, but Agee was vague.

The meeting broke up. Allied had to put together a formal proposal. The lawyers and bankers would work over the weekend to filter out the glitches and draft the documents.

Ed Hennessy stopped by Allied headquarters early Saturday afternoon to see how the work on the Bendix bid was coming along. Gleacher, Kearns, Hill, and the Allied staff were sitting around the table in the windowless conference room reviewing the financials; the Allied legal team was next door studying the business overlaps between the two companies.

"What do you think is going to happen?" asked Hennessy.

"I think Allied is going to have the opportunity to buy both companies," said Gleacher.

"That's what I want," said Hennessy.

Gleacher suggested that Allied look at three possible scenarios so that it would be ready if something unexpected happened. Allied buys the proposed stake in Bendix. Allied buys all of Bendix but Marietta doesn't buy Bendix; Allied buys Bendix after Martin Marietta has bought 50 percent of the shares.

"Is there anything more that we need to discuss?" asked Hennessy about four o'clock when he got up to leave.

"We've got to talk about a fee," said Gleacher. "I don't think we are going to buy any shares under this offer. The fee should be based on buying all of Bendix."

"I agree with that," said Hennessy. "How much do you want?"

Gleacher had talked to Kearns and the senior Lehman executives about the bill the night before. He pulled out a sheet of numbers.

"I don't want to see your sheet," said Hennessy. "How much is Salomon getting paid?"

"Four million," said Gleacher.

.

.

"How much is First Boston getting?" asked Hennessy.

"They signed on for $2.75 million," said Gleacher. "The Bendix total is $6.75 million."

"How much do you want?" asked Hennessy.

"Five million," said Gleacher.

"You've got it," said Hennessy.

"It's normal to have a minimum fee for a banker if a tender offer is filed," said Gleacher. "How about $500,000?"

"No way," said Hennessy. "I want to do it all or nothing. Is Lehman in it with me all the way?"

"Yes," said Gleacher.

"Fine," said Hennessy. "How much do you want if this partial tender goes through?"

"One and three-quarters million for the common and a quarter of a million for negotiating the preferred," said Gleacher.

"That's two million," said Hennessy. "I'll pay you $2.25 million if the offer goes through with no minimum. In fact, I'll pay you $2.5 million with no minimum."

"We want to represent you on all the divestments and financing relating to the deal if we don't have a minimum," said Gleacher.

"We'll be glad to call," said Hennessy.

That night Hennessy, his wife Ruth, and his father went to dinner at the Morris County Golf Club. The three were having a before-dinner cocktail when Kearns, his wife Pat, and Gleacher came over to say hello. The bankers talked to Hennessy about the deal and about Hennessy's goals for Allied. "I want both companies," said Hennessy. "It's a great opportunity that I don't want to miss."

Kearns introduced Gleacher to Mrs. Hennessy and to Hennessy's dad. Gleacher shook hands with Hennessy, Sr. He had a grip like a steel vise.

"What was Ed like when he was a kid?" asked Kearns.

"Ed was always the toughest kid on the block," said

Hennessy, Sr. "As long as he got the first punch in, Ed said he never had to worry about anything."

By Sunday morning, the Allied lawyers were beginning to get nervous about antitrust. Allied and Bendix made some of the same products, and it looked like the overlaps might be so serious that they would kill the deal. There were two potential showstoppers. First was timing. The Justice Department might ask Allied for extra time to approve the purchase. United Technologies had already been negotiating in Washington for two weeks; once UTC bought Bendix, Allied couldn't. And even if Allied got cleared to buy before UTC did, there could be a problem. If Allied had to sell millions of dollars of its own assets to get that clearance to buy a $600 million stake in Bendix, the deal was off.

So the first thing that Hennessy heard about when he got to Allied at noon was antitrust. An Allied lawyer said that he didn't have enough information from Bendix to tell just how serious the problem was. Both Allied and Bendix made electrical connectors.

"I don't think that's a significant problem," said Hennessy.

Allied made Prestolite spark plugs. Bendix made Autolite spark plugs.

"Prestolite is small and profitable," said Hennessy. "I could sell it in a day."

Gleacher and Wasserstein had scheduled a meeting at three o'clock to tie up the last loose ends on the negotiations. Gleacher didn't want to do that until the antitrust question was answered. He called to reschedule for six.

By five o'clock, the Allied lawyers still didn't have the information they needed on antitrust. Gleacher called Wasserstein to reschedule the meeting again.

"Can we move it to nine?" he asked.

"I'll look into it," said Wasserstein. "I don't know."

.

.

Wasserstein was supposed to meet with Agee at nine.

"I think the deal that makes most sense for all concerned is for Allied to buy both companies," said Gleacher. "The sooner we negotiate that the better."

"You may be right," said Wasserstein. "That's what we originally contacted Allied about. But this isn't the time."

Hennessy decided to go home. "I'll see you at the party this evening," he told Kearns as he left.

On the way to his apartment, Gleacher stopped to get some take-out Chinese food. When he walked in the door, the phone rang. It was one of the lawyers from Skadden, Arps.

"Art Fleischer is here now," he said. "This is the time to talk."

Gleacher left his dinner and hurried to Skadden, Arps. Both Fleischer and Wasserstein were waiting. So were Morris Kramer and Tom Hill. The five talked for a few minutes. Gleacher said that they had to finish negotiating the terms. Kramer said there was an antitrust problem.

"You know, if you guys don't want to go ahead with this, then fine, let's not go ahead," said Wasserstein. Fleischer didn't volunteer any antitrust information.

"I can't understand your attitude," said Gleacher. Bendix had to be bluffing. Wasserstein and Fleischer were acting as if they had a lot of alternatives. The way they were talking, Allied was on the bottom of the list.

A Skadden antitrust lawyer came into the room. "This problem is pretty serious," he said. "We haven't got the information we need from Fried, Frank."

Fleischer knew that Bendix was worried about an antitrust problem too, and he wasn't going to cooperate until Bendix had done its own investigating. "I'll look into that." Fleischer called an antitrust lawyer at Fried, Frank. He put her on the speaker phone. The Skadden lawyer asked some questions. She said she would try to get the answers.

"Art and I have to go to dinner," said Wasserstein. "We'll be back."

"When?" asked Gleacher. It was already eight o'clock.

"Eleven," said Wasserstein.

Wasserstein and Fleischer stopped downstairs at P. J. Clark's for dinner before their meeting with Agee. P.J.'s is Fleischer's favorite hamburger joint. He ordered two burgers. So did Wasserstein. When they had finished, they walked to the Helmsley Palace. They talked to Agee about the negotiations with Allied. They talked about what Bendix could offer to seduce Martin Marietta into doing a merger deal.

After Wasserstein and Fleischer had gone to dinner, Gleacher, Hill, Kramer, and the other Skadden lawyers kept talking about the antitrust problem. Gleacher called Hennessy to say that the terms of the agreement seemed to be changing. Fried, Frank was still stalling on antitrust. Then Gleacher, Hill, and Kramer went out to get some dinner. They stopped at P. J. Clark's, but the restaurant was crowded. They put their name on the waiting list and walked up the street to find another place. They couldn't agree on where to eat. About ten thirty, they came back to P.J.'s. They had hamburgers. They didn't see Fleischer or Wasserstein.

Ed Hennessy and his wife threw a cocktail party on Sunday night for the benefactors of the Morristown Memorial Hospital. Hennessy is a hospital trustee. Bill Kearns and his wife were among the 175 guests. The night was clear and warm. The hospital donors mingled on the rolling lawns below Hennessy's hilltop house. While Hennessy was chatting with his guests, Gleacher called. Hennessy looked around for Kearns. He was on the patio. Hennessy pulled Kearns into the den. Hennessy tried to reach Agee.

Two of the party guests drifted into the den. "Oh, look

at the boat racing trophies," said one. "Isn't that lovely?"

"Ask those people to get out of here so we can have a private conversation," said Hennessy to Kearns.

Kearns tried to push the guests politely out the door. Another guest wandered in. Kearns removed him as well. Hennessy called his team in New York. He kept trying to reach Agee but couldn't locate him. He talked to Kearns. He talked to Gleacher.

The party ended. Kearns and his wife went home. Hennessy finally reached Agee near midnight.

"We've got to have a meeting tomorrow," said Hennessy.

THE PRINCIPALS
MEET

Wasserstein had called Siegel Sunday afternoon to talk about continuing negotiations.

"We have figured out a way for you not to buy," said Wasserstein. "Bendix is going to indemnify the Marietta directors. They won't have any liability."

Siegel was dubious. "I'll talk it over with our lawyers," he said.

"Agee wants to present the idea to Pownall himself," said Wasserstein. "We've got to set up a meeting."

"Pownall isn't a lawyer," said Siegel.

"We need a meeting," said Wasserstein.

"Okay," said Siegel. "I'll see what I can do."

Pownall and Agee were scheduled to meet at Dewey, Ballantine's midtown office at ten o'clock. Before he faced Agee, Pownall discussed with his team what to say. Siegel stressed that Pownall should focus on how the two companies could be put together rationally. It looked as if there was no way to avoid a merger.

"This is a very complicated situation," said Siegel. "Agee may not have total authorization from his board.

Bendix didn't call back on Thursday night. Be careful with him. Make him put anything he offers in writing."

"Watch what you say," said Fullem. "Agee may be wired to record this."

Pownall was startled. "You've got to be kidding."

•

Pownall and Agee sat facing each other in a corner office. "We're somewhat known to each other." Pownall broke the ice. They had met once before. Agee, an active Republican, had thrown a birthday party for Jack Kemp during the Republican National Convention in Detroit in 1980. Pownall is a close friend of Kemp's—he once dislocated his shoulder in a wrist wrestling match with Kemp—so Agee had invited him. Pownall flew out to Detroit for the party. He had been introduced to Agee. He had been introduced to Cunningham.

Agee and Pownall talked for a few minutes about the party. Agee said that he had a house in Idaho. He talked about it for half an hour. Finally, Agee and Pownall got down to business.

"We have a responsibility to make sure that this collision course doesn't happen," said Agee. "We have a responsibility to work it out between ourselves so that your company doesn't end up in a crippled position, nor mine. Under no circumstances am I going to let Bendix end up in a crippled position."

"I don't want that to happen either," said Pownall. "It will be very bad for us to have $900 million of debt and for us to spend the next x-number of weeks fighting over who runs who and so on. It doesn't make any difference who comes out on top. Whoever it is will be running a financially less viable company."

"We're agreed on that," said Agee. "I will go to any

•

•

lengths that are reasonable and prudent to make sure that we avoid that. Why don't you schedule a board meeting, and I will give you an offer that is much better than what you have."

"The problem isn't economics," said Pownall. "We have a serious legal problem because of the obligation our directors feel they have to the Bendix shareholders who have tendered to us. We have to buy your stock."

"You simply can't spend that money to buy our stock," said Agee. "Clearly Bendix is going to wind up in the driver's seat here and your buying is just going to emasculate what might otherwise be a fine organization."

"Have you read our tender offer?" asked Pownall.

"Yes," said Agee.

"Well, there have been some revisions that I think you've missed," said Pownall. "Somehow what you've said makes me think that you don't understand some of what we've said. We have waived the conditions of our offer. We do not know how we can avoid buying your stock. I admit that what you say about finances is true. It's a sort of double jeopardy situation we find ourselves in. Thursday is coming upon us and unless something changes which I just do not now contemplate, I think that the die is cast."

Agee said that he thought that Bendix would win the legal battle. He thought that the Bendix employees would tell Citibank to withdraw SESSOP shares that Citibank had tendered.

"We will buy unless the shark repellent amendments pass," said Pownall.

"Well, we just can't let that happen," said Agee. "We will indemnify you against all. We will improve our offer."

Agee started to explain how an indemnification would work, but Pownall stopped him. "I'm not a lawyer," said Pownall, "but I can't imagine how we can avail ourselves of that."

·

·

Agee paused. "I'd like to bring in my lawyer to help explain this," he said.

Pownall nodded that that was fine. Agee walked to the telephone. A few minutes later, Fleischer arrived. Pownall was surprised that he had come so quickly. Fleischer had been waiting outside in the Bendix limousine. Agee had called the car radiophone.

Pownall called Fullem into the office. Fleischer laid out the terms of the indemnification. Fullem pointed to what he thought was a legal flaw. Martin Marietta would have to breach a contract to buy the shares; Bendix could indemnify the Marietta directors against that. Not buying might also be a violation of the securities laws; the SEC had always said that it was impossible to indemnify against a violation of public policy.

"At first blush, I can see some questions," said Fullem. "I'm not sure that this will hold up. I'll have to think about it."

"I think it will be adequate protection," said Fleischer. He started to give the legal details.

"There is no need for Mr. Agee and Mr. Pownall to participate in our legal discussion," said Fullem. "Let's step into the office across the hall and let these two concentrate on the business questions."

Fleischer and Fullem walked into an empty office across the hall. Fleischer talked about the technicalities of what he had in mind.

Agee and Pownall kept talking about the new package that Agee had put together. Agee repeated his offer to indemnify the Marietta directors. He listed the other terms: Bendix would raise the value of the stock swap to $53 a share. "I'll give you four seats on the board," said Agee. "You can pick your four best board members."

"Hell, we don't *have* any such things," said Pownall. "Our board members are all of high standing."

Agee tried to talk about Pownall's role in the merged company.

"Please," interrupted Pownall. "I am not a factor in this thing. I'm just the front man for the company, and nothing that is going to happen here tomorrow or the next day or at some time in the future has anything to do with me personally. I am individually not a factor here. I am just acting for Martin Marietta at the moment. I am here trying to understand what it is you're offering and whether there's anything in that offer that could entice us to do something different from the course that we've already indicated to you that we intend."

"Then let's talk about the offer," said Agee. "I will go to any length to avoid this collision course."

"Has this offer been approved by your board?" asked Pownall. Agee hadn't mentioned that it had been. "Before I can conceivably take anything like this to our board, I have to know that it has the full sanction of your board. I'm not saying that our board will do anything as a result of this offer, but we will consider it."

"This does have the approval of the board," said Agee. He explained that he had a committee of three directors who sanctioned his negotiated decisions.

Pownall didn't quite understand that arrangement, but he didn't really care how the offer had been approved as long as it had.

"How soon can your board consider this?" asked Agee.

"The soonest I can intelligently call together a board meeting is tomorrow afternoon," said Pownall. "This is important, so we won't do it by telephone. I'd appreciate having your offer in writing. I understand what you've offered, but I don't want to just go into a board meeting with a handful of notes. Simply so that I know that this is being offered officially by the Bendix Corporation, I'd like it in writing."

"I'd like to come and present the offer to your board," said Agee. "I'd like to bring my attorney with me."

Pownall was surprised at the request. "I can't assure you that there will be an opportunity for you to address the board," he said. "There may not be any need for us to hear you. We've got our own counsel, so I don't know that we'll need to hear yours. The only thing we'll need is a written proposal. But I will indicate to the board your willingness to talk to them."

"Well, I will be there *anyway*," said Agee. "I will be in Bethesda. Could you arrange accommodations for me?"

"Yes," said Pownall.

The two got up and shook hands. "I feel encouraged by the meeting," said Agee.

After Agee left, the Marietta team sat down to talk about the meeting and about what they would say to United Technologies later that afternoon. Now that Martin Marietta was going to be able to buy the Bendix stock before United Technologies could, the two partners had to negotiate a new agreement. Both sides had worked feverishly over the weekend to put together a list of alternatives.

At four o'clock, Pownall, Adams, Leithauser, Menaker, and Siegel assembled in the large conference room at Wachtell, Lipton with Gray, Large, Brown, Rohatyn, and Lipton to talk through the possibilities. The most obvious deal was the reverse of what they had negotiated two weeks before: Martin Marietta would sell United Technologies the Bendix industrial and automotive divisions at a fixed price. Marietta thought it might be able to get a better price selling assets individually and UTC didn't like the idea of its buying assets before it saw the books.

Siegel suggested a stock swap: Marietta would sell control of Bendix to United Technologies for $75 a share; after UTC took over Bendix, UTC would sell Martin Marietta part of the 70 percent block of Marietta that Bendix owned. The logistics would be complicated. UTC would pay for the balance of Bendix with UTC notes convertible into new Martin Marietta stock. That would give Martin Marietta some equity. If the swap were done at the price each side had paid, United Technologies would still have a big block of Marietta after the deal was complete. There would be a legal hitch: once UTC bought Bendix, Martin Marietta would be a United Technologies subsidiary. The two companies had to find a new buyer for fuel controls.

"We've been talking to Rockwell International about fuel control," said Gray. "A swap could be a possibility, but I don't think the numbers will work because, in my view, you are paying too much for Bendix now that Bendix has spent its cash. However, I have got a different approach. UTC can make an investment in Martin Marietta. We'll buy a block of a new preferred stock that you will issue. That will give you some cash to pay down debt. We can dilute Bendix's control below 50 percent."

"That sounds interesting," said Pownall. "How big a block are we talking about?"

"We want to structure this so that UTC doesn't have to put Martin Marietta debt on its balance sheet," said Gray. "We're thinking of say half a billion. We want enough to have working control, but we want to limit our risk."

"Isn't that asking us to sell control to you at a good price without our getting much in return?" asked Siegel.

Lipton's secretary came into the conference room with a sheet of paper. Lipton read it carefully. "There is a rumor that Joe Flom is getting involved," said Lipton. Joseph Flom, a name partner at Skadden, Arps, was a close friend and rival of Lipton's; the two had lunch together once a week. "The rumor is that he's representing Allied and that Allied is having a board meeting right now."

"Bendix is probably trying to line up a white knight," said Siegel, "That may change the situation."

The teams talked for another half hour. Then the meeting broke up. "Let's keep in touch," said Pownall. "Let's talk about this when we have more information."

Gray leaned back in his chair and spread his hands on the table in front of him. "I wish I could do more for you, Tom," he said. "But that's my best offer. I'm sorry."

•

Agee went straight from his meeting with Pownall up to Skadden, Arps to finish his negotiations with Allied. Hennessy and his team were waiting.

"There are five points," said Kramer. He listed them. Allied wanted an indemnification against possible losses in an antitrust fire sale. Allied wanted to firm up the conditions of the offer. Allied had some technical objections to the wording of the agreement.

Agee listened. He talked the points over for five minutes.

"If I understand you correctly," said Kramer, "you just said no, no, no, no, and no."

"That's not right," said Agee. He went over the points again.

"I see," said Kramer. "No, no, no, no, and three-quarters no."

"That's not right," said Agee.

Kramer turned to Fleischer. "I seem to be having trouble understanding your client. Could you explain the Bendix position?"

The Bendix team went out to caucus. They came back. Agee agreed to the $20 million indemnification. Bendix negotiated some of the other points.

Agee looked at his watch. "I've got to go," he said.

"I'm in a hurry too," said Kramer. "We haven't finished."

The teams solved a few more points. There was only one issue outstanding: the kind of "sister" investment that Bendix would make in Allied.

"I've got to go," said Agee. "I've got a board meeting."

Hennessy and Agee agreed to let the lawyers settle the investment. Agee left. Hennessy stayed for a few minutes, then he left.

The Bendix directors sat around the table in the General Motors building. "Let me tell you that there are a lot of things going on," Agee said. "A lot of things including talks with Tom Pownall and several great extenders. I want to tell you first about my meeting with Tom this morning."

Agee said that he and Pownall had talked. Pownall had seemed more flexible. Pownall had invited Agee to Bethesda. Agee hoped to be able to talk to the Martin Marietta board. The crux of the new Bendix offer to Martin Marietta was to pay for any legal problems that Martin Marietta might have if it didn't buy. Fleischer thought that the maximum that Bendix would have to pay in damages was $300 million.

"Now I want to talk to you about my great extender with Allied," said Agee. "The principal interest of Allied is to take over Bendix. Ed Hennessy said to me in our first conversation that all else being equal, his preference was to buy Bendix. I said that my first preference was to go ahead with Marietta, but that I would welcome him as a shareholder."

Wasserstein listed the terms of the Allied investment. Then he handed out copies of the Allied 10K and other financial information and made a short presentation on its businesses.

"This sounds good to me," said a director, "but isn't it inconsistent for us to endorse an Allied offer at $80 a share when we just rejected a United Technologies offer at $85?"

"The United Technologies offer was in effect $62," said Wasserstein. "Gray was going to pay $85 on the front end and offer stock on the back end that was worth less than $50. Now we are selling only part of the company, and for a much higher price."

"How do we know that Allied will give us a good price for the company if Allied decides to buy the rest?" asked a director.

"We'll worry about that later," said Wasserstein. "Normally a company would not want to do a deal like this. Normally it would avoid it for fear of being taken over. But I have discussed that extensively with Agee and he says that that is not a concern."

"It is possible that we will still be a target for someone," said Agee. "We might have to fight another raid from UTC. But now we have built in someone to be helpful to us. I have no problem with Bendix being bought at our time at the right price."

"There are two other potential extenders," continued Agee. "There is a potential of swapping for the RCA stock. There is another company that is prepared to invest and in turn exchange for a subsidiary, a division. The overriding objective is the Marietta merger. These are the options that we're looking at, and I'm going to work like hell to solve the Marietta situation."

The directors talked. They agreed that Marietta was the top priority. They approved a raise to $52 a share on the back end. Then they endorsed the Allied proposal. Bendix had a safety net.

●

The Allied board meeting began at four o'clock in the boardroom of the St. Regis Paper Company on Lexington

Avenue. The chairman of St. Regis is an Allied director. Harold Buirkle, Allied's chief financial officer made a slide presentation on the financials of the Bendix investment. He said that Allied hoped to negotiate an asset swap.

"I think that this is an attractive opportunity because it is the first step towards buying both companies," said Gleacher. "The investment on its own is attractive because the standstill period is so short. Sooner rather than later, Allied will acquire two very attractive companies on a good economic basis. The price that Bendix paid for 70 percent of Martin Marietta was fair. The price we are paying for Bendix is a good one relative to the value of Bendix."

Hennessy said that he endorsed the idea of an investment in Bendix but that the deal had changed so much since that morning, that he didn't have a firm proposal. There was nothing to vote on. It was clear that the board didn't like the idea anyhow.

"I may come back to you with a proposal to buy all of Bendix," said Hennessy at the end of the meeting. "Are you interested in that?"

Yes. Then some of the directors talked informally about the kind of person Bill Agee is and what it meant to invest in a company he controlled.

Agee and Wasserstein were sitting in Agee's office when Gleacher called at six o'clock.

"The Allied board won't make an investment in Bendix," said Gleacher.

"I understand," said Wasserstein. "We'll see what happens from here."

Agee and Wasserstein talked about the Allied rejection.

"I know it isn't Ed's fault," said Wasserstein. "As you know Bill, you're quite controversial."

"Should I call Hennessy?" asked Agee. "What should I do now?"

"There's a good chance that if we needed it, Allied

.

.

would be a white knight," said Wasserstein. "Let's wait for the wounds to heal."

●

Late Monday afternoon, Jay Higgins had called John Gutfreund. Higgins had found out that there had been a Bendix board meeting that afternoon. Salomon Brothers had not been invited.

"I think we should resign the Bendix deal," said Higgins. "Technically, Agee is violating our agreement. He is having substantive discussions with other parties without informing us. He doesn't listen to our advice. I'm deferring to you, but I think we ought to withdraw."

"We are gentlemen," said Gutfreund. "We don't walk out on a client in the heat of the battle. If Agee gets beaten up, we will get the blame."

At ten thirty Monday night, Al McDonald called Jay Higgins.

"Jay," he said. "I'm wondering if you have any ideas about extenders for us."

"What?" asked Higgins incredulously.

McDonald started to explain what an extender bidder was.

"I know what an extender is," laughed Higgins. "But we don't have one for Bendix. You can only take the fact that we don't have an extender in the context in which you and Agee asked us to approach this assignment. You told us to butt out. Salomon Brothers have been on you for weeks to talk to Allied and Esmark, and you and Agee told us that you didn't want to talk. Then we find out that you're talking behind our backs to the same companies we told you to talk to. We had nothing to do with your decision to buy the stock last Thursday night. I begged Agee to go down to Bethesda and talk to Pownall on Friday. Now, I've heard that you guys had a board meeting today to which we

●

●

weren't invited and that the deal fell apart a couple of hours ago. All I can say is that we've been following
this with interest."

"Jay, I don't deny anything you say," said McDonald.
"Bill is his own man. He likes to do things himself. I just
wanted to know if anybody had sort of walked in off the
street that you think might be able to help us."

"No, Al, no one has."

A TRIP TO
MARYLAND

•

1 2 Donald Trump is a real estate developer. He lives in a posh apartment overlooking Central Park. He belongs to all the right clubs. Thirty-six years old, six-foot-two with sandy blonde hair, Trump is a striking figure. He staked out the site for New York's new convention center. He rounded up the backing for the tall Trump Tower on Fifth Avenue, which may just become the city's most expensive address. He is also controversial. He razed the old Commodore Hotel beside Grand Central Station to build his glittery glass Grand Hyatt. One New York City official says he will not negotiate with Trump without a witness; the Metropolitan Transportation Authority has sued him for allegedly not keeping his promises.

Trump wants to do deals outside of real estate. He tried to buy the *New York Daily News*, but lost out. In the months before the Bendix bid for Martin Marietta, Trump had bought a lot of stock in RCA; he wanted to add the Bendix block of RCA shares to his hoard. He asked his investment banker, Paul Hallingby, Jr., of Bear, Stearns & Company, to talk to Bendix about the idea. Hallingby had done that;

•

•

the Tuesday that Agee had seen Don Kelly and Roger Briggs from Esmark, he had also met with Hallingby. Hallingby told Agee that he had a client who was interested in the RCA stock and who was willing to bid for Bendix and swap blocks to get it. Agee told Hallingby that he might be interested; he said he would give Hallingby a call.

Monday night, Agee summoned Hallingby and his client to the Helmsley to talk about the sale.

Trump and his team of investment bankers and lawyers got to the hotel for their seven-thirty appointment Tuesday morning, the day after the Allied rejection. They met with Agee, Cunningham, Fleischer, and McDonald. Trump agreed to tender for about 7 percent of Bendix and swap that for the RCA stock. He also wanted to have an option on the block: if the tender for Bendix didn't work out, Trump would buy the RCA stock for the same price in cash. Agee and Trump made an appointment to negotiate the price of the block at ten o'clock that night.

"This offer has got to start tomorrow," said Fleischer.

"We'll do it," Trump assured him.

As soon as Trump left, Agee hurried out to have breakfast with the president of the company that was thinking about tendering for Bendix and swapping the stock for some Bendix automotive assets. Wasserstein and Grassi came up to the suite from their office at First Boston. Stephen Fraidin, a corporate lawyer from Fried, Frank, walked in. Fleischer had called Fraidin near midnight the night before to ask him to come down to Bethesda. Fleischer thought that he might need a second attorney. Agee came back from breakfast. He said that the price that the company was offering for the assets was too low. He wasn't sure that he wanted to break up Bendix anyhow. Agee talked to his strategists about the Trump deal. He talked about the possibility of an Allied deal. He talked about what he would say to the Martin Marietta board. The team packed up for the trip to Maryland.

Wasserstein called Gleacher.

"I'm sorry things fell apart," said Gleacher.

"There's a lot going on," said Wasserstein. "My advice is that you keep working on the papers for a 100 percent deal. I can't promise anything, but I feel it will be worth the time and effort."

The strategists took the elevator down to the lobby. They went out to the street to catch the limousine to Newark Airport.

"Mary's coming," said Agee, "and so is Fleischer." Agee hadn't mentioned the possibility of taking Cunningham to Bethesda before.

"Steve Fraidin's coming," said Fleischer.

There were only five seats on the Bendix plane. If Agee, Cunningham, Wasserstein, Fleischer, and Fraidin all went to Maryland, Grassi couldn't come.

Agee looked at Grassi. "Maybe Fraidin doesn't need to come," he said.

"Fraidin's coming," said Fleischer.

Grassi looked at Wasserstein. Wasserstein shrugged.

At Newark Airport they boarded the Bendix plane. The Martin Marietta jet was parked alongside. The Bendix strategists watched the Kidder and Dewey, Ballantine advisers climb aboard.

Agee sat across a small table from Cunningham. Fleischer sat next to Agee; Wasserstein was next to Cunningham. Fraidin sat behind them. After takeoff, Cunningham got out a legal pad and pencil to write a letter to Tom Pownall. She passed draft sentences across the table in front of her to Agee. Agee penciled in his own changes and passed them back. Every few minutes, Agee or Cunningham read a draft sentence out loud. Wasserstein,

Fleischer, and Fraidin made comments. Cunningham re-
wrote. When the team was finally satisfied, Agee read the
longhand copy of the letter over the radio phone to a Bendix secretary in Washington.

Then Agee and Cunningham started to discuss their options. Agee decided not to do the assets deal. "I want to
make a clear decision," he said. "I want to settle with Marietta or sell Bendix. I just don't think the extender is the
right thing to do. I don't like the idea of selling part of the
company. Tactically it may be good, but I've got to sleep
at night."

Agee talked through what he wanted to tell the Martin
Marietta board.

"Don't get your hopes up," said Wasserstein. "It's highly
unusual for the board of a target company to invite the
chairman of a raider to talk. I can't think of a time it has
happened. You might not get in there."

"I think I will," said Agee. "Do you think our proposal
is going to work?"

Wasserstein, Fleischer, and Fraidin were noncommit-
tal.

"I think it will," said Agee. "I think we are right. I think
we will be able to make a deal."

The Bendix jet landed at Dulles Airport. A Bendix car
was waiting. The strategists rode down the Capital Beltway
to the Pook's Hill Marriott a mile down the road from Martin Marietta. Three suites had been reserved in Art Fleischer's name for Agee and the team to wait in. A Martin Marietta lawyer was already in the lobby to take Agee's written
proposal to headquarters. The Bendix secretaries in the suite
were still typing it up. Agee checked into the hotel in his
own name, and went upstairs to call Pownall.

"Tom, I want to read you a letter that I will be sending
over to you shortly," said Agee. He read the draft copy of
the letter over the phone.

.

.

"I will call you back as soon as the board decides whether it wants to accept your proposal to come and talk to us," said Pownall.

Fleischer was hungry and someone ordered lunch. The advisers talked about their options. Wasserstein paced up and down the red carpet. A waiter arrived with a tray of sandwiches. Fleischer hurried him out the door. Cunningham put the cold cuts on the table. As the five ate lunch, Fleischer talked about the alternatives that he and Fraidin had thought up to get around the "legal problem" that Martin Marietta kept talking about. "I can't promise that any of these will work," he said, "but they are worth trying. If Marietta wants a way out of buying the Bendix shares, we can find one."

The secretary came in from the room next door with a typed copy of the letter. Agee read it through. He pointed out a typo. The secretary took it back and corrected the mistake. She brought the letter to the table. Agee signed it and sent it downstairs to the Marietta lawyer.

•

While Agee and his advisers waited, the Marietta directors gathered in the boardroom for their meeting. Pownall summed up what had happened since the board meeting the previous Thursday. At that point Bendix had not yet bought any Martin Marietta shares. Then he set the stage for the new Bendix proposal. "Agee and I sat down in New York yesterday," he said. "Our meeting lasted two hours. Thirty minutes of platitudes, thirty minutes of verbal sparring, thirty minutes on the issues, and thirty minutes to end the meeting."

Menaker left the boardroom. He came back with the Bendix letter. He handed it to Pownall. Pownall set it down on the table in front of him. "Mr. Agee outlined to me a new proposal which he believes will bring this episode to a

•

•

conclusion," continued Pownall. "He has described the terms of the proposal in a letter to our board and he is waiting at a nearby hotel should you wish to discuss the offer with him."

Pownall paused. The directors shook their heads no. They would hear the offer first. Pownall passed Calvin a note and Calvin left the boardroom to call Agee. Then he picked up the letter from the table and flourished it in front of the directors. "This is the letter from Mr. Agee," he said. "I will read it to you."

Dear Tom:

The time has come for us to put any disagreements behind us. Let us return to operating our businesses.

The original proposal for the merger between our two companies was intended to create a combined entity that would be financially stronger and more capable of servicing our national defense needs. It was with this objective in mind that we purchased our 70 percent interest in Martin Marietta.

We have a plan which can be implemented in the very near term that will fully achieve these objectives which are clearly in the best interests of our shareholders, employees, and our country.

Tom, without getting into the intricacies of the legal discussions, I believe that our proposal presents the most prudent course for your board. The benefits of a combination are obvious. The dangers of proceeding with the purchases of Bendix stock are, in our view, dramatic:

1. Sufficiently impaired financial condition;
2. Forced divestitures of assets under disadvantageous circumstances;
3. Significant prolonged distraction and disruption to the joint employees and management;

4. Potential weakening of our ability to service key customers including the U. S. Government;

5. Material reduction in shareholder value.

Any decision by your directors must clearly balance the benefits of our proposal against the enormous risk of not working together. Therefore, I want to set forth in more detail for you and your fellow directors the various points which I had the opportunity to discuss with you yesterday. The Board of Directors of Bendix has authorized me to make the following proposal.

The letter then listed eight terms to the offer, some highly technical. Bendix would pay $54 a share in securities for the remaining Martin Marietta shares; Bendix would indemnify the Marietta directors against any damages resulting from not buying the shares; Bendix would give Martin Marietta four seats on the board of the merged company. Bendix would allow Martin Marietta to leave its headquarters in Bethesda. The letter concluded:

Tom, I believe that we have an opportunity and an obligation to do something very outstanding for our two companies, our shareholders, our employees, and our country.

Sincerely,

William M. Agee

Pownall asked his secretary to make copies of the letter for the directors. He recessed the meeting so that Kidder could consider the terms of the revised offer and make a recommendation to the board.

Siegel took the letter into the war room. He called his office. Siegel read the terms of the letter to one of his staffers. He asked him to run the calculation on the Kidder computer. Then Wasserstein called to say that the offer in the letter was supposed to be a package of securities worth

$55 a share, not $54 a share. Siegel called New York with the update. Siegel's assistant called back a few minutes later with the results and Siegel scribbled down the numbers.

The directors were waiting in the boardroom when Siegel came back.

"Given that Bendix already owns 70 percent of Martin Marietta, the $55 a share offer is fair," said Siegel. "However we can't recommend that you accept the offer. There are real legal problems with it. Bob Fullem talked about that at the board meeting when we launched ASCAP. And if we don't buy, there is going to be a potential liability of at least $300 million."

Leithauser nodded that he agreed.

"I outlined what a double buy does to the balance sheet at the last board meeting," said Siegel. "Bendix has now bought 70 percent of our stock instead of the 50 percent I was talking about and that changes the numbers. I want to just give you a quick update." Siegel explained that things were worse—but still manageable.

A few of the directors started to ask questions about the fairness of the new Bendix offer.

"We can't consider this," said Bradley. "We made a contract with the Bendix shareholders last Monday that we would buy their stock unless Bendix withdrew its offer or the shark repellent charter amendments passed. Bendix did not withdraw its offer. The charter amendments have not passed. Nothing has changed. We have to buy. Agee is saying: abrogate your contract and I will insure you against this wrong act. That is morally wrong. It is clear to me that we made our decision a week ago."

"Did we?" asked Byrne. "That is clearer to you than it is to me. Is there some way that we could agree not to buy if Agee started talking about a more reasonable price?"

"The Bendix shareholder meeting has been postponed," said Menaker. "The shareholder amendments won't

·

·

be considered until tomorrow if ever. There is still the possibility that Bendix will find a friendly bidder and delay our purchase by ten days. But even if Bendix buys 99 percent of our stock, Bendix has to call a special shareholder meeting to change control. And Bendix now has to give thirty-days notice to do that. If this corporation buys more than 50 percent of the Bendix stock, the court will probably not interfere. A negotiated settlement is the most likely result."

"That's right," said Fullem. "Short of a reorganization under the bankruptcy laws, the courts are not going to get involved in this settlement. And if the courts do not block Marietta from buying and if the shareholder amendments do not pass in Southfield, then the failure to take down the Bendix stock will constitute the breach of a valid contract. If that is correct, then the indemnification as proposed by Mr. Agee might be unenforceable as contrary to public policy."

"It is almost as if they've got a plan," said one of the directors. "They're following the plan without any regard to changes in conditions."

"But can you do that?" asked Mel Laird. "Can you indemnify directors?"

"You can do that, yes," said Fullem. "You can indemnify directors and a corporation, and unless what you are indemnifying them against is a violation of public policy, the indemnification would be valid. But many millions of dollars have changed hands on the basis of our statements. A courtroom or a jury could come out and say we were playing around with the securities laws. Bill Agee is trying to push the problem off on his shareholders. They aren't going to like that. People who thought we were going to buy are going to scream. If we announce that we aren't going to buy, half the Bendix stock will go on the block. Trading won't open for days. The price will go through the

·

·

floor. I asked an investment banker friend, an outsider, not Kidder, what he thought the trading price of Bendix stock would be if we didn't buy. He said in the twenties a share. The liability could easily be more than $500 million."

"Where are we legally if we don't accept this?" asked a director.

"Once we buy we will be legally equal to Bendix," said Fullem. "We will be a Bendix subsidiary. Bendix will be a Martin Marietta subsidiary. The most realistic outcome is that both sides will be in the same boat. We may have a Mexican standoff. While everything that I have read makes me think that Agee thinks that he is in the driver's seat, if anything, *we* have an edge. The Maryland corporate statutes give us a time advantage."

"Agee is waiting to come and discuss the letter with you," Pownall reminded the directors.

"It would be unprecedented for you to invite him in," said Menaker. "But I can't think of a legal reason not to."

"What is your pleasure?" asked Pownall.

"This is Griff Bell," said Bell over the speaker phone. He was in Georgia for another board meeting. "Tom, have you asked them to meet with their board?"

"No," said Pownall.

"Well, then I don't understand why Agee thinks he ought to be meeting with our board," said Bell. "He can meet with you."

"Didn't Napoleon like to deal with an alliance?" asked one director.

The board agreed. Only Tom would see Agee. They voted unanimously to reject the terms that Bendix had offered in the letter to Pownall.

After the meeting, Pownall asked Roy Calvin to draft a letter to Agee. Calvin sat down at his old manual typewriter.

Dear Bill:

The proposal that you forwarded on authority of the Bendix Board was received today while our Board was in session and was found to be unacceptable on several grounds.

It must be stated that the Martin Marietta Board finds it impossible to accept your key proposition—that is, "no shares of Bendix stock would be purchased under the Martin Marietta offer without Bendix's consent . . ."

In our September 13 and subsequent statements, we were explicit about the conditions of our tender for 11,900,000 shares of Bendix stock for $75 cash if Bendix proceeded with its tender for Martin Marietta shares.

By your action on September 17, when Bendix not only proceeded to purchase the tendered Martin Marietta shares, but also purchased substantially more, you eliminated the possibility for us to withdraw the Martin Marietta tender for Bendix. The only other remaining condition attached to our tender is that our obligation to purchase Bendix shares would be eliminated if your stockholders vote for your proposed charter amendments.

I should tell you also that we absolutely reject the responsibility for creation of any of the disadvantageous conditions you now say may arise if we consummate our tender for Bendix. Our view is that Bendix was, or certainly should have been, aware of the potential for such consequences before it began purchasing Martin Marietta shares. Also, we can see no evidence of such concern in your increased offer to acquire 70 percent of our shares instead of the simple majority originally sought.

For all of these and other reasons the Martin Marietta board did not find your propositions of today to be timely, constructive, adequate, or otherwise in the interests of stockholders.

It may yet be possible somehow to implement a plan under which Martin Marietta and Bendix can be combined. I sincerely doubt that any such plan would be acceptable to our board which did not treat the two companies as equals in order to protect adequately our remaining shareholders.

Sincerely,
Thomas G. Pownall

While Calvin wrote, Pownall talked to his advisers about what he should tell Agee. Pownall wanted to explain that the board had rejected Agee's offer and Pownall wanted to invite Agee over to Martin Marietta headquarters to talk. Some of the advisers didn't like that idea.

"If the press finds out that you talked to Agee here," said one, "there's going to be all kinds of speculation that you're about to reach an amicable settlement."

"I don't give a damn," said Pownall. "If we're going to meet, does it make any difference whether we meet here or in a hotel? The only respectable thing to do is to invite him over here. He's only five minutes away. I feel better about that than saying to him: stand by, I'll come over and talk to you at the hotel."

Agee had thought that he would be asked to appear before the Marietta board at two fifteen. He sat at the Marriott and waited for Pownall to call. When the phone rang, Agee picked it up on the first ring.

"Mr. Fleischer?" said the voice on the other end.

"Just a minute," said Agee. "I'll get him."

"This is Roy Calvin from Martin Marietta," said the voice. "I'm really trying to reach Mr. Agee. Can you get him instead?"

"This *is* Bill Agee," said Agee.

"Oh, well, Mr. Agee, I'm calling on behalf of Mr. Pownall," said Calvin. "The board meeting is running a little late and the board hasn't decided if they are willing to hear you. I'll call when they've made a decision."

Agee hung up. The phone rang again. This time it was for Fleischer. It was one of the litigators. The Delaware Supreme Court had just said that Martin Marietta had a moral duty to Bendix because Bendix was its majority shareholder.

Fleischer called Larrabee at Martin Marietta to make sure that he had heard about the decision. Fleischer wanted Larrabee to tell the Marietta board what the Delaware court had ruled. Then Fleischer and Agee talked about what the decision meant. Martin Marietta might still be allowed to buy Bendix stock the next night, but if Marietta had a moral duty to Bendix it probably couldn't vote the shares. If Marietta could not vote, Marietta could not take control. As Fleischer saw it Bendix had a leg up in the legal battle for control. Bendix just had to convince the court that Marietta had a legal duty to Bendix as well as a moral one. Then it wouldn't be rational for Marietta to buy.

At three fifteen, Roy Calvin from Martin Marietta called Agee again.

"I've got another message for you from Mr. Pownall," said Calvin. " 'The jury is out on the invitation. Wait until four.' I'm sorry about the delay. I'll call you again."

"Can you bring Mr. Pownall a message from me?" asked Agee.

"Sure," said Calvin.

"Have him tell the jury that is still out on the invitation that there's a witness over here who is very eager to testify," said Agee.

"Will do," said Calvin.

Cherno, the Fried, Frank litigator, called from Baltimore. The hearing before Judge Young on the Bendix motion to block Marietta from buying had gone very badly. Young seemed to be annoyed that Bendix was back in court asking for more time after Bendix had appealed his order of the week before giving them more time. At the end of the hearing Young had said that he "was inclined to deny the motion."

At four o'clock, Wasserstein called Gleacher.

"Time is running out," said Gleacher. "Marietta will be able to buy at midnight tomorrow. We have got to set up a meeting between Hennessy and Agee to negotiate this deal."

"I don't know if we're ready to do a deal," said Wasserstein. "Keep your people working. I can't guarantee anything. I will call you by seven."

The hotel phone rang again at a quarter to five. This time it was Frank Menaker.

"Frank, how are you?" said Agee.

"Bill," said Menaker. "The board has just met. Tom has asked me to invite you over here to talk to him."

"The board has met?" said Agee. "What do you mean? The board meeting is over? Is the board waiting for me to talk to them?"

"The board meeting is over." said Menaker.

"Over?" asked Agee. "Aren't I going to get to address the board?"

"No," said Menaker. "The board members have left. But come over. Tom wants to talk to you."

Agee paused. "I'll bring my crew over," he said. "I'll be happy to talk to you."

"Good," said Menaker. "I'll send the cars."

•

•

•

Agee and his team arrived about fifteen minutes later. Pownall came out to the elevator. Agee introduced them. Pownall assumed that Cunningham had come along because she and Agee were flying out together to Southfield that night for the Bendix shareholder meeting the next day. Pownall reminded Cunningham that they had met at Jack Kemp's birthday party. Then Pownall and Agee walked across the corridor to Pownall's office. Frank Menaker took the others into the boardroom to wait.

Cunningham walked around the long polished table to the window. She pulled back the curtain and looked into the courtyard. "This looks a lot like the Bendix building in Southfield," she said. "But Bendix doesn't have the grounds."

"We don't want you to get too enamored of the place," said Menaker. "You won't get to own it."

Cunningham laughed and sat down at the center of the table. Wasserstein took the chair to her right. Fleischer and Fraidin sat to her left. Menaker offered them a snack, and they chatted for a few minutes. Then Menaker went back into his office to work. Fullem and Larrabee wandered into the boardroom. The lawyers talked about the indemnification. Fullem and Larrabee were worried that the breach of contract for not buying the shares would violate the federal securities laws—Martin Marietta would be charged with having manipulated the market with a fake offer—and that the indemnification would therefore be unenforceable. Fleischer thought that the idea was ridiculous. So did Fraidin. They talked about the problem. Fullem and Larrabee seemed unimpressed.

"Is there any risk that your indemnification will be unenforceable?" asked Larrabee.

"Of course there is," said Fraidin, "there is always a

•

2 1 9

•

risk that an indemnification will be unenforceable. This is a low-risk indemnification. I don't think there will be a problem."

"But can you tell us that there is no risk?" asked Fullem.

"No," said Fraidin. "You know I can't. No lawyer could."

"Our board believes it has a moral responsibility to the people who tendered," said Fullem.

Pownall's office is spartan. There is a large desk often stacked high with papers. There are hunting prints on the wall: a charging elephant, a cape buffalo, an eagle. In the corner there is a small table with a Martin Marietta silver bowl award on the shelf. There are two stiff armchairs beside it. There is a large round table at the window overlooking the duckpond.

Agee and Pownall sat facing each other at the table.

"My wife has been working very closely with me on this," said Agee. "I have a lot of respect for her intellect and her judgment."

Pownall was puzzled that Agee had volunteered that. He said that the Marietta board had carefully considered the Bendix proposal and that they had turned down the indemnification because they believed that they had a legal and an ethical responsibility to buy. The idea of an indemnification was anathema.

"Well, Tom," said Agee. "Let me talk about this for a minute. I'm very disappointed that I didn't get a chance to speak to your board. I wasn't going to take much of their time. But I was going to say that I thought there were three issues. One is a business issue. One is a legal issue. One is a moral issue.

"As it relates to the business issue, there is no doubt in my mind that our business combination that we started out on in the first place was the right one. Obviously you must have felt that way or you wouldn't have come back at us. So it was only a matter of price. I offered you $55 a share for your 30 percent minority shareholders which is $7 a share more than the other people received, so that is fair."

"It isn't a question of economics," said Pownall. "The board's decision focused on the legal side."

"Let me speak to the legal side again," said Agee. "Because our lawyers feel very strongly. I talked with insurance companies and where we can indemnify you to the extent that there are legal problems and there probably will be, we're prepared to assume them. So now it is our problem, and not your problem."

Pownall shook his head no. Martin Marietta had a legal and moral responsibility to buy the Bendix shares. According to its reading of the law, it was not possible to indemnify someone doing violence to the law.

Agee said that his lawyers thought that the indemnification would work. "I don't quite understand that part," he said. "But I was prepared to bring the lawyers in so they could discuss in front of us what the legal differences are, if any."

Pownall repeated that the directors could not ethically accept the indemnification.

Agee reminded Pownall that the Delaware Supreme Court had suggested earlier that day that Martin Marietta had a moral responsibility to Bendix, as its largest shareholder.

"Martin Marietta has a responsibility to all its shareholders," said Pownall.

"Let's discuss two other aspects," said Agee. "First of all, did your board consider the legal liability that they have to the 30 percent minority shareholders who were precluded from any opportunity to receive $55 in securities. There is a legal obligation to those people. Would you please consider that particular legal exposure."

"As I said in my letter to you," he continued. "Consider the moral obligations that we have to shareholders, our employees, and to the communities that we serve. If we stay on this collision course and you buy the stock, there is a serious consequence.

"And that's all I was going to tell them," said Agee. "In addition, I was going to say that if there are any other problems or any other things I'm not aware of that you want to negotiate, I'm very much prepared to do that. I would be in front of your board. I am here now. I honestly believe that it is not in your interest or our interest to end up in a stalemate. I'm going to do everything I can. I've already shown in good faith how far I'm prepared to go to make sure that this happens."

Agee circled around the same points again and again. Pownall felt that he never really focused on what bothered Marietta: an indemnification against an illegal act. Finally, after talking for an hour and a half, the two agreed to break.

"Well, let's get some creative lawyers," said Agee. "Maybe we have got the wrong lawyers here."

"We have talked about this," said Pownall. "Our board has considered it. I have said that I will look at it again. Maybe we can get started now."

Pownall called Menaker into his office. "Frank, is there any way that this indemnification can work?" he asked. "Can you take a look at it now?"

Menaker said that he would take a look and that he would hire a second outside counsel to study the question. He would meet with Agee's lawyers in New York the next morning to talk the question through once more.

"You made a real mistake buying 70 percent of Martin Marietta," said Menaker.

"Don't talk about what's happened," said Agee. "Let's talk about going forward."

Menaker left for his office.

•

•

"You have rejected the indemnification on very narrow grounds," said Agee. "You are looking at this with tunnel vision, I want you to think about it again."

Pownall promised again that he would. The two shook hands. "I'm not going to release my letter tonight," Agee promised.

The five Bendix negotiators took the elevator back down to the garage. As they were about to leave the building, Agee decided to go back. He left Wasserstein and Fraidin to wait, while he, Fleischer and Cunningham took the elevator back upstairs. The three met Pownall in the corridor. "Keep thinking about this Tom," said Agee. "I'm going to have my lawyers work on alternatives."

"I'm willing to consider anything you think will work," said Pownall.

The Bendix team was finally ready to leave. Agee, Cunningham, and Wasserstein climbed into the Marietta slate-gray Olds; Fleischer and Fraidin rode in the dark blue Chevy station wagon. The drivers headed down the Capital Beltway toward the airport. Agee briefed Wasserstein on his meeting. Wasserstein could hardly believe that the two had focused on legal questions.

"You're very close to an agreement," he said. "You really ought to think again if you want to leave when you're this near a settlement."

Agee, Cunningham, and Wasserstein talked about going back. As the car crossed the Cabin John Bridge into Virginia, Agee signaled to the driver. "I need to make a phone call," he said. "Where's the nearest place with three phones?"

The driver thought for a minute.

"The Exxon station on Route 123."

"Let's go there," said Agee.

The two cars pulled into the Exxon station. "We'd like to talk in the car before we make our phone call," said Agee.

·

·

The driver got out. It was a warm night so he left the engine running and the air conditioning on. Fraidin and Fleischer got into the Olds with Agee, Cunningham, and Wasserstein. The five talked for a few minutes. Suddenly they got out of the car and walked up the hillside that overlooked the road. They talked. "We've got to go back," said Agee. "If it's only a legal problem and that is all that is keeping them from agreeing to the merger and that is all it is, then we've got to sit down and get this figured out. It can't be that complicated. If there's a will there's a way and things can be worked out."

Fleischer and Wasserstein walked over to the phone booths.

Wasserstein called Gleacher to make sure that Allied would be ready. "Are you drafting papers?" he asked. "It's up to you. I want to make it clear, I'm not encouraging or discouraging you; I don't know what is going to happen."

"What do you mean, Bruce?" asked Gleacher. "You've changed gears."

"I've got to go," said Wasserstein. "It's a very fluid situation."

Agee came over to the booths to call Pownall. "Look, Tom," he said. "We've been talking about this all the way to the airport and I continue to be perplexed. If it's a legal problem, I'll bring my lawyers back. Let's get your lawyers and our lawyers together and let's wrestle this thing through."

Pownall put his hand over the receiver. Siegel was standing next to him. "Agee wants to come back," he said.

"I don't think you'll get anywhere," said Siegel. "But tell him to come. The worst thing that could happen is that you'll keep him tied up so that he can't talk to another white knight."

Pownall took his hand off the receiver. "If you want to talk, then come on back, I'm willing to listen."

•

•

Cunningham walked up to the driver of the Olds. "There's been a change," she said. "We're going to Martin Marietta."

"Fine," said the driver.

"Would you mind riding with the other driver in the station wagon and giving us your car so that we can ride together and discuss matters in private?" asked Cunningham.

"I really can't do that without getting prior permission," said the driver. "The car was assigned to me and I'm responsible for it."

"I'll check with our attorney," said Cunningham. "I'm sure that there won't be any problem." She walked over to Fleischer and talked to him for a minute. Then she walked back to the driver. "We will assume all responsibility," she said. "So don't worry about it."

"That's fine," said the driver, "but I still have to get approval from someone in our headquarters before I can do this."

Cunningham walked over to the phone booths to talk to Fleischer again. Agee joined them. Cunningham walked back to the driver. "It will be all right," she said. "You can drive us to headquarters."

This time Agee went to the boardroom first. He sat down in the center of the table with his back to the window. It was just where Cunningham had sat earlier. Cunningham was at Agee's left and the other Bendix advisers lined up along the same side of the table. The Marietta strategists faced them. Agee spoke.

"I'm not going to go into the past," he said. "I want to focus on the future." Agee recounted the story of what had happened. He stressed that he had tried to communicate with Martin Marietta. He had not succeeded. He told this same story of his attempts three times.

"We are where we are and I don't see the point of casting blame for any of this," he continued. "When Bendix started with its offer, we wanted to create a company that was stronger financially and technologically. Now we are going to end up with a company that is very weak financially. I am very concerned about that. I am very concerned for my employees. I have no concern for the arbs, who don't deserve the money. I understand that you guys are going to buy because you think you have a 'legal problem.' Let's get around that legal problem."

The Martin Marietta strategists were dumbstruck. Menaker came into the boardroom and sat down across the table from Agee. Leithauser left. Agee continued to talk about how the merger would be good for America, good for the national defense, good for the Bendix employees. Cunningham took notes in a small spiral book. She nodded at each point that Agee made.

Agee said that the Citibank tender had been in gross violation of Citibank's agreement with Bendix and of its duty to SESSOP participants. "Citibank did not act in the best interests of the employees when it tendered the shares," he said.

Menaker interrupted. "If we buy the Bendix shares tomorrow night, it will certainly have been in the best interests of the employees that the SESSOP shares were tendered and that they had stayed tendered."

Agee glared across the table at Menaker and continued his speech.

"Let's get down to business," said Menaker. Agee had been talking for twenty minutes.

"I think that there is a way around this legal problem," said Agee. "Art here has been thinking about some alternatives."

Agee left the boardroom to meet with Pownall. Wasserstein and Cunningham went into the conference room where Pownall had been when Agee called the day the battle began. The others stayed in the boardroom to listen to Fleischer.

"I don't agree with you on the indemnification," said Fleischer, "but I find it difficult to understand how you can hold up a major business deal on a technicality. Let's talk about some ways around this."

Fleischer explained that he and Fraidin had thought of three possibilities. They were just ideas; one of them might work. First: seven of the thirteen Martin Marietta directors would resign; Marietta would then appoint seven Bendix directors to the board; the new board would decide whether or not to buy the Bendix shares; there were thirteen Marietta board directors: Bendix would have a majority.

The Martin Marietta lawyers just stared at Fleischer.

Two. The sides could go to Judge Young on Wednesday morning. Both would explain that they were negotiating and needed time. Young might issue a temporary restraining order blocking Marietta and United Technologies from buying Bendix shares; the Bendix shareholder meeting would be postponed. Marietta and United Technologies would not be allowed to solicit proxies. Bendix would.

"Did I hear you right?" asked Katcher, Marty Lipton's partner. He didn't like the idea.

"Can't we find some way to amend the offer to add a condition that will occur and then withdraw?" suggested Fleischer. "I think the way that the text was drafted you could do that."

Fullem thumbed through his copy of the offer. Fraidin pointed to where he thought the language was fuzzy. Fullem read it. It was boilerplate to him. "I don't think that's a fair reading of the offer," he said.

Fraidin read it through on his copy. "It's hard to tell what that boilerplate means," said Fraidin. "If it means anything, it means this."

Pownall and Agee had gone into Rauth's office. Pow-

•

•

nall's office was being used for another meeting, and Rauth's office was more comfortable anyway. It was the same size as Pownall's, but there was an orange and blue print sofa against the wall with a blue arm chair on each side. There was a coffee table in front of the sofa. There was a Norman Rockwell on the wall. Agee settled on the couch. Pownall sat down in an armchair. Agee repeated the arguments that he had made in the first meeting. He said that Martin Marietta had admitted that the merger made sense when it had countertendered; it was irrational for Martin Marietta to ruin the financial structure of the joint company by buying Bendix shares. He said that his lawyers didn't believe that there was any problem with buying, but that he was offering an indemnification to cover the directors if it did turn out that they had a liability.

Cunningham knocked on the door and Agee left the room. A few minutes later, he came back.

"We ought to broaden the discussion," said Agee. "Let's bring the lawyers in. I'll get Arthur."

Agee left the office again and came back with Fleischer. Fleischer sat down in the second blue armchair opposite Pownall. Agee took his place on the couch.

Fleischer outlined the reasons he felt Martin Marietta could accept an indemnification. Pownall knew that what he was hearing was coming from a prestigious attorney, and he respected that—but it still didn't make sense to him. He called Menaker in to help him evaluate what Fleischer was saying. Menaker sat down on the couch beside Agee and the four talked through the indemnification again and again.

Agee repeated that the merger made business sense and that the indemnification would solve the problem of the legal liability that the Martin Marietta directors thought they had. Pownall said that Fullem had told the Martin Marietta board that they could not be indemnified in this situation.

·

·

They had made a contract with the Bendix shareholders.

Fleischer launched into an elaborate analysis of the legal issues. He said that the Martin Marietta directors faced a greater liability for buying than for not buying. If Martin Marietta bought, shareholders might sue for breach of fiduciary duties; they might try to collect damages of $900 million, the amount that Martin Marietta was going to spend to buy Bendix. If Martin Marietta didn't buy, the Bendix shareholders might sue for the amount they lost, the difference between the $75 a share that Martin Marietta was offering to pay and the $50 a share that the stock might trade for when the battle was done. That totalled only $300 million, and Bendix was promising to pay it. The Martin Marietta *directors* didn't have to worry. "The Delaware Supreme Court stated very clearly this afternoon that you have a moral duty to Bendix," he said.

"We have an opinion of counsel that such an indemnity agreement may violate public policy," said Menaker. "It could be void under the provisions of the securities laws."

"Look, Tom," said Agee. "I'll indemnify the directors and all these problems will be irrelevant. You won't have to buy and the two companies will be combined."

"Bill," said Pownall. "It's a shame that we have to spend $900 million tomorrow night, but we're going to buy the shares. Bill, you brought us to this point. The board went over your letter and we have rejected it. The $55 a share that you are offering is fair, but it doesn't solve the legal and moral problems. There is no point in just repeating that offer. I can't go back to my board with an offer they have already rejected. They are willing to listen. They don't want to buy. They have to have something new to listen to."

Agee repeated his offer to indemnify.

The four negotiators circled around and around the same issues. Agee and Fleischer thought that the Martin

•

•

Marietta team was being inflexible. Pownall and Menaker thought that the Bendix team was being unrealistic.

Agee and Fleischer went out to caucus. They still didn't understand what stood in the way of a deal. Agee decided that he was prepared to offer six directorships.

Agee and Fleischer came back into Rauth's office and took their places. They talked about the legal responsibility of the directors. They went through the rationale behind the indemnification.

Menaker decided to sidetrack Agee. "Assuming the two companies are going to merge, let's talk about the board."

Agee was surprised. "Is the quid pro quo here that if I give you more directors, the legal problem will go away?"

"No," said Menaker.

Agee started to talk about how the board would be put together. Agee would be chairman. Pownall would be vice-chairman. "I said you would get four directors in the letter—Mr. Pownall, Mr. Rauth, and two others—but if board seats matter, heck, we can give you six or seven or whatever. Let me tell you, I feel so strongly about putting this thing together on a rational basis that if you want more directors you can have them. I don't know if the board is going to be fifteen or sixteen or whatever, but if you want seven directors fine."

"I think we should have a split board," said Menaker.

"If it's an even kind of deal, maybe we could do it," said Agee. "But I don't see that it's an even kind of deal. Bendix owns 70 percent of Marietta. We will have 70 percent of the joint board."

Menaker didn't understand the rationale of that statement. Marietta would buy 50 percent of Bendix the next night. He didn't ask about it, though. "What will Pownall's role in the merged company be?" asked Menaker.

"He'll be one of the most principal guys," said Agee. "He'll be running this business. He'll be an integral part of

·

·

the management team. He'll be on the board. He'll be the number-two paid guy in the company. He'll be very important."

"Have you thought about a co-CEOship?" asked Menaker.

Agee wouldn't discuss that. "I am the chairman of Bendix and have been for six years. I know how to do a chairman's job. You're here to be the lawyer and talk about the legal side." He looked at Pownall. "Are we talking about a legal problem or does the legal problem go away if we resolve the management problems?"

The four talked for a few more minutes.

"Let's break," said Agee. "I want to talk to my advisers."

•

While Agee talked to Pownall, Cunningham and Wasserstein sat in the boardroom and waited. Cunningham walked into the hallway. Roy Calvin and Bill Harwood were chatting in an office. She walked in.

"Hi," she said. "I haven't met you fellows." She shook their hands. "What do you think is going to happen?"

"We are going to buy the shares," said Calvin.

"It is too bad that this had to happen," said Cunningham. "Bill really admires Tom, and I know Tom likes Bill. This could have come out differently if the bankers and lawyers hadn't kept the principals from talking to each other. That is what bankers and lawyers do. I know. I used to work at Salomon Brothers."

"I didn't know that," said Calvin.

"This was such a straightforward deal until United Technologies came in," said Cunningham.

Calvin assumed that Cunningham meant that the UTC offer had destabilized Bendix.

"Unity Day was great for the employees," said Cunningham. Bendix had held a pep rally in support of management the day before. "It uplifted their morale. It made Bill feel wonderful. They rallied around their management."

Calvin thought Cunningham sounded like the Bendix Unity Day press release. He couldn't think of anything appropriate to say.

Wasserstein called Eric Gleacher to find out how the papers were coming. Wasserstein had a new investment idea for Allied. Allied and Bendix would jointly own the Bendix aerospace division and the 70 percent stake in Martin Marietta. Wasserstein was a little vague on how the deal would work.

"I don't know whether Allied is going to be interested in this," said Gleacher. "We are losing a lot of time. If we are going to talk about a 100 percent deal, we have got to start."

"Give this some consideration," said Wasserstein. "Talk to my people at First Boston."

Gleacher had assumed that Wasserstein was at First Boston. "Where are you?"

"I can't tell you," said Wasserstein.

Agee and Fleischer sat down with Wasserstein, Cunningham, and Fraidin in the boardroom to talk about strategy. There was a big bowl of potato chips in the middle of the table. There were some Cokes on a small table in the corner. Agee and Fleischer were baffled as to what was really bothering Martin Marietta. Bendix had increased its price. Bendix had increased the number of directors that it was offering. Bendix had worked out an indemnification. Wasserstein suggested that Bendix offer a package of Bendix securities to Martin Marietta for Marietta to use to pay the Bendix shareholders who had tendered. Agee said he'd think about it. Fleischer told Agee to stress the ego parts of the Bendix offer. Bendix would change the name of the joint company. Bendix would leave Martin Marietta headquarters in Bethesda.

Siegel and Katcher went into Rauth's office for a briefing. They were worried that Agee would fast-talk his way around Pownall and Menaker.

"Do you know how to boil a frog?" Menaker asked Katcher.

Katcher was puzzled.

"You don't put him in hot water, Dick," said Menaker. "He'll jump out. To boil a frog, you put him in cold water and slowly turn the heat up."

Fleischer came into Rauth's office. He walked over to Siegel and suggested that Bendix might be able to solve Marietta's legal problem by offering a package of securities to Marietta to pay the Bendix shareholders.

Agee came into Rauth's office. Cunningham followed him with a Coke.

"Can I have one too?" asked Menaker. Cunningham walked out to the boardroom to get it.

Agee and Fleischer sat down. "Look," Agee said to Siegel, "I really would like to have a conversation with Tom. Art and Frank can stay. Could you leave?"

Siegel went into the Kidder war room.

Agee and Fleischer repeated their offer. Bendix would indemnify the directors. The indemnification would work. The price was fair. They had made concessions. They didn't understand why Martin Marietta didn't seem to be responding. They didn't understand why Martin Marietta didn't seem to be able to articulate its objections.

Pownall and Menaker listened. Pownall thought that Agee sounded like a wind-up doll: each time Agee finished his speech, he turned around, jerked his arm and started again. Pownall and Menaker kept trying to explain why they couldn't accept Agee's offer: their lawyers thought that the indemnification wouldn't work. Martin Marietta had a contract with the Bendix shareholders. There was no good reason to break it.

Finally, after midnight, Menaker suggested that it was time to break up the meeting. "We're all tired," he said. "We've gone round this thing. I understand what you are saying, but I don't agree. I will analyze the issue in depth. I will have a team working on it all morning. We will start now, but there is no point in the four of us continuing."

Agee and Fleischer agreed. "Think it over, Tom," said Agee. "I'll call you in the morning. If there is anything you need me for, just call me in New York."

"New York?" asked Pownall.

"Yes," said Agee. "Our shareholder meeting is postponed."

Agee and his team left for the airport. Pownall walked into Calvin's office. He hadn't yet gotten around to signing the letter to Agee. He told Calvin that Agee had promised not to release the letter he had written to the Marietta board. Martin Marietta did not need to send Agee a formal reply.

SETTLEMENT

On the plane ride back to New York, Agee talked through his options. He could put his chips on a breakthrough with Martin Marietta. He could go with Trump. He could try a joint venture with Allied. He could sell the company. Agee didn't know which road to take. He didn't want to commit himself. He would try to play them all.

When the Bendix jet landed, Bruce Wasserstein called Eric Gleacher. It was three in the morning. Wasserstein wanted to talk about the white-knight deal. He wanted to talk about the joint venture deal. He didn't know which Agee wanted to do. Gleacher asked some questions about the new investment scheme. He thought that the idea was interesting, but that it was too complicated to negotiate given the time that the two companies had to do their deal before Marietta could buy.

"Allied will consider this joint venture," said Gleacher. "But we are wasting time. The only way to proceed is with the sale of the company."

Wasserstein thought so too. He had to talk to Agee before he set up a meeting. "Call me first thing in the morning," he said.

At seven o'clock, Wednesday, Gleacher called Hennessy. Gleacher told him about Wasserstein's joint-venture idea. Hennessy wasn't interested. The Allied board had already said that it didn't want to make an investment in Bendix. Hennessy wanted to buy the whole company. He told Gleacher to set up a meeting.

Gleacher called Wasserstein again. Then he called Hennessy. The Allied team would caucus at Skadden, Arps at nine o'clock. Hennessy would negotiate with Agee at ten.

Agee got a little sleep. He thought about the options he had. He was ready for a new round of negotiations. While Agee talked to Pownall in Bethesda Tuesday night, Donald Trump had been meeting with Al McDonald, the president of Bendix, to talk about the RCA stock; the price was still up in the air and the lawyers were beginning to have some problems with the fine print on the terms. There had been a series of phone calls in the early hours Wednesday morning. Trump had agreed to a final negotiating session at eight thirty Wednesday morning.

When Trump and Paul Hallingby arrived, Wasserstein, Fleischer, and Fraidin were in the Helmsley suite with Agee and Cunningham. Agee asked Wasserstein and Fraidin to wait in the bedroom. Fleischer and Cunningham stayed.

"Look Donald," said Fleischer. "There are two or three things open on this: the price and the legal terms. We have got to negotiate those."

Trump looked embarrassed. "I didn't realize that these things were so complicated," he said. "My bank called back yesterday after I had the credit lined up and asked what I wanted the money for. I told them that I was going to tender for Bendix, and they pulled out. They have a policy of not financing competitive bids. They already do financing for United Technologies. I didn't know banks were so sensitive."

Agee called McDonald into the room. "Al, get your boys and name the banks that are close to Bendix."

McDonald left the room again. A few minutes later he came back with a list. Agee handed it to Trump. "Try one of these," he said. "Maybe they can help."

"When are we going to negotiate the price?" asked Trump's lawyer.

"Coordinate that with Al," said Agee. "Let me know."

After Trump left, Agee talked to his advisers. His resolve had stiffened. He was worried that Martin Marietta would buy.

At a few minutes after nine, Agee called Pownall in Bethesda. Pownall had driven to his office early that morning to work over the legal question with Menaker. The two had not gotten very far.

"I have a last offer," said Agee. He explained that Bendix would give Martin Marietta a package of Bendix securities that Martin Marietta could use to pay the Bendix stockholders who had tendered to Martin Marietta. Agee said that he would stand by his offer of six directors out of eighteen. "You have to let me know in forty-five minutes," said Agee. "Your answer has to have board approval. My preference is to do a deal with Martin Marietta."

"I doubt that I can get board approval for anything in forty-five minutes," said Pownall.

When Agee hung up, Wasserstein called Siegel with the technical details of the new Bendix securities offer. Then the team sat down on the brown couches in the living room. They talked while they waited for Hennessy.

"Why don't Ed and Bill meet privately," suggested Cunningham as soon as the Allied team arrived.

Everyone except Agee and Hennessy went into the bedroom to wait. Agee told Hennessy that he was willing to sell Bendix. Hennessy told Agee that Agee would be president of Allied and remain chairman of Bendix. Hennessy would continue to look for a new chief operating officer for Allied. Then the advisers came back into the living room to negotiate the terms of the deal. The price had been agreed to: $80 a share. Allied would offer to buy 55 percent of the Bendix stock for $85 a share and pay securities worth $75 a share for the rest of the company. Hennessy said that he wanted a crown-jewel option on the aerospace division, so that even if Allied were outbid or blocked from buying Bendix, Allied would get it. Wasserstein and Fleischer said that a crown-jewels option could be a legal headache and could sabotage the entire deal. Hennessy wouldn't budge.

Gleacher had told Wasserstein when he called the night before that Allied wasn't drafting papers. When he hadn't been able to get a commitment from Wasserstein at seven the night before, Gleacher had called Buirkle to discuss whether Allied should keep up the drafting. They had decided that it was silly to waste the time and the $100,000 in printer's fees to work up the formal documents for a deal that might never be. But the Allied strategists thought that even if they couldn't block Marietta from buying by making an offer—it was now logistically impossible to file by the SEC's five-thirty deadline—they might still be able to keep Marietta from buying control of Bendix. Bendix could put out a press release as soon as its board approved the deal, announcing that a new offer for Bendix would start the next day. The arbs would pull their stock out of the Marietta pool so that they could tender to Allied for an extra $10 a share in cash.

While Hennessy and Agee talked about the merger, Wasserstein went into the bedroom to call Siegel.

"Have you decided on the package yet," he asked.

"I'm not sure that it solves the legal problem," said Siegel. He had talked it over with Fullem. Fullem thought that Bendix still didn't understand the problem.

"You have to make a decision pretty soon or we are going to sell," said Wasserstein.

"What?" asked Siegel. "You mean you are going to sell the Marietta block?"

"No," said Wasserstein.

"You are going to sell Bendix?" asked Siegel.

"It's complicated," said Wasserstein.

Wasserstein went back into the dining room. The teams were discussing the crown-jewels options. After twenty minutes, Agee and Wasserstein went into the bedroom again. Agee called Pownall. It was close to eleven thirty. Time was running out.

"I've been waiting for your call," said Agee. "If you don't act by noon, we will act. You can believe it."

Pownall wasn't sure what Agee meant.

Agee hung up. He walked back into the dining room.

"Look, Bill," said Hennessy. "It's almost noontime and I have a board meeting set for this afternoon. We have a lot to do if we are going to get this offer out and we just don't have any more time. I am offering $80 a share. I need an answer."

"I will need some time," said Agee. "I will have an answer for you by one o'clock."

"Okay," said Hennessy.

"There is a risk that Marietta will buy," said Agee. "My first preference is to get the Marietta deal settled amicably. That's my first priority. When I come back to you, subject to board approval, I will be saying one of two things: either we have settled with Martin Marietta and we are proceeding on that basis or we have a deal with you."

"Well, don't come back and say you've got a deal with another white knight," said Hennessy.

"I won't," said Agee. "We've been negotiating with you in good faith. You'll get one of two answers. Either we've settled with Martin Marietta and are proceeding on that, or you and I have a deal."

The Allied team left for Skadden, Arps to wait. The Bendix team started to talk about the Allied offer. At quarter to twelve, Wasserstein called Siegel. "Have you made a decision yet?" he asked.

Siegel wasn't sure that Marietta's using Bendix securities to pay Bendix shareholders for their Bendix stock made sense. "Is Bendix serious about this?"

"We are serious about this," said Wasserstein. "Fleischer and I are running things. We're in control here and we want to work out a deal, but we are getting bearhugged. Bill Agee will do very well." Bearhugged is bankers' jargon for getting an offer that squeezes the board into accepting.

Siegel called Pownall. "I just talked to Wasserstein," he said. "He says he's in control. He says he's being bearhugged. I think Allied is going to move to buy all of Bendix. There is a rumor that Allied is coming in. Can you slow down your talks with Agee? Maybe you should suggest a stock swap."

"I promised I would call at noon," said Pownall. "I will call."

•

The Bendix team stood around the dining-room table eating oatmeal cookies and talking. Trump called to negotiate a price. He had lined up his financing. Agee stalled.

"Does it look like we're going to have a deal with Martin Marietta?" asked McDonald.

"We're not going to lose," said Fleischer. "We may not win, but we're not going to lose. They can't vote those shares."

"Wait a minute," said Grassi. "You have to think about whether the shareholders are better off pursuing Marietta to the end or selling to Allied."

"In a strict sense, you can't lose with Marietta," said Wasserstein. "They can't vote the stock. But what you may have if you win is a great deal of debt. You could end up in a straightjacket. You could still be bought by United Technologies if Gray can figure out how to spin off Martin Marietta. The other option is to sell to Allied. That's not guaranteed. There may still be problems from United Technologies. A deal with Allied may not work out on a personal basis, but you have a hell of a price."

Agee polled around the table to find out how each of the advisers felt.

"I don't think there is a clear answer here," said Wasserstein. "On the one hand, I would have to be less than candid if I didn't tell you that if I were running a company at my age, I'd have to think seriously about continuing. If Marietta can't vote, Bendix can 'win' and I might care about winning in a conventional sense. On the other hand, this is a hell of a price. Do you care what people think?"

"I think it's a good deal," said McDonald.

"You can win," said Fleischer. "But the Allied deal may be the right thing to do. That is a management and a board decision."

"I want to talk to Mary and Al about this," said Agee. Agee went into the bedroom with Cunningham and McDonald. They talked about what was happening. Agee was worried that if Martin Marietta was allowed to buy Bendix now that Bendix had already bought Martin Marietta, Bendix might end up financially weakened. He was worried that if United Technologies bought Bendix, Bendix would be dismembered. Allied was offering a far higher price and the promise that Bendix would remain intact.

Tom Pownall dialed Agee's number at noon. The line was busy. He tried again. Still busy. He called Siegel. "I can't get Agee," he said. "Can you tell Wasserstein that I want to talk about swapping shares?"

Siegel called Wasserstein. "Tom's been trying to call Agee," he said.

"Have Pownall call again," said Wasserstein. "We'll stand by."

Agee walked back into the dining room. "I've decided to do the Allied deal," he said. "It's the right thing to do. I don't want to make the company a financial cripple. I can't think about what people think."

The phone rang. It was almost one o'clock. Cunningham answered.

"Hi, Mary. This is Tom Pownall. Is Bill there?"

"Tom, he's not here right now," said Cunningham. "Oh, he's coming in right now. Here's Bill."

Agee got on the line.

"I've been trying to reach you," said Pownall. "Your line was busy."

"I was under the gun," said Agee. "My line was open."

"Bill, have you thought about a stock swap?" asked Pownall.

"No, I haven't," said Agee. Wasserstein passed him a note: find out what Pownall has to say. "The situation has been taken out of my hands. I was stretched. It's out of my hands. It's been taken out of my hands. I am withdrawing the offer that I made this morning. You'll be hearing about it soon."

Agee hung up. Pownall couldn't imagine what was going on. Menaker thought that Agee had been fired. Leit-hauser thought that the board had taken the matter into its own hands and that the board might be willing to negotiate.

•

Early Wednesday afternoon, Martin Marietta vice-president James Simpson called Frank Menaker. Simpson was in Michigan for the Bendix shareholder meeting. He gave Menaker a report. The shareholder meeting had already been moved from yesterday to today and was now rescheduled for the following week, but Simpson explained that Bendix had to formally open and recess the meeting. The day before, a Bendix vice-president had strode across the stage, read a press release, and then strode off. He had not called for a quorum count. He had not seemed prepared to handle anything unusual. Joe Morrow, Marietta's head proxy solicitor, who was also in Michigan, thought that if Martin Marietta tried, it might be able to take control of the meeting and call for a vote on the amendments. If Bendix had postponed the meeting, it must mean that Bendix didn't yet have the votes to get the amendments passed.

Simpson and his team drove out to Bendix headquarters with their boxes of proxies. A guard at the front door was handing out press releases. "The meeting has been adjourned until next week," he said. "Why don't you just go home."

The team walked into the building. Behind the shareholder registration desk was a cordon of armed guards. The Martin Marietta representatives were issued red name tags. The United Technologies staffers got gray tags. Everyone from Bendix was identified in blue and white.

The armed guard asked the Martin Marietta people to put the box of proxies through the metal detector. They did. Then they marched into the auditorium for the meeting. Jim Simpson sat on the aisle.

At ten o'clock the chairman of the meeting strode across

the stage. Bang. He hit his gavel beside the microphone.
"This meeting is called to order." He introduced himself as
Donald G. Speyer from Bendix. He began to read the press
release that the guard had been handing out at the door.
Simpson read along on his copy. When Speyer got about
halfway through, Simpson stood up and raised his hand.
"Mr. Chairman."

Speyer ignored him.

"Mr. Chairman."

Speyer read on. Simpson waved his hand for attention.
"Mr. Chairman. I would like to call for a quorum count
please." If there was a quorum of shareholders present
either in person or by proxy, the meeting could only be recessed by formal vote.

Speyer kept reading. He finished the release. "I now
declare the meeting adjourned . . ."

"Mr. Chairman, I call for a quorum," said Simpson.

". . . until ten A.M. on Monday, September 27," said
Speyer.

Bang. Speyer hit the gavel again. He strode off the stage.
Simpson walked to the podium. "It's my belief that there
is a quorum present and that this meeting should proceed
as originally scheduled," said Simpson. "Since there is no
chairman, since the chairman has departed, I would like to
call for a vote on electing me, James D. Simpson, as chairman of the meeting."

The team from Marietta and United Technologies voted
aye. The team from Bendix was silent.

"I hereby declare myself chairman of the meeting," said
Simpson. He began to discuss the shark repellent amendments, but the Bendix lawyer interrupted him. Simpson
continued. The lawyer from Bendix kept interrupting.
Simpson recessed the meeting for an off-the-record conversation with the Bendix lawyer.

They met at the side of the stage. "What do you think

you're doing?" asked the Bendix lawyer. "This is silly. We have got a quorum here and if you call for a vote on the amendments, we will defeat you."

"You say you have got a quorum," said Simpson.

"Yes, of course we have a quorum," said the lawyer.

"Then we will reconvene the meeting," said Simpson.

Simpson returned to the podium. He said that Bendix had conceded that there was a quorum present. The Bendix team got up and walked toward the door. Someone in the audience joked that if the lights went out, the meeting should be moved to the Michigan Inn. Then, the lights did go out. Simpson officially adjourned the meeting to the Michigan Inn.

Simpson and the proxy solicitors walked to the parking lot. As the solicitors loaded their boxes into the car, a Bendix employee walked over to them. "That was it," he said. "I've had it. That meeting was the end. I can't stand any more of this nonsense. I want to tender my shares."

The employee took a stock certificate out of his briefcase. One of the Marietta lawyers found a copy of the tendering form. The employee signed it.

When the Marietta team arrived at the hotel, the woman at the reception desk said that there were no conference rooms free. A proxy solicitor had noticed a group coming out of the Erie room. "We'll take that," said Simpson.

The woman said that there were no tablecloths on the tables.

"That won't bother us." said Simpson.

There were indeed no tablecloths on the five round tables in the Erie room. There was a half-assembled portable wall in the corner. Simpson reconvened the meeting. He called for a vote on the Bendix amendments. He recessed the meeting while two lawyers inspected the proxies. Simpson reconvened the meeting. He announced that the amendments had been overwhelmingly defeated. No one had presented the Bendix proxies.

●

Pownall had called the Marietta board meeting at four thirty Wednesday afternoon so that the directors could have a final update on buying the Bendix stock. He began the meeting with a recap of everything that had happened since the meeting the day before. He recounted the tale of Agee's visit and the series of phone calls that morning. He said that trading had been halted in Allied, Bendix, and Martin Marietta stock at two thirty. He explained that Katcher had overheard the Bendix pilot talking about a board meeting. "I can't guess what is happening at Bendix anymore," he said. "Wasserstein told Marty Siegel this morning 'I'm in control here.'"

"We've got Haig back," said Bell. "Haig's been reincarnated."

Pownall smiled. He continued with his recap of events. The Bendix shark repellents had been defeated at the shareholder meeting. Jim Simpson had taken control. The directors laughed. Pownall turned to Menaker. "Can you give us a legal summary."

Menaker explained that there were three courts still out on whether Marietta could buy the stock. It was still possible that Martin Marietta would not be allowed to buy. Jack Byrne was called out of the boardroom. One of his investment staffers was on the line. Byrne came back with a page of notes. "My people say that Allied and Bendix have agreed to merge," he said. "Apparently Allied is going to pay $85 a share on both ends and Allied wants to buy the rest of Martin Marietta as well."

Then one of Leithauser's financial staffers came into the boardroom with a copy of a Dow Jones wire. Pownall read it out loud.

●

●

New York. William Agee, chairman of Bendix Corp. said that Bendix and Allied Corp. have agreed in principle to a merger in which Bendix shareholders will receive cash and securities of Allied. The transaction has been approved by the Bendix board of directors.

Edward Hennessy, chairman of Allied Corp., said that he intends to recommend approval of the transaction to the Allied board at its meeting this afternoon. . . .

The Martin Marietta directors were surprised that Bendix would issue an announcement before Allied had approved the deal.

"The point of the announcement is to get stock out of our pool so that even if Allied doesn't file this afternoon, we can't buy control," explained Siegel. "We have got to put out a press release immediately saying that we are going to buy. If Allied wants to buy Bendix, we might be able to strike a deal to sell Allied all of the Bendix stock that we buy, in exchange for the Martin Marietta stock that Bendix has already bought. But we can't do a swap unless we can buy the stock."

Pownall's secretary buzzed to say that Bill Agee was on the phone. Pownall left the boardroom to take the call. Katcher went into an empty office to write a press release saying that Martin Marietta would buy.

"I have just made a deal with Allied," Agee told Pownall. "I am going to be president of the company. The announcement is on the wires, but I wanted to tell you personally."

"Thank you for calling," said Pownall. "And good luck. I hope it works out well for you."

Pownall walked back to the boardroom. "Agee just called to confirm the press release," he said. Pownall recessed the meeting until five thirty. If Allied managed to file with the SEC before the doors closed that day, Martin Marietta could not buy for another ten days. If Allied filed by five thirty tomorrow, the offer would be retroactive until one minute after midnight. Martin Marietta would only be able to buy between 12:00 and 12:01.

Siegel called his office. "Get everybody in the building on the phone to Bendix shareholders who have tendered," he said. "Every arb has got to get a personal call to say that Marietta will buy at midnight."

At 5:32, the Marietta lawyer waiting at the doors of the SEC called to say that Allied hadn't filed. The office was closed. The directors began their meeting again. A financial staffer came in with the Allied press release. Allied had approved the merger. Pownall's secretary buzzed again. Paul Thayer of LTV was on the line. Pownall left the boardroom to take the call in his office.

"Tom," said Thayer, "you remember I'm on the board of a company called Allied? Well, Allied has just made an agreement to merge with Bendix. It is all wrapped up. The boards have approved it. And that brings you into play. As I understand it, Bendix owns rather a lot of Martin Marietta."

"Yes they do, Paul," laughed Pownall. "But I didn't think you and I would get together this way."

"I think it would be a good idea for you to talk to Ed," said Thayer. "You two probably could work something out."

"I think that's a good idea," said Pownall. "We don't have much time."

Hennessy got on the line. Pownall explained that the Marietta board was in session, but that if Hennessy wanted to talk, Pownall would recess the board meeting until later that evening. Hennessy said he was coming down from New York. Pownall guessed that Hennessy wanted to buy Martin Marietta. "I promise you that no one at Marietta will report to Agee," said Hennessy.

Pownall went back into the boardroom to say that Hennessy was on his way. Rauth recessed the meeting until ten thirty. The directors left for dinner at the Congressional Country Club. Just before they left, Jim Simpson arrived from Michigan. The board members patted him on the back. "Welcome home, Chairman Jim," they laughed.

Leithauser began to make arrangements for Marietta to buy the Bendix shares within fifty-nine seconds. He sent Bob Powell, the corporate treasurer, to New York on the company plane. Leithauser put the assistant treasurer on the Metroliner train to New York. Peter Wood asked Rauth's secretary Diana to be sure that there was champagne available that night. Siegel called New York. Most of the Bendix stock was still in the Marietta pool.

•

When the Bendix board meeting began in the General Motors building in New York, Fleischer and Fraidin were at Skadden, Arps negotiating the legal terms. Flom refused to budge on a crown-jewel option. Fleischer agreed to work out the terms.

Agee opened the meeting with a capsule history of the past twenty-four hours. "I am totally convinced that Martin Marietta is going to buy tonight," he said. "I am worried that the extender may only be a short block and even in spite of that they may challenge it. Now Hennessy is interested in, and in a position to buy, the whole company. I reported that this was his intention when he started. We are in a position where, if we don't accept this, we are going to be in a stalemate situation."

Agee told the board that Hennessy would pay $80 a share for Bendix and that he wanted a crown-jewels option on the aerospace division.

"Gentlemen," said Wasserstein, "you have to understand that there are no right answers here, only wrong answers. You can go after Martin Marietta. You can merge with Allied. The lawyers say that the worst outcome on Marietta will be a stalemate where neither side can vote. On the other hand, this is a hell of a price."

"Let's appoint a committee to study the Allied proposal," suggested a director.

"No," said Agee. "I want to make a decision now."

"Wait a minute," said Tavoulareas of Mobil. "We've just been told by the lawyers that we can't lose and we may win. The Allied deal is new. What are we rushing for?"

"Why are we selling the company?" asked another director. "What has changed since we decided to go ahead and buy the stock. Didn't we know that this could happen from the beginning?"

"I don't want to sell the company," said Agee. "I didn't set out to sell the company. But I think we're blessed because we have a situation where we have a company that's a very fine company, one that knows us and is interested in our strategy, is interested in the businesses we're in. We don't have to dismember Bendix as we would if the Marietta deal happened. We are getting a very substantial premium over what we have been offered before."

"You mean you don't want to run Marietta if you have to work your way out of a difficult financial situation?" asked a director.

"No," said Agee. "As I told you before, we'd be prepared to try and work ourselves out, but I don't think that's fair to our shareholders and our employees because this combined enterprise has $900 million more debt and the basic businesses aren't any different. And while it could be done, it will be difficult."

"Well, you answered me before that you could do that," said a director.

"Yes, I did," said Agee. "I was responding to the fact

that it wouldn't be a bankrupt situation, it would be one that we had to work our way out of."

Fleischer came into the meeting. He was forty-five minutes late. He outlined the terms of the crown-jewel option he had just negotiated with Flom. Allied would get the Bendix aerospace division for $720 million if someone else bought Bendix. The directors asked so many questions about the crown-jewel agreement that Fleischer sensed that the terms were unacceptable. He left the boardroom. He called Flom. He negotiated a new deal.

"What is going on over there?" asked Fraidin from Flom's office.

"I'll tell you about it later," said Fleischer.

Fleischer went back into the boardroom to say that he had got a better deal from Allied. Now Allied had agreed to pay $800 million; Allied would get the aerospace division only if a company other than Martin Marietta bought 51 percent of Bendix for more than $80 a share.

Jack Fontaine of Hughes Hubbard called Agee from Miami airport. He had talked to Agee early in the afternoon and Agee had told him about the Allied offer. Fontaine asked if the deal had been approved. Agee said that there were some questions.

"Gentlemen," said Agee when he came back into the boardroom, "we're running out of time. We have to make a decision."

"We started out in a situation where we were going to buy Martin Marietta," said a director.

"What happens now is critical to our shareholder employees," said McDonald. "The Allied deal is by far the best from their point of view. For many of the Bendix employees, the SESSOP shares are the most important asset they have along with their houses."

"I don't want to go ahead with a merger that will make Bendix a financial cripple," said Agee.

"This is a no-win choice," said a director. "How did we get here?"

"That was someone else's creation," said Wasserstein.

"Gentlemen," said Agee, "we're running out of time."

Agee called for a vote on the Allied deal. Agee, McDonald, and the other three inside directors voted in favor. Two of the six outside directors voted in favor; one abstained; three, Hugo Uyterhoeven, a Harvard Business School professor, Don Rumsfeld of Searle, and Bill Tavoulareas of Mobil, voted against. The merger was approved.

Tavoulareas and the other three directors who had not voted with Agee stood up and walked out of the boardroom. They caucused in the small conference room down the hall. They talked about what had happened. They drafted a statement for their fellow board members. They drafted a statement to the press. They stood up and left the building for the last time. They had resigned.

•

The Allied board meeting began at four o'clock in the boardroom of the St. Regis paper company. Hennessy had just begun to explain what had happened when Agee called to say that the Bendix board had approved the deal. The press release had been read over the telephone to Dow Jones. Flom told the directors that the point of the release was to get the stock out of the Marietta pool before Marietta could buy. If Marietta bought, the Allied deal didn't make sense. Gleacher said that Allied had negotiated a fair price. The directors began to ask Buirkle what buying both companies meant for Allied's financials.

Gleacher was standing to Hennessy's right at the head of the table. Suddenly he realized that Allied was planning to buy Martin Marietta and that Allied had no idea what Marietta was really going to do at midnight. He scribbled a note to Hennessy on the yellow legal pad in front of him.

"You've got to go down to Bethesda tonight."

Hennessy read the note. He nodded yes. "I'm going to try to see Tom before twelve," he told the board.

Paul Thayer offered to come along.

"I'm going to need all the help I can get," said Hennessy.

"This is a tremendous opportunity for Allied," said Robert Kilpatrick, chairman of Cigna insurance. "I move that we approve the deal."

After the Allied board voted to buy Bendix, Thayer and Hennessy went to call Pownall. Gleacher called his office. There was a message to call Marty Siegel in Bethesda.

"We want to come down there tonight," said Gleacher. "We want to talk about buying Martin Marietta."

"Come on down," said Siegel. "We want to talk about selling Bendix."

When the Allied board meeting was over, Hennessy, Thayer, Gleacher, and Flom piled into the LTV limousine for La Guardia Airport. On the way, they talked over Allied's options. Gleacher and Flom were certain that Allied would be able to negotiate buying both Bendix and Martin Marietta—and that that was possible even if Martin Marietta went ahead and bought the Bendix stock at midnight. Allied could also make an agreement with Martin Marietta to swap the Martin Marietta shares that Bendix owned for the Bendix shares that Martin Marietta was about to buy. Swapping the stock would freeze out another Bendix bidder—like United Technologies—and it would put Hennessy in a no-lose situation on Martin Marietta. A cost-for-cost swap would leave Allied holding a big chunk of Martin Marietta. If Martin Marietta managed to recover after spending $900 million in borrowed cash to buy Bendix, its stock price would rise and Allied could sell its shares at a handsome profit. If Martin Marietta plunged near bankruptcy, Allied could take over.

.

.

Hennessy liked the sound of the swap. Swapping meant less debt. Hennessy had spent his first years at Allied working off debt. He didn't want to start over again. And he did want an option on Marietta.

The team talked all the way down to Washington. The pilot had brought some Kentucky Fried Chicken on the plane for dinner.

"If we want a swap," said Flom, "Martin Marietta is going to demand a premium."

"No way are we paying a premium," said Hennessy.

The LTV jet landed at National Airport about nine o'clock. Hennessy couldn't find the Martin Marietta car. Thayer called Pownall. The car was on the way. While Hennessy waited, Alexander Haig walked over to say hello. He had just got in from Chicago. Haig knew Hennessy. He knew Paul Thayer. He seemed to know about the deal. And he wanted to talk.

"Congratulations," he said to Hennessy. "You've got the people in Hartford a little upset."

Hennessy and Haig chatted. C. William Verity, chairman of Armco Steel broke into the circle. Verity and Hennessy were old friends—Verity had given Hennessy his eagle—and Verity knew Haig and Thayer. Verity wanted to know about the deal.

Hennessy was nervous to go. He had a deal to cut that night and time was running out. The Marietta car must have gone to the wrong airport. Gleacher walked out to find a cab.

●

At six o'clock, Tom Hill from Lehman Brothers called Bruce Wasserstein.

"What about Martin Marietta?" asked Wasserstein.

"Don't worry," said Hill. "We've got everything under

control. We have been in contact with Martin Marietta. Everything is going to be all right."

Hill stopped by Wasserstein's office on his way home from Skadden, Arps. He had just talked to Siegel. Siegel wanted to know what had happened to Hennessy and Gleacher. They hadn't got to Martin Marietta. Hill didn't know where they were. They hadn't called him.

"What's going on?" asked Wasserstein.

"Hennessy and Gleacher are on their way to Bethesda," said Hill. "But they aren't there yet."

As soon as Hill left, Wasserstein called Agee. He had talked to Agee earlier in the evening about the possibility of Hennessy going down to negotiate with Pownall. He wanted to tell Agee that that had happened. Agee had gone to bed early and Wasserstein woke him up.

"Hennessy is down in Bethesda," said Wasserstein. "He may be negotiating a swap."

Morris Kramer and Bill Kearns were waiting at Skadden, Arps. They sat with several other lawyers at a conference table stacked with cigarette butts, empty coffee cups, and stale sandwiches.

"I'm just a lawyer, Bill. I don't know these companies," said Kramer. "But, does Bendix still make washing machines?"

•

At half past eight one of the Delaware litigators called Larrabee to say that the Court of Chancery had just ruled that Marietta could buy the Bendix shares but it could not vote them. That meant that for the moment, Marietta could not take control of Bendix. Katcher said that Marietta could always appeal the ruling. Larrabee expected that Bendix wouldn't be able to vote either: there would be a Mexican standoff.

Harry Gray called Pownall. Gray had just talked to Haig

and he knew that Hennessy was on his way to Marietta headquarters. He told Pownall that Pownall had better negotiate with Hennessy. "Allied is paying you more than we can, Tom," he said.

Then Gray gave Pownall some bargaining tips.

Just after Gray's call, Ed Hennessy finally arrived. Thayer introduced everyone and the team sat down in the brick-walled lounge next to Rauth's office.

"Our board is going to meet as soon as you and I conclude our conversation," said Pownall. "Hopefully not later than ten thirty, because I have asked them to reconvene at ten thirty. We have people standing by in New York to execute the documents and take down the stock. We've been through the question of not buying with Mr. Agee and his attorney, and we see no alternative but to do what we have set out to do. We are going to buy the stock between 12:00.01 and 12:00.59. Do you want to swap?"

"I would consider a swap," said Hennessy, "but I would prefer to negotiate buying the whole company."

"We are only interested in a swap," said Pownall. "We are not going to sell the whole company."

"I'll do the swap," said Hennessy.

"Great," said Pownall.

Everyone in the room all started to talk about numbers. Gleacher and Siegel walked into the hallway. They needed someplace quiet to bargain. The storeroom across from Pownall's office was free. They went inside. Siegel leaned against a file cabinet and started to explain why the two companies should swap the stock block for block.

"That's bullshit," laughed Gleacher. "It's after ten. You've got a board meeting at ten thirty and that premium is just not going to be. We will deliver you your independence but cost for cost and not a penny more." Gleacher pulled out his pocket calculator. "Okay," he said. "Your cost is $75 a share. Bendix's cost was $48."

"Wait a minute," said Siegel. "Bendix's cost wasn't $48. They bought 5 percent of our stock for $27. Their cost was $46.66."

"Okay," said Gleacher. "We'll give you $46.66."

Gleacher punched the tabs on his calculator. Agee had bought $1.2 billion worth of Martin Marietta. Fifty percent of Bendix would cost Martin Marietta $890 million. That meant that Allied would end up owning $300 million worth of Martin Marietta. At the Bendix cost of $46.66 that was 38 percent of the stock.

"We'll need a standstill," said Siegel.

"We'll give you a standstill," said Gleacher.

"Ten years," said Siegel.

"Okay," said Gleacher. "You've got to drop the litigation against Bendix. We'll negotiate the rest of the terms later."

The directors came back from their dinner at the Congressional Country Club. Pownall and his advisers went into the boardroom to explain the Allied swap.

"This is really a partial-leveraged buyout," said Siegel. "Your remaining stockholders should actually do very well."

"I'm recommending it," said Leithauser. "It takes the uncertainty out of continuing the fight."

"What will Bill Agee's role at Allied be?" asked a director.

"He will be president of the company," said Pownall. "But no one at Allied will report to him."

The directors voted to swap stock with Allied.

Leithauser went into his office. He called in the entire Martin Marietta financial staff. Citibank had just withdrawn almost all of the SESSOP shares. Only 44% of the stock was still in the Martin Marietta pool. At a few minutes after eleven, Leithauser and Pownall telephoned Bob Powell, who was waiting at the bank. They authorized him to buy. Powell and the bankers synchronized their watches.

At one second after midnight, Powell looked across the counter at the teller. "Buy all of the Bendix stock in our pool and keep buying until you have bought 11,900,000 shares," he said.

The teller pressed a button on his terminal and the checks began to shoot out of the printer. Powell called Leithauser.

"Do you realize that you just spent $890 million?" asked Leithauser.

"Yes," said Powell.

The Martin Marietta staff cheered. Someone popped a champagne bottle. It felt like New Year's Eve. Leithauser took a couple of bottles of champagne down to Rauth's lounge where the directors were waiting. He told them that Marietta had bought. Judge Bell slapped his thigh. "I'm so glad we won," he said. "I just hate to lose."

Pownall was in his office working. He heard the noise in the hallway and walked out to see what was going on. Leithauser told him that Martin Marietta had bought. Pownall nodded and went back to his office to work.

•

At quarter to seven the next morning, Hennessy called Gleacher. Hennessy hadn't got home until four o'clock; he had a headache from the champagne. He had just shaved and showered and changed his clothes. He hadn't had any sleep.

Allied was going to have to negotiate a new deal with Bendix now that Martin Marietta had bought. Hennessy and Gleacher talked about Allied's bargaining position. Allied in effect owned 44 percent of Bendix. Gleacher thought that Allied could force Bendix to accept the same $75 a share on the back end that it had agreed to take the day before. Gleacher couldn't believe that Bendix would continue to fight for control of Martin Marietta now that Marietta had bought half the Bendix shares. Even if Bendix had won a single victory in the Delaware courts, Bendix's legal battles weren't over. If Bendix kept fighting, it would be months before anyone took control of the merged companies and the financial structure would be atrocious in any case.

Hennessy and Gleacher agreed that they would give Agee $85 a share on the back end, since that would leave the price that Allied paid for the whole company unchanged. Then Gleacher called Wasserstein. He explained that Allied had agreed to swap.

"We still want to do a friendly deal," said Gleacher.

"We won in court yesterday," said Wasserstein.

"Come on Bruce," said Gleacher. "We could force you to $75."

"If you say $75, we say $95," said Wasserstein. "We're going to be tough."

"We'll give you $85," said Gleacher. "The cosmetics are right."

When Hennessy, Brian Forrow, Allied's general counsel, and Hal Buirkle, Allied's chief financial officer, arrived at the General Motors Building for their eight o'clock meeting, Agee and Wasserstein were in Agee's office. Hennessy and his team sat down to wait in the glass-walled conference room behind the Bendix reception desk.

Wasserstein explained to Agee that although Allied had agreed to swap and Allied thought that Allied had leverage, Bendix had won an important legal battle and it was Bendix that had the leverage. Martin Marietta could not vote the shares that it had bought the night before. Allied could not swap them without the agreement of Bendix.

"We've locked in $85 a share," said Wasserstein. "I spoke to Gleacher this morning. There may be some posturing, but they are going to give us $85."

Wasserstein walked out to the conference room where Hennessy was waiting. Wasserstein took Hennessy to Agee's office for a one-on-one conference. Agee told Hennessy that he wanted Allied to raise the price on the back end to $95.

Hennessy and Agee walked out of Agee's office. The teams were waiting in the Bendix boardroom to do the final negotiations.

"Unless you make a deal with me," said Agee, "the shares you agreed to swap last night belong to Bendix. I can go ahead with this and take over Martin Marietta, but you can't sell Martin Marietta back the Martin Marietta stock unless you make a deal with me."

"Bill, be reasonable," said Hennessy. "I can buy control of Bendix from Martin Marietta for $75 a share. Once I have control I can do whatever I want."

"You can't buy that stock for thirty days," said Wasserstein. That was true. A company had to wait for a month after announcing a handshake to buy such a large block in a private deal. "Martin Marietta can't vote the stock. Once stock becomes nonvoting, it may stay nonvoting forever. You might not be able to get control."

"You're lucky to be getting $75," said one of the Allied staffers. "We don't need to give you a dime more."

"You've got to be kidding," said Wasserstein. "Is that meant as a threat?"

"Can we meet privately for a minute," said Gleacher to Wasserstein.

The two bankers went into the small conference room across the hall. "This deal is going to get done at $85," said Gleacher. "Let's stop this."

"That's what I thought," said Wasserstein. "Can't you control your guy?"

"Ed's on board," said Gleacher. "Don't worry about it."

Gleacher and Wasserstein walked back into the boardroom. Hennessy and Agee were talking about price. Fleischer and Flom were working out the technicalities of how Allied would pay for Bendix. The teams bargained.

They caucused. A small group went into Agee's office. They ironed out the last details. They had a deal.

Agee looked at his watch.

"It's getting late," he said. "Mary and Al and I are having dinner tonight at six thirty with President Carter in Southfield. It would save me fifteen minutes if you could lend me your helicopter to get to Newark Airport."

Hennessy signaled to Gleacher. The two walked into the hallway. "What in the hell is this guy up to?" asked Hennessy.

"I don't know," said Gleacher. "He's on another wave length. Give him what he wants. Let him have the helicopter. Let him have two: one for him and one for Mary. Offer him the plane if he wants it."

Hennessy and Gleacher walked back into the boardroom. "We've got a deal," said Hennessy. Agee and Hennessy shook hands. Agee went into his office for the Bendix board meeting. Hennessy and his team went to Skadden, Arps for a telephone meeting of the Allied board.

•

The Bendix directors were waiting for Agee in his office. Agee explained that Marietta had bought the stock the night before and had agreed to sell it to Allied. He had negotiated a new deal. Allied and Bendix would agree to merge. Martin Marietta would keep buying Bendix stock until it owned 50%. Then Martin Marietta and Bendix would swap blocks of stock through Allied. That would give Allied control of Bendix plus 38% of Martin Marietta. Allied would buy the rest of Bendix with securities worth $85 a share.

"Let me try to put this into perspective," said Wasserstein. "We were trading at $45 when this started. UTC tried to raid you at $65. You now have an offer of $80. This is a great deal for your shareholders and your employees."

The directors unanimously approved the package.

•

•

At three o'clock, the lawyers for Bendix, Martin Marietta, and Allied met at Skadden, Arps to draft a peace agreement. Agee, Pownall, and Hennessy had settled on the financial terms, but the lawyers had to work out the mechanics and write up the fine print. Agee was in Michigan, but Hennessy came with his team and Pownall stayed until late that night. Larrabee kept trying to convince Pownall to go to the Waldorf and get some rest.

"I've come this far," said Pownall. "I want to see it through."

After twenty-seven hours of bitter negotiations, the lawyers had completed the draft documents. Harry Gray called Tom Pownall.

"I'm going to Europe," said Gray. "I am scheduled to take off at seven thirty tonight, but if there's anything you need me for, if there's anything I can be helpful with, I will cancel the trip and come to New York."

"It's very generous of you to offer," said Pownall. "But I think that this is moving toward its proper conclusion and I won't need your help."

"I can be there in forty-five minutes," said Gray. "Just call me if you need me."

"I will," promised Pownall. "Thank you."

When the final drafts of the papers were ready late in the afternoon, Bendix held a special board meeting in Southfield to approve them. Then the lawyers and investment bankers gathered in a Skadden, Arps conference room for the signing. The documents were spread on the table. Pownall signed. Hennessy signed. The lawyers and bankers cheered.

Hennessy called Agee. "It's signed," he said. "It's done. I'm looking forward to working with you."

•

E P I L O G U E

•

As soon as the three-way peace pact was signed, Bill Agee tried to explain what he did and why he did it. He released a version of the letter that he had written to Tom Pownall the night he was in Bethesda; he granted half a dozen interviews. Agee told the *Wall Street Journal* that negotiating with Martin Marietta had been "like dealing with the Russians." He told a group of businessmen that the battle had taught that "you should never overestimate the rationality of your foes." In December, Agee and Cunningham were named the "Most Intriguing Couple of the Year" by *People Magazine*. The award article featured a page and a half photograph of Agee kneeling before Cunningham. In early February, just days after the marriage between Allied and Bendix was made formal, Agee resigned as president of Allied. Agee said that he had wanted to become the chief operating officer of Allied and that Hennessy had said no. Agee will receive $4.1 million from his golden parachute.

•

Tom Pownall held a press conference when the battle was done. A few weeks later, Pownall returned the Don't Give Up The Ship Tie to Jack Byrne. The tie is mounted in a red frame with a small hammer dangling along the side. Byrne put the frame on the wall outside his office door. The instructions read: "Break Glass. Open In Emergency Only. To Be Worn When Under Attack." In January, Pownall was elected chairman of Martin Marietta. By March, Martin Marietta had retired half its Bendix debt by selling off a small chemical division and four older cement plants and by issuing new stock. By the end of April, its share price soared to $54, more than Bendix had ever offered. Pownall wishes that the whole fight had never happened: "It was an unpleasant event in an otherwise inglorious year."

•

After he bought Bendix, Ed Hennessy quickly hit the acquisition trail again. He bought Instrumentation Laboratories, the maker of medical and analytical equipment; he bought Semi-Alloys Inc., a supplier to the semiconductor industry; he bought the specialty chemical division of GAF. In February, Hennessy was elected to the Martin Marietta board of directors. At the end of March, Allied sold the RCA block owned by Bendix to Salomon Brothers for $129 million. A few weeks later, Hennessy announced that he was reorganizing Allied's corporate structure. He had not been able to find a chief operating officer outside Allied; he is now looking inside. In the first quarter of 1983, Bendix added $17.8 million to Allied earnings. Hennessy makes no bones about how he sees the merger battle: "It was a pretty sorry spectacle. It has given American business a black eye. I hope that history remembers Allied kindly."